The Law and Practice relating to Oil Pollution from Ships

The Law and Practice relating to

Oil Pollution from Ships

by David William Abecassis, M.A.,
of the Middle Temple, Barrister,
Legal Adviser to Shell International
Petroleum Company Limited

The views expressed in this work are those of the
author alone and do not necessarily represent those of
any section of the oil or tanker industry, or of Shell
International Petroleum Company Limited.

London · Butterworths · 1978

England London	Butterworth & Co (Publishers) Ltd 88 Kingsway WC2B 6AB
Australia Sydney	Butterworths Pty Ltd 586 Pacific Highway, Chatswood, NSW 2067 Also at Melbourne, Brisbane, Adelaide and Perth
Canada Toronto	Butterworth & Co (Canada) Ltd 2265 Midland Avenue, Scarborough MIP 4SI
New Zealand Wellington	Butterworths of New Zealand Ltd 77–85 Customhouse Quay
South Africa Durban	Butterworth & Co (South Africa) (Pty) Ltd 152–154 Gale Street
USA Boston	Butterworth (Publishers) Inc 19 Cummings Park, Woburn, Mass 01801

ISBN 0 406 10105 1

Printed in Great Britain by
Thomson Litho Ltd, East Kilbride, Scotland

Preface

The sea is one of man's most precious resources, and its pollution by oil is being increasingly recognised as a serious threat to its good management. Oil finds its way into the sea from three main sources: from the land, via rivers and via the atmosphere; from offshore installations; and from ships. The source which has attracted by far the greatest attention from international and national legislators is ships, and it is this body of law, and the practice connected with it, which forms the subject of this work.

There have been many works compiling legal texts on this subject, but so far none has attempted a systematic analysis of them. Hence this work has the following main objects:

1. To consider the problem of oil pollution from ships and to evaluate the law relating thereto in terms of the contribution it makes to the remedy of the problem.
2. To set forth a systematic exposition of the development of that law.
3. To examine, where possible, the practice of those involved in the administration or working of that law.
4. To suggest, where appropriate, the best direction in which further development should take place.

In order to see the law in perspective, it has been necessary to set forth certain facts concerning the nature of the problem of oil pollution from ships. In so doing I have had to rely largely upon the work of others, although the use to which their conclusions are put and any views expressed on the significance of their results are my own. However, no attempt has been made to set down the state of man's knowledge as to exactly what damage oil does do[1]: it is assumed throughout that the problem is sufficiently undesirable to require its eradication.

Since going to press two important international legislative developments have taken place which require mention here. The more important of the two is the adoption on 7th July 1978 at a Diplomatic Conference organised by IMCO of the Convention on Standards of Training, Certification and Watchkeeping for Seafarers. The Draft Convention forming part of the Conference documentation is mentioned in section 3.3.1. The Convention contains a chapter, not in the draft, dealing with mandatory minimum requirements for the

---

1. Such information is available elsewhere: see e.g. D. F. Boesch et al., *Oil Spills and the Marine Environment*, 1974, Cambridge (Mass.), which also contains an extensive bibliography at pp. 47–55; see also *Study VI*. The main types of damage are mentioned in section 9.8.1.

training and qualification of masters, officers and crew of oil, chemical and liquified gas tankers. This new chapter is clearly in response to Resolution 8 of the International Conference on Tanker Safety and Pollution Prevention. Resolution 10 of the Conference outlines in some detail how in practice the rather basic provisions of Chapter 5 relating to oil tankers should be implemented. Resolution 17 deals with additional training for masters and chief mates of large ships. Article X, dealing with enforcement, provides a limited right of port states to detain a vessel for infringement of the Convention, but significantly the posing of a danger to the environment is now part of the criteria for authorising detention, and, perhaps even more so, the provisions on detention 'shall be applied as may be necessary to ensure that no more favourable treatment is given to ships entitled to fly the flag of a non–Party than is given to the ships entitled to fly the flag of a Party' – see Article X(5). Such a provision is clearly in line with the approach of the 1973 Convention (see section 4.1).

The other development is the adoption on 23rd April 1978 at a Regional Conference of Plenipotentiaries convened by UNEP of the Kuwait Regional Convention for Co-operation on the Protection of the Marine Environment from Pollution, with a Protocol Concerning Regional Co-operation in Combating Pollution by Oil and Other Harmful Substances in Cases of Emergency. The intention to adopt such an instrument was noted in section 6.6. The Convention and Protocol between them set up an administrative structure to deal with communications and assistance in cases of marine emergency. A marine emergency is defined in Article I(2) of the Protocol as 'any casualty, incident, occurrence or situation, however caused, resulting in substantial pollution or imminent threat of substantial pollution to the marine environment by oil or other harmful substances and includes, inter alia, collisions, strandings and other incidents involving ships, including tankers...'. There are now familiar provisions on the reporting of incidents and requests for assistance. Concepts from pre-existing Regional Conventions have clearly been used in the development of this Convention and Protocol, and it is notable that among the matters in respect of which the parties agree to co-operate and co-ordinate their activities is the distribution and allocation of stocks of material and equipment.

Since preparing the manuscript for press, the *Amoco Cadiz* ran aground on the rocks off Ushant, releasing not only her entire cargo of oil, but, in its wake, an unprecedented howl of public anguish. The question of what to do about accidental oil pollution has been raised afresh at IMCO and in the EEC[2], which have reacted with commendable alacrity. It has been possible to mention the developments in IMCO until 30th June 1978 in a new chapter (Chapter 13),

2. See Marine Pollution Arising From the Carriage of Oil ('Amoco Cadiz'), EEC. Doc. COM (78) 184 fin., of 28 April 1978.

but other treatment of the incident has had to be confined to brief references in footnote and text. The Liberian and French inquiries into the incident are still proceeding, and so it is still not possible to say with confidence exactly what did happen. Only one thing is certain: there will be a renewed impetus at IMCO and elsewhere, just as there was following the *Torrey Canyon* incident.

I have stated the law on the basis of materials available to me at 31 December 1977, but in some cases, notably in Chapters 2, 3, 12 and 13, it has been possible to provide more up to date information.

This work would have been impossible without the willing help and encouragement of many people in industry, government and international organisations. To mention every individual who has freely given time, advice or information would be to extend an already long work, but I feel that I must mention the following.

To Dr. C. F. Kolbert, of Magdalene College, Cambridge, I owe a debt of gratitude which, sadly, it will be impossible ever to repay. He has read the entire manuscript (in various stages of revision) making many valuable comments, and has encouraged me throughout the long process of writing. I am grateful to Mr. P. G. F. Leader, of Messrs. Charles Taylor & Company, for allowing me to work as his assistant for six months during the preparation of this work. That experience enabled me to come to grips with the law relating to civil liability, and led to my being able to attend the 1976 Conference on Limitation of Liability for Maritime Claims. I am also indebted to Mr. R. Maybourn, of the B.P. Tanker Company Limited, for permission to sail aboard the M.T. *British Laurel*.

The preparation of the manuscript would have been impossible without Miss Halina Libera and my wife, who did the typing, and Mr. Hugh Lake, of I.B.M. Limited, who kindly arranged for the use of a sophisticated electric typewriter.

D.W.A.

Selbourne
21 August 1978

Contents

PART THREE. SALVAGE

Abbreviations

BIICL	British Institute of International and Comparative Law
BIMCO	The Baltic and International Maritime Conference
BYIL	*British Yearbook of International Law*
CLC	The International Convention on Civil Liability for Oil Pollution Damage 1969
dwt	Deadweight. The deadweight tonnage of a vessel is the cargo capacity of that vessel in tons.
grt	Gross registered tons. The grt of a vessel is a measure of the volume of space occupied by the vessel.
ICS	The International Chamber of Shipping
ILM	*International Legal Materials*
JBL	The *Journal of Business Law*
J Mar L & Comm	The *Journal of Maritime Law and Commerce*
LNTS	*League of Nations Treaty Series*
NDLS	*New Directions in the Law of the Sea*
OCIMF	The Oil Companies' International Marine Forum
OR	The *Official Records* of the International Legal Conference on Marine Pollution Damage 1969 (IMCO Sales No. 1973. 7. (E)).
SOLAS (1960 and 1974)	The International Conventions on Safety of Life at Sea 1960 and 1974.
Study III	Final Report on Study III, 'Retention of Oil on Board', submitted by the U.K. to the International Conference on Marine Pollution 1973, IMCO Document MP XIII/2(a)/5.
Study IV	Report on Study IV, 'Clean Tanks for Ballast Prior to Vessel Sailing', submitted by France to the International Conference on Marine Pollution 1973, IMCO Document MP XIII/2(a)/6.

Study VI	Final Report on Study VI, 'Environmental and Financial Consequences of Oil Pollution from Ships', submitted by the United Kingdom to the International Conference on Marine Pollution 1973, IMCO Document PCMP/2/Add. 1.
UKTS	*United Kingdom Treaty Series*
UNTS	*United Nations Treaty Series*

Table of Statutes

References in this Table to "*Statutes*" are to Halsbury's Statutes of England (Third Edition) showing the volume and page at which the annotated text of the Act will be found.

Table of Statutory Instruments

Table of Cases

In the following Table references are given where applicable to the English and Empire Digest where a digest of the case will be found.

D

E

F

G

H

I

O

P

Q

R

S

Y

Table of Conventions and International Conventions

Part one
Prevention and clean-up

1 Introduction

Marine-based oil pollution can emanate either from ships or from offshore installations. Natural seepages also cause oil pollution, in the widest sense of the words, but are not studied here because there is very little, if anything, that man can do about them. It is also more usual to use the word pollution in a sense which excludes natural seepages; perhaps the most helpful and most widely used recent definition is that adopted at the 1972 United Nations Conference on the Human Environment: '...the introduction by man, directly or indirectly, of substances or energy into the marine environment (including estuaries) resulting in such deleterious effects as harm to living resources, hazards to human health, hindrance to marine activities including fishing, impairment of quality for use of sea water, and reduction of amenities'[1].

1.1 The size of the problem

Oil pollution of the sea began with the introduction of oil fuel in ships, it increased with the carriage of oil cargo in bulk, and it has probably been increasing ever since. While it might be of academic interest to know how much oil is discharged to sea, and how much is floating on the surface at any one moment, the figures which are of most use are those which break down oil pollution into its relevant parts. Such figures can give an insight into the priorities which should be adopted when setting out to solve the problem.

1. UN Doc. A/CONF. 48/8, para. 197. National anti-pollution statutes contain a wide variety of definitions, but most involve the concept of harm to marine life or detriment to man's use of the waters.

A large number of studies have been done to try and assess the relative importance of the main sources of oil pollution, and although a fairly wide spread of results has been obtained, it is notable that estimates of the total oil loss to sea from marine sources nearly all come within the range of one to two million tons per annum[2]. Table 1.1 reproduces the results of a United Kingdom study[3], which gives some idea of the relative importance of the various sources.

TABLE 1.1 Estimated annual loss to sea of oil from ships and offshore installations

Mode of Discharge	Quantity discharged (tons)	Percentage of Total
OPERATIONAL		
Tanker deballasting and tank washing – Load on Top	105,000	6·6
Tanker deballasting and tank washing – non-Load on Top	529,000	33·5
Tanker tank washing pre-maintenance	360,000	22·8
OBOs[4] and bulk/ore carriers	46,000	2·9
Tanker bilge pumping	23,000	1·4
Other ships	180,000	11·4
Offshore installations	negligible	
ACCIDENTAL		
Tankers (crude and products)	200,000	12·6
Tank barges	32,000	2·0
OBOs and Bulk/Ore carriers	16,000	1·0
Other ships	9,000	0·6
Offshore installations	80,000	5·1
TOTAL	1,580,000	99·9

These figures are admittedly inaccurate, but they are good enough to enable us to draw certain important conclusions. The first of these, which is readily apparent from Table 1.1, is that in terms of the total oil discharged to sea, by far the most important problem is operational (i.e. deliberate) discharges. Why ships need to discharge oil to sea at all

2. Ten studies are compared in *Study VI*, Appendix 1, 40 (Table XVII).
3. *Study VI*, Appendix 1, 21, 22 (Table VIII), 24, 25.
4. An OBO is a ship capable of carrying either oil or ore in bulk.

is dealt with below in section 2.1. The important point at this stage is that, contrary to popular belief, dramatic accidents account for less oil discharged to sea than do routine discharges of small quantities. It must be remembered, however, that accidental spillages often release large quantities of oil all at once, and so cause more intense and localised damage.

Breaking down the operational sources, it can be seen that the most important one is the tanker which does not operate Load on Top (LOT for short), and which discharges its dirty ballast and tank washings to sea. It is noticeable that the ten estimates made previous to the one above and summarised in the United Kingdom's Report[5] all reached the same conclusion. It is for this reason that special attention is focussed on LOT in this work.

Next in importance it seems are tankers which clean their tanks before entering the repair yard or dry dock, and discharge the dirty washings and ballast to sea. The Report based its figure on information provided in another Report prepared for the same Conference[6], namely that half of all ships enter repair yards with no residues aboard and with clean tanks. In view of the fact that most major repair yards have now got adequate port reception facilities for these dirty mixtures, this proportion seems too high – and so the corresponding figure in Table 1.1 may be too high. Nonetheless, the problem is real in that a tanker cannot enter a repair yard unless her tanks are well cleaned, and so this matter is also dealt with below[7].

Three other items in the operational sphere need special mention at this stage. First, ships other than tankers: Table 1.1 clearly indicates these vessels as an important source, and it will be seen[8] that there are international standards relating to them. Second, Table 1.1 shows that even tankers which do operate LOT still discharge a significant quantity of oil. It must be remembered, however, that if the LOT system is operated well, discharges from the ship are made in an environmentally acceptable way, and so they do not cause unacceptable pollution[9]. Third, contrary to popular belief, offshore installations do not cause significant operational oil pollution at all.

Turning to accidental discharges, it can be readily seen that tankers are by far the most important problem. However, other ships, while directly contributing a small amount, are integrally bound up in the problem of accidents to tankers, for they collide with tankers and are often at fault. This explains the approach taken in Chapter 3, where shipping accidents are dealt with in detail. Perhaps the most surprising figure of all to the layman would be the relatively low one for offshore

5. *Study VI*, Appendix 1, 40.
6. See *Study IV*.
7. Sections 2.2.2 and 2.2.3.5.
8. Section 2.3.3.
9. See further section 2.2.1.

installation accidents. The low figure does not surprise the industry, which is pleased with its relatively good oil pollution record[10].

1.2 Is the problem worsening?

To make any accurate statements about future trends in oil pollution incidence is impossible, but certain facts can indicate likely patterns for the future sufficient to enable us to establish priorities for action. One of the most influential forces is, of course, the law and its effectiveness, yet it is unfortunately difficult to predict how these will change.

Turning to Table 1.1 again, it is clear that the first four operational sources mentioned are likely to bear a direct relation to the amount of oil carried over the world's seas. This has risen steadily over recent years, although at varying rates. The average yearly increase in 1975 over 1970 was 3·5%; if 1965 is taken as the base year, the figure is 7·2%[11]. Despite changing patterns in oil production and consumption, economic considerations and political structures, there seems little reason to suppose that world seaborne crude trade will not continue to increase for some time yet – say until the 1990s[12]. It follows that unless a change in anti-pollution practice takes place, these four sources of oil discharge will give rise to increasing quantities of oil lost to sea in the foreseeable future. It is one of the functions of this work to plot the change in this practice, whether voluntary or in response to legal norms. While it is true that considerable progress is being made[13], the rise in world crude trade expected in the future underlines the need for continued efforts.

With respect to operational discharges from ships other than tankers, these too are likely to be directly related to levels of world trade, and so without a change in anti-pollution measures, discharges from these vessels too seem likely to increase.

On the accidental front, there is no reason to suppose that the rate of tanker casualty will decrease in the short term, but there are more positive longer-term hopes[14]. There is definitely room for optimism

10. See D. H. Falkingham, 'Environmental Protection in Offshore Exploration and Production Operations', *Report of the Proceedings of the IPIECA Symposium 'Petroleum and Environmental Conservation'*, 1975, 215.
11. *B.P. Statistical Review of the Oil Industry, 1975*.
12. This conclusion is supported in *Study VI*, Appendix 1, 42, 47; estimated crude production is shown as rising until the year 2000, and the proportion of crude production transported by sea rising from about 45% p.a. in 1976 to about 56% p.a. in 2000.
13. See section 2.4.
14. See section 3.5.

that offshore anti-pollution measures will improve[15], despite the expected increase in world offshore crude production[16]. It may be tentatively concluded therefore, that accidental oil discharges may actually decrease in the long term.

The general conclusion must be that oil pollution from all marine-based sources taken as a whole is likely to increase, both in the long and short terms, unless adequate anti-pollution standards are increasingly adhered to from now on. The subject of this study is therefore of primary importance to the prospects for cleaner seas in the future.

15. See generally *Accidental Oil Pollution of the Sea*, Department of the Environment Central Unit on Environmental Pollution, HMSO, 1976.
16. *Study VI*, Appendix 1, 46, shows offshore production increasing from about 27% of world crude production in 1976 to over 40% in 2000.

2 Operational Discharges

2.1 The problems

2.1.1 THE CRUDE OIL TANKER

After the tanker has discharged its cargo, a proportion of it remains in the tanks, caught mainly on the horizontal surfaces of the joists which give the tank its structural strength. Such clingage varies largely according to the type of cargo carried, varying from 1·0% to 0·1% of the total cargo, the average for crudes being about 0·4%. If the clingage were to remain, a number of consequences would follow. For instance, the risk of an explosion would increase; the heavy fractions would accumulate to impede drainage, to make inspections impossible and to reduce the cargo capacity of the tank; and the residues may be incompatible with the next cargo to be loaded, thus making it unacceptable to the consignee. The clingage must therefore be regularly removed, and this has traditionally been done by washing the tanks with sea water. The problem this creates is that the water must itself then be returned to the sea and before the early 1960s this was done without separating it from the clingage. The oil was thus deliberately discharged to sea, and an average of 0·4% of the crude oil transported over the oceans therefore reached the sea.

Exactly the same problem arose with those tanks filled with ballast. Since discharge of dirty ballast water close to the shore has for some years been prohibited in most jurisdictions, the tanker had to take on ballast into a cleaned tank before arriving at the loading port. The dirty ballast was therefore discharged out at sea before arrival.

The tanker shares with other vessels the problem of disposal of oily bilges and of sludge from fuel oil purification. Both these are described in the next section.

2.1.2 OTHER SHIPS

Vessels which burn Bunker C or other heavy fuel oils face the problem of fuel oil purification. During the course of a voyage the purification of the fuel oil produces a quantity of sludge which varies with the rate of fuel consumption and quality of fuel burned. Normally these sludges are kept in sludge tanks, but eventually the contents of these tanks must either be discharged to a shore reception facility, or to sea.

Another problem is that pumps, tanks and machinery almost inevitably leak small quantities of various types of oil (mainly lubrication oil). These can amount to an appreciable quantity, and are normally fed via special drainways to separate bilges, or are collected in the normal bilges. There are three possible methods of dealing with these bilges. The oldest and least desirable is to discharge them to sea. A second method is to discharge them to shore reception facilities where they are available. The third is to install an oil/water separator of appropriate capacity; the separated oil may be either stored in a special tank or fed into the fuel oil tanks. The oil content of the water discharged to sea through the separator can be kept within legal limits[1] if the separator is operated properly[2]. However, if the oil which has been separated out is stored rather than burned with the bunkers, it will eventually need to be discharged to a shore reception facility – or to sea.

A serious problem faced by many dry cargo ships is the disposal of oily ballast. This arises where the vessel has to use its bunker tanks for water ballast to ensure stability. The oily ballast is normally discharged only when the vessel is nearing port, but, as with bilges, this may be done via a separator; alternatively shore reception facilities may be used if they are available.

2.2 Practical solutions

2.2.1 LOAD ON TOP

Following the 1962 Conference to revise the International Convention for the Prevention of Pollution of the Sea by Oil 1954, the oil industry was asked to see if it could not come up with a technical solution to the oil discharge problem, which the 1962 Conference had failed to solve[3]. The solution was to separate the oil and water on board,

1. Section 2.3.3.
2. Performance and specification of separators is dealt with in *Study III*. A more recent report is contained in D. Cormack, Oil-Water Separation and Oil-in-Water Monitoring, SYMP V/1 (Paper delivered at the IMCO Symposium on Prevention of Marine Pollution from Ships, Acapulco, 22–31 March, 1976). See also IMCO Resolution A.233 (VII), adopting the Maritime Safety Committee's Recommendation on International Performance Specifications for Oily-Water Separating Equipment, and MEPC VI/17, Annex II for a Revised Recommendation to be submitted to the 10th IMCO Assembly.
3. Per J. H. Kirby (then Managing Director, Shell International Marine Ltd.), 'The Clean Seas Code: a Practical Cure of Operational Pollution', *Proceedings of the International Conference on Oil Pollution of the Sea, 7–9 October, 1968, Rome*, 201 at 204.

discharge the water to sea, retaining the oil residues aboard. The next cargo could then, in most situations, be loaded on top of the residues – hence the system was christened Load on Top (LOT for short).

The LOT procedure basically consists of the following events[4] (see Figure 2.1):

1) After discharge of cargo from the cargo tanks, sea water is taken on as ballast into some of the tanks (Nos. 1, 4, 7, 9 and 11). Other tanks are washed with sea water (Nos. 2, 3, 5, 6, 8 and 10).

2) The cargo tank washings are transferred through 'stripping' pipes to a slop tank (No. 12), (which may be just another cargo tank). These washings settle in the slop tank.

3) a) Clean ballast water is pumped into the cleaned tanks (Nos. 2, 3, 5, 6, 8 and 10).
   b) The dirty ballast water taken on at the start has by now partially settled, so the lower layer of water is discharged to sea (from Nos. 1, 4, 7, 9 and 11), and
   c) the residual oil and water is stripped to the slop tank (No. 12) to settle.

4) After settling in the slop tank the water layer is discharged to sea (from No. 12) or to port reception facilities when available.

5) A new cargo is loaded on top of the slop tank oil residues (not shown).

By operating LOT a tanker can save nearly all the oil which it would otherwise have discharged to sea[5], and what it does put over the side can be discharged in an environmentally acceptable way. The discharge will be close to the side of the ship and so the oil and water mixture will usually be further dispersed by passing through the wake. Some of the oil will remain beneath the surface, but some will rise to form a thin film (from 0·002 mm to 0·005 mm thick) which will normally be degraded within two to three hours. The system is, therefore, an excellent anti-pollution device, and has undoubtedly saved millions of tons of oil pollution since its introduction.

Since its introduction in 1963 and 1964, adherence to LOT quickly reached about 80% of all tankers[6], but there, it seems, it has stayed[7]. LOT has not been accepted by 100% of the tanker industry because not all tankers can in practice operate the system – or not all tanker owners for some reason want to. The problems associated with LOT

4. Detailed and practical explanations are contained in *Clean Seas Guide for Oil Tankers: The Operation of Load on Top*, Joint ICS/OCIMF publication, 1973, and in *Study III*.

5. Ways of improving the operation of LOT to achieve the minimum oil discharge possible are mentioned below, section 2.3.2.4.

6. J. H. Kirby, 'The Clean Seas Code: a Practical Cure of Operational Pollution', *Proceedings of the International Conference on Oil Pollution of the Sea, 7–9 October, 1968, Rome*, 201.

7. *Study VI*, Appendix 1, 18 (1973); MEPC VI/8/5, page 4 (1976).

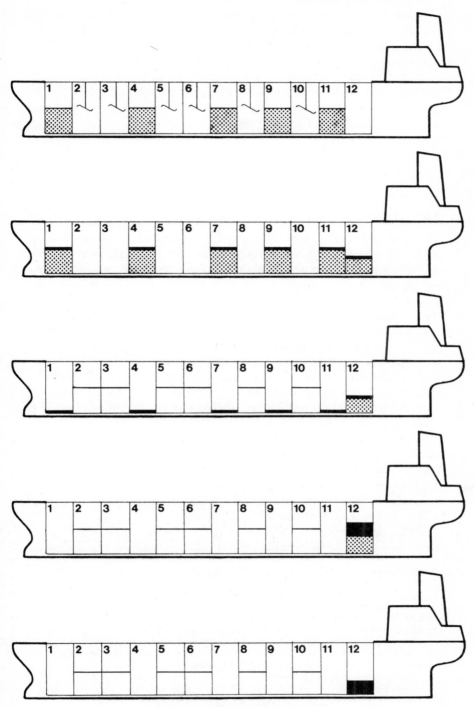

Figure 2.1   Diagram of LOT procedure

which cause this situation are discussed below. It should be pointed out here, though, that Table 1.1 shows that of all the oil discharged operationally by tankers, OBOs and Bulk/Ore carriers, tankers operating LOT account for just under 10%[8]. Hence, 80% of the world's tankers cause a small proportion (say 10%) of operational oil discharges in a non-polluting way, whereas 20% of the world's tankers produce the vast majority (say 90%) of such discharges in a polluting way. It is therefore of primary importance to see why those 20% do not operate LOT.

2.2.2 PROBLEMS ASSOCIATED WITH LOT

One problem is that the oil retained on board in the slop tank has inevitably got a higher salt content than some refineries can tolerate[9], and so a tanker whose next cargo is destined for such a refinery will be unable to use the system. Another problem is that the system takes time to operate[10] because of the settling necessary to separate oil and water, and so vessels on short-haul voyages cannot use it. A similar problem is encountered by vessels on coastal voyages: because even LOT means discharging some oil, there would be a contravention of the total ban on all oil discharges imposed within 50 miles of the coast by most jurisdictions and by the 1954 Convention. Again, if a tanker is to carry as its next cargo a white oil, or some other oil incompatible with the persistent oil just carried, then it too will be unable to operate LOT.

A special problem for the tanker arises before it is to enter the repair yard: its tanks must be specially well cleaned to remove oily residue and sludge. Although some yards permit tankers to inert the atmosphere in the slop tank[11], and so allow the vesel to enter with residues on board, this will not always be the case, and so the tanker will be unable to retain oil on board.

OBOs and Bulk/Ore carriers[12] have a special problem connected with their operational peculiarities. When it is desired to change over

8. 105,000 tons out of 1,063,000 tons. C. A. Walder concurs in, 'The Response of the Oil Industry to the Problems of Pollution of the Sea from Ships', *Report of the Proceedings at the IPIECA Symposium, Petroleum and Environmental Conservation, 7–9 April 1975*, 199 at 202.

9. K. G. Brummage, 'The Consequences of Load on Top in Petroleum Refining', *Proceedings of the International Conference on Oil Pollution of the Sea, 7–9 October 1968, Rome*, 183.

10. The time varies with the weather encountered on the ballast voyage, the size and construction of the tanker, the efficiency of the crew, the type of equipment used on board, and with other factors. The minimum time for a tanker of, say, 65–95,000 dwt would be about 50 hours. A more usual time would be 72 hours.

11. A process of removing all the oxygen in the tank above the oil surface and replacing it with a special, inert gas.

12. The distinction between the two types of vessel for oil pollution purposes is immaterial – both can carry both dry and wet bulk cargoes.

from carrying an oil cargo to carrying a dry cargo (say coal or ore), the tanks must be cleaned of all residues. There is no question of the dry cargo being loaded on top of the slops in the slop tanks! On the last voyage before taking on dry cargo, therefore, these vessels have an oil disposal problem.

The last problem connected with the operation of LOT concerns the charter market, but it is related to some of the previous problems. If a charterer wishes to voyage charter a vessel to take a cargo from, say, the Gulf to Rotterdam, he will not necessarily discover whether or not the vessel chartered has slops aboard incompatible with the cargo he wishes to load until inspection is made at the loading terminal. Of course, if there are adequate shore reception facilities at the loading terminal, there is no problem; however, as we shall see[13], many countries have yet to provide reception facilities in their loading ports adequate for the traffic using them. The result is that an owner chartering out his vessel on the open market may well be reluctant to operate LOT on the ballast voyage (during part of which the vessel may be on offer in the market): he will not know where the vessel will be going to for loading until a charter is agreed, and so he cannot be sure that any slops aboard can definitely be discharged ashore. The owner will therefore be under pressure to put the residues over the side.

Further pressures of a financial nature operate on the owner of such a vessel. Where residues have been retained on board, the charterer may well be unprepared to pay freight in respect of the slops or deadfreight in respect of the space above them (assuming cargo is not loaded on top of them). If the residues can be discharged ashore at the loading terminal, the charterer may well be unprepared to allow the time taken for such discharge as laytime.

There are also similar difficulties concerning the distribution of financial burdens in time charters, both of oil tankers and of OBOs and Bulk/Ore carriers.

2.2.3 CURRENT SOLUTIONS TO THE PROBLEMS ASSOCIATED WITH LOT

2.2.3.1 High salt content

There is nothing that the tanker owner can do about this problem except to operate LOT as efficiently as he can, thus reducing the salt in the residues which collect in the slop tank. The efficiency which can be achieved will depend on the weather on the ballast voyage (calm weather being best), the care which the officers and crew involved devote to the operation, and, to a certain extent, the availability of

13. Section 2.2.5.

equipment on board which aids the operation – for instance, slop tank heating coils.

Really the problem is one for the refining branch of the industry. Any refinery can accept LOT cargoes if it has adequate desalting equipment: of course, the installation of such equipment is costly. However, it is fortunate that since the early 1960s more and more refineries have been building desalting equipment, and it is now a minority which do not have them[14].

2.2.3.2 The short-haul tanker

The International Chamber of Shipping and the Oil Companies International Marine Forum have recommended four possible solutions to the problems of the short-haul tanker[15], which are worth attention.

(a) Eliminating tank washing and discharging dirty ballast at the loading terminal. The trouble here will often be that the tanks will have to be washed to enable acceptance of the next cargo, and even if such washing is not necessary, the loading terminal may not have adequate dirty ballast reception facilities. This is the first case where the importance of adequate reception facilities at all the world's leading terminals becomes apparent.

(b) Washing ballast tanks at the discharge terminal and sailing with clean ballast. This again relies on there being available reception facilities for the washings either at the discharge terminal or at the next loading terminal. In addition, washing ballast tanks at the discharge terminal may in some cases involve the vessel spending more time in port than she can afford to – or than the terminal authorities want her to.

(c) Segregating ballast in some cargo tanks as a temporary trading measure. For the tanker on regular short voyages, this normally will be expensive, in that it reduces the cargo capacity of the vessel. Particularly in times of recession, shipowners are sensitive to the great need to make every voyage a commercial success, and so will be reluctant to take such drastic steps. It does, however, represent a real alternative for a tanker which only occasionally, or rarely, makes short voyages.

(d) Re-routing the ship or slowing down to allow enough time for proper LOT procedures. This is acceptable for the occasional short

14. Private communication from Capt. A. T. Thompson, OCIMF, dated 16 February 1977:
'... as a general rule there are few, if any, private enterprise oil refineries which will not now accept cargoes which have been loaded on top. Some of the national refinery companies of the newer States are still reluctant to receive such cargoes as are few of the very old refineries which do not have de-salters'.

15. *Clean Sea Guide for Oil Tankers: The Operation of Load on Top*, Joint ICS/OCIMF publication, 1973, 10.

voyage, but, again in the case of the regular short-haul voyager, the position is different: in times of prosperity such measures would normally prove costly, in terms of lost profit, but in times of recession this may be for some owners an acceptable procedure. The kind of owner who could do this would be the large fleet owner who does not want to lay up the vessels (as a result of decreased demand) but prefers to keep them in service. By slow steaming, the capacity of the fleet to transport oil is reduced down to current demand levels, while allowing for a quick response to increased demand when world trade starts to pick up. In this way losses can be mitigated.

From this it may be concluded that the only really acceptable solution to the regular short-haul tanker's problem is the provision of adequate port reception facilities.

2.2.3.3 The coastal voyage

The problems of the tanker making coastal voyages, or voyages within the 'prohibited zones'[16] (e.g. within the North Sea) are identical to those of the short-haul tanker, with the exception that it is not possible to slow down so that LOT can be operated, because LOT will still involve a discharge of *some* oil, and this is prohibited. It is therefore even more important to the alleviation of this problem that adequate reception facilities be provided. It is fortunate that many of the vessels in this category are in the white oil trade – i.e. carrying non-persistent oils. At the moment the problem does not arise for these vessels because discharges are usually only prohibited within a certain distance from the coast if they are of persistent oil. However, as will be seen[17], when the 1973 International Convention on Prevention of Pollution from Ships comes into force, discharges of white oils will also be prohibited within 50 miles of land.

2.2.3.4 Cargo incompatibility

The problem here is not one of time in which to effect the LOT operation, but is that the new cargo cannot be loaded on top of the settled out and separated slops because it is of a different type: for instance, where the tanker has been carrying Kuwait crude and next cargo she is to carry Fuel Oil[18]. The only possible way to retain the oil

16. As defined by the 1954 International Convention for the Prevention of Pollution of the Sea by Oil. These zones are described below, section 2.3.2.1.
17. Section 2.3.2.4.
18. A related problem arises when the next cargo cannot by its nature tolerate the extra salt content: for instance, Low Cold Test crude oil (used to manufacture particular types of lubricant) must be carried without any contamination whatsoever since even a small amount of impurity can ruin the Low Cold Test properties of the oil.

on board would be to reserve the slop tank space exclusively for the crude slops; this, however, reduces the capacity of the vessel[19] and is therefore unpopular. The most effective solution is to discharge the contents of the slop tank to reception facilities at the loading port – following that, to wash all tanks at the discharge terminal, discharge the washings to reception facilities there, and sail with clean ballast. Here again the importance of reception facilities is seen.

2.2.3.5 Pre-maintenance washing

Although the burden of this problem can be mitigated by cleaning tanks more intensively as the repair period approaches and by carrying on the last cargo voyage a crude which helps to dissolve sludge, such measures do not remove the problem altogether. The slops from washing all tanks have to be discharged to shore somewhere (either at the last discharge terminal, or at a port between there and the repair yard), or permission must be sought to enter the yard with slops in an inerted tank. Happily, the provision of reception facilities at yards has improved greatly in recent years. The practice of yards on allowing entry with slops aboard varies from yard to yard and according to the repairs to be done.

2.2.3.6 OBOs and bulk/ore carriers

These vessels have to clean their entire cargo system when changing from oil to dry bulk cargo. There are only two possibilities for such vessels to avoid discharging the residues to sea; one is to retain them in the slop tank(s) throughout the dry cargo voyage, and thus incur deadfreight in respect of the slop tank(s), and the other is to discharge them to shore reception facilities.

2.2.3.7 Chartered vessels

On 28 April 1976 the International Chamber of Shipping published its *Pollution Prevention Code (Oil Tankers)*[20]. This Code, which applies only to tankers (including OBOs and Ore/Oil carriers) has been prepared to enable the operable provisions of the International Convention for the Prevention of Pollution from Ships 1973 relating to oil pollution to be practised fully without further delay, despite the

---

19. The more technical term is incurring or suffering 'deadfreight' in respect of that part of the vessel's capacity which is unused.
20. Brought to the attention of IMCO's Marine Environment Protection Committee (MEPC V/INF. 12) and approved (MEPC V/19, para. 101).

fact that entry into force of that Convention is not expected until after 1980. As one of its specific objectives it takes the provision of 'a means whereby any Owner and any Charterer may voluntarily signify agreement to conduct all tanker operations under their respective control in accordance with the standards recommended in the Code'. Owners and charterers may declare their acceptance of the Code (on payment of a fee of £10) but this does not create a contract: Clause 5 states that 'Acceptance of this Code does not constitute a binding agreement between those who have signified their acceptance, but is an expression of intent by an Owner or Charterer to abide by the Code and to incorporate its provisions by reference or otherwise into relevant existing and future charters'.

It seems however, that the Code may infringe United States anti-trust legislation, which is why so many US Charterers and Owners are absent from the 96 companies who had declared their acceptance by 31 January 1977. The Code has been registered under the UK Restrictive Trade Practices Act. It may therefore be thought that the Code is of little use, but that would be quite wrong. Although there are still many smaller operators who have not accepted it, the effect of the two European 'sisters'[1] and other large companies joining is that the market is considerably affected. If it is known that they accept the Code, it is easier for owners to induce others to accept it. Indeed, it is this effect which makes the Code possibly a breach of the US legislation.

a) *Voyage charters*
In Clause 7 the Code deals with the problems of the voyage charter market mentioned above:

'A Charterer shall recognise the problems, including those associated with any lack of appropriate reception facilities, which the Owner may have in ensuring that his ship complies with the provisions of paragraph 6 (load-on-top for black oil) and will offer a Charter Party the terms of which are compatible with such compliance. In particular, the Charterer shall offer a Charter Party which:
(a) In the case of a voyage charter, requires the retention of any residue which remains on board from the previous cargo and
(i) if the residue collected in the course of tank washing and ballast changing is co-mingled with the cargo loaded, provides that the Charterer will pay freight on the collected residue, and also on the water associated with it provided that this water has

---

1. Royal Dutch/Shell and British Petroleum. The international majors who make up the 'seven sisters' – the seven largest oil companies in the world – are Exxon, Standard Oil Company of New York (Socony-Mobil), Standard Oil of California (Chevron), Gulf Oil, Texaco, Shell and B.P.

been reduced to a minimum consistent with the ship's compliance with paragraph 6; or

(ii) if the Charterer instructs that collected residue and minimum associated water be segregated from the cargo to be loaded, provides that the Charterer will pay freight on the residue and on minimum associated water and will pay any deadfreight so incurred; or

(iii) if the Charterer instructs that collected residue and minimum associated water are to be discharged ashore before cargo is loaded, provides that time so used shall count as laytime;

(b) . . .'

It can be seen that this puts the financial burdens involved in the operation of LOT, where there is a voyage charter, onto the charterer. However, these burdens are more apparent than real. In cases (ii) and (iii) of Clause 7(a) the burdens cannot be described as onerous, especially when viewed on a per ton basis, and in case (i) can lead the charterer to a profit. It is worthwhile illustrating how this profit arises as it is an example of an anti-pollution measure being economic, and as the profit would accrue not only in a charter situation but also where an owner transports his own cargo (a common situation in large oil companies).

Suppose a 100,000 dwt tanker is chartered to carry crude from the Gulf to Rotterdam at a freight rate of $5.00 per ton. If the ship is clean on arrival at the Gulf because all her slops from the previous voyage have been discharged to sea, the charterer will have to load 100,000 tons of oil, on all of which he will pay freight. When the vessel discharges at Rotterdam, anything from 0·1% to 1·0% of the cargo will cling to the tanks: say for purposes of this example the figure is the average, 0·4%. The out-turn will therefore be only 99,600 tons, 400 tons remaining as clingage. This oil, whose c.i.f. Rotterdam value is, say, $115.00 per ton, is lost to the charterer. His costs are therefore as follows:

$500,000	Freight.
$ 46,000	Lost oil.
$546,000	TOTAL

Now suppose the same ship arrives in the Gulf having operated LOT on the ballast voyage. She will therefore have about 0·4% of her previous cargo aboard as separated slops – i.e. 400 tons. This means that the charterer can load only 99,600 tons on top. On arrival in Rotterdam, again 0·4% of the total 100,000 tons aboard will remain as clingage, so that the out-turn will again be only 99,600 tons. This is the quantity the charterer put in. If Clause 7(a)(i) of the Code applies, the charterer's costs are as follows:

$498,000	Freight.
$ 2,000	Clause 7(a)(i) Freight.
$500,000	TOTAL

The charterer has therefore saved $46,000. The owner has received the same freight as he would have received had the ship been clean, so he has lost nothing.

b) *Other charters*

Clause 7, paragraphs (b), (c) and (d) make similar provisions in respect of time charters both for oil tankers and OBOs and Ore/Oil carriers, none of which require separate treatment here. It is enough to note that with these provisions Clause 7 constitutes a real attempt to cope with the pollution difficulties of the charter market. It is greatly to be hoped that, even if the US companies feel legally unable to accept the Code formally, they will nonetheless incorporate its provisions in charterparties whenever they can: certainly, there is no US law against that. If this happens, the Code will make a significant contribution to cleaner seas.

2.2.4 CRUDE OIL WASHING[2]

There is no reason why water has to be used to clean tanks if another substance can be found to do the job. The only substance which would not create problems of separating it from the oil after the washing had been done is oil itself. This is one reason why for some years there was interest within the tanker industry in crude oil washing, which uses the cargo itself as the washing agent instead of seawater. It was found, however, that portable washing machines could not be used to effect crude oil washing, and so it was not until fixed washing machines became available that research on the method could start. These machines are supplied with crude from the cargo by permanent pipes, and the washing cycle is controlled by the drive units. Following almost two years of trials and evaluation, crude oil washing was introduced into some VLCCs in 1974, and it is now a routine procedure for many ships. Tanker owners are increasingly taking up the system in suitably equipped vessels.

Put simply, the process involves part of the cargo being diverted through the fixed tank cleaning system into the tanks as they are being

2. A brief description of the method of crude oil washing is contained in MEPC VI/6/2, pages 2–3. A more detailed description is contained in R. Maybourn, 'Crude Oil Washing', SYMP VI/3 (Paper delivered to the IMCO Symposium on Prevention of Marine Pollution from Ships, Acapulco, 22–31 March 1976). An operational guide is published by OCIMF/ICS: *Guidelines for Tankwashing with Crude Oil*, 1976. Detailed information is also contained in MSC/MEPC/INF. 17 and MSC/MEPC/10, Annex XIX.

emptied, so that the exposed surfaces where cargo and sludge collects are washed by powerful jets of crude oil. The residues on these surfaces are thus washed down into the cargo as it is being discharged.

However, the system is not a cure-all. There are three situations where a tank needs a subsequent water-wash (albeit a shorter one than would otherwise have been needed): (1) where the tank is needed for clean ballast; (2) where the tank has to be gas-freed for entry or repair; and (3) where the next cargo is incompatible with crude oil.

Because less water is used, there is less water and oil separation to be done, and so there is less risk of pollution during discharge. Also, the system means that there is less oil remaining on board, for much of the oil which would have clung to the tank and which would have ended up in the slop tank in a LOT operation is now discharged with the cargo. The system therefore has considerable economic advantages[3]: cargo out-turn is increased, the cost of routine tank cleaning is reduced, and where the vessel is chartered but Clause 7 of the ICS Code[4] is not in operation, there may be increased freight due to the smaller quantity of oil retained on board. The two main disadvantages are that cargo discharge time is increased, and there is an increased workload in port.

The system is only suitable for vessels equipped with the fixed washing machines and with flue gas inerting systems[5], and so cannot be adopted by all existing ships. Conversion can of course be effected, but then the costs thereof must be balanced against the economic gains of operating the system. It is undoubtedly one of the most exciting anti-pollution developments of modern times and was included in international regulations for the first time in 1978.[6]

2.2.5   RECEPTION FACILITIES

It was seen in section 2.2.3 how important the existence of reception facilities for tank washings and dirty ballast is to the solution of the problems faced by those tankers which cannot, for one reason or another, operate LOT. They are also important to all ships for the handling of oily bilges, sludges and dirty ballast, and to tankers for the handling of oily residues and sludges. It will be apparent that the ports where they are most in need are those where short-haul tankers end

3. Other advantages include less salt discharged to refineries, potential reduction in corrosion from water washing, and reduction of manual desludging.
4. See section 2.2.3.7.
5. A necessary safety measure to prevent the possibility of an explosion caused by water in the crude giving rise to an electrostatic discharge. However, some believe that it is perfectly safe to operate the procedure in an over-rich atmosphere.
6. See sections 2.3.5 and 2.3.6.

their ballast voyages, where repair yards are sited and generally where oil is loaded into tankers.

At its ninth session in May 1971, IMCO's Sub-committee on Marine Pollution requested information[7] on facilities in ports for the reception of these residues. A questionnaire was sent to all IMCO member states, and states then party to the 1954 Oil Pollution Convention. The replies were published in 1973[8], and they indicated a serious lack of adequate facilities. Although the need for them was appreciated by the international community as long ago as 1954[9], it is still true in 1977 that 'dirty ballast and slop reception facilities are almost non-existing in major oil exporting areas, such as the Arabian Gulf, West and North Africa, and in major oil importing and trans-shipment ports in Northern Europe'[10]. It is these areas, of course, which are most in need of these facilities. In addition, there is a general lack of them at ore loading ports where OBOs load after discharge of an oil cargo, and at ports handling dry cargo vessels which wish to dispose of dirty ballast or fuel oil purification sludges. While the position at repair yards is much better (if not ideal) there is a total lack of facilities at offshore loading terminals: the only solution here seems to be for short-haul tankers to use segregated ballast[11].

IMCO's Marine Environment Protection Committee has had a review of the matter in hand since 1974, and has now reached the stage of producing 'Guidelines on Means for Ensuring the Provision and Maintenance of Adequate Reception Facilities in Ports'[12]. Such guidelines are extremely helpful in enabling a state to decide what facilities to provide at its various ports, but it is regrettable that the present inadequacy of reception facilities creates the need for such a document. The failure of many governments to take the necessary action on the provision of these facilities, despite recommendations by IMCO[13], is in sharp contrast to the efforts made by the oil and tanker industries over the last fifteen years to overcome pollution. IMCO, in collaboration with UNEP, also has in hand now a scheme to help developing countries meet the cost of providing these facilities[14].

7. OP IX/12, para. 9.
8. *Facilities in Ports for the Reception of Oil Residues*, IMCO, London, 1973, IMCO Sales No. 1973/4. The publication is in the course of review, and a new questionnaire has been drawn up: MEPC VI/17, para. 59; MEPC VII/19, para. 35.
9. The 1954 Convention contains an Article relating to the provision of reception facilities: see below, section 2.3.4.
10. Per INTERTANKO, MEPC VI/8/5, page 4; see also MEPC VII/19, para. 32 where this point was made again, this time by the UK.
11. Section 2.2.6.
12. MEPC VI/17, Annex III. It is to be published separately by IMCO – see MEPC VI/17, para. 57. The methodology is clearly based on Paper VII/2 given at the IMCO Symposium on Prevention of Marine Pollution from Ships, Acapulco, 22–31 March 1976, 'Methodology for Determining Adequacy of Reception Facilities in Port for Treatment of Ship-generated Oily Wastes', by G. C. Steinman, K. J. Randall and C. F. Propp.
13. Resolutions A235 (VII) of 12th October 1971, and A348 (IX) of 12th November 1975.
14. See MEPC VII/19, paras. 33, 34.

In fact, the provision of these facilities need not necessarily involve undue expense. One proposal, made in 1976 by INTERTANKO[15], that the problem be solved quickly and economically by using converted elderly tankers as reception facilities, would have the added advantage of mopping up much of the current surplus of such tonnage. There are two further advantages: first, the use of redundant tankers is an excellent way of providing facilities at offshore loading terminals and deepwater ports; second, their use provides a flexibility which land installations cannot offer. When eventually all large tankers have segregated ballast tanks[16], the capacity of reception facilities needed at the ports and terminals used by them will be dramatically reduced. A land installation, which represents a long-term capital investment, would become redundant, but a ship can either be moved elsewhere, sold or scrapped. Ships of smaller capacity can be used as demand decreases, or if demand is increasing (due perhaps to recent discoveries in a particular area) more or larger ships can be bought.

Further, whatever type of facility is installed, the means of paying for it can be partly offset by the value of the oil residues it accepts. The rest of the cost may be covered either by charging a fee for their use, or by increasing port dues[17].

2.2.6 SEGREGATED BALLAST TANKERS

If oil and water never mix, there is no problem of having to separate them. This is the principle behind the segregated ballast tanker, which is specially constructed so that in certain tanks only ballast is carried, and in the remainder, only cargo is normally carried – there being an exception in favour of very rough weather, when extra ballast must be taken on to maintain safe navigation. This type of tanker has separate piping and plumbing arrangements for the cargo and the ballast, so that the ballast tanks are truly segregated.

The provision of segregated ballast tanks was first made a requirement in the International Convention on the Prevention of Pollution from Ships 1973: that provision was limited to new tankers of 70,000 dwt tons and above[18]. Clearly the provision of such tanks has a role to play in the fight against marine pollution. The extension of the mandatory fitting of segregated ballast tanks which was achieved in

---

15. MEPC VI/8/5. The Committee left the choice of type of facility to each authority without special recommendation – MEPC VI/17, para. 58.
16. When Regulation 13 of Annex I of the 1973 Convention enters into force, all new tankers of 70,000 dwt tons and over will need such tanks: as to segregated ballast, see sections 2.2.6 and 2.3.5.
17. MEPC is studying the question of the desirability of charging fees: see MEPC VII/19, paras. 46–48. See generally Chapter 7.
18. See sections 2.3.5 and 2.3.6.

1978 by the adoption of the Protocol to the 1973 Convention forms the most important part of that Protocol[18]. It is worthwhile here briefly summarising the arguments for and against widespread fitting of segregated ballast tanks, because otherwise the compromise actually adopted by the International Convention on Tanker Safety and Pollution Prevention 1978 cannot be understood.

Those who favoured some extension of the 1973 provisions relating to segregated ballast tanks (notably the United States, Greece, Norway and Sweden) saw the admitted environmental benefits and regarded them as technically and economically feasible. They regarded an extension of the mandatory provisions as being a superior method of achieving a significant reduction of operational pollution to alternatives such as the mandatory operation of crude oil washing procedures. Some states were undoubtedly in favour of such an extension, not so much because of the environmental benefits, but because if the world fleet of existing tankers had to be fitted for segregated ballast, a given quantity of oil would take more ships to carry it than without such extension. The effect of this would be to stimulate demand in a severely depressed tanker market.

Those against extension to existing tankers (for instance the United Kingdom) took the view that the environmental benefits were too small to justify the enormous costs involved[19].

These costs are suffered not only in having to pay for the retrofitting, but are suffered in time lost during the carrying out of the works. Thereafter, there is a permanent cost due to the increase in bunkers that is needed to transport a given quantity of oil. There is also the difficulty of seeing that the application of the provisions is uniform, and so fair[20].

One alternative to the mandatory fitting of segregated ballast tanks is the operation of crude oil washing (which does not involve such serious economic consequences); another is to carry ballast in existing, unaltered cargo tanks which are dedicated exclusively to the carriage of ballast (so that on the laden voyage they are empty)[1]. While this does not involve the retrofitting costs of segregated ballast tankage for existing tankers, all the other arguments against segregated ballast apply to these dedicated ballast tanks (or 'clean ballast tanks').

As we shall see[2], the 1978 Conference adopted a compromise whereby certain existing tankers may dedicate ballast tanks or operate crude oil washing as an alternative to fitting segregated ballast tanks.

---

19. OCIMF estimated $1.5 to 2.5 million for a VLCC (MEPC VI/6/3); Italy, Lira 1.5 billion (say $1.7 million) for 'a vessel' (MEPC VI/6). Taking the lowest figure, this would create a world conversion cost for ships over 70,000 dwt tons of about $1,600 million.
20. The papers by OCIMF give detailed and cogent reasons why the notion is misconceived: see MEPC VII/5, MEPC VI/6/3, MEPC V/INF. 13 and 16, MEPC IV/4.
 1. First suggested (as an interim measure) by Sweden: see MEPC VI/6/4, MEPC VII/5/1, TSPP II/2 para. 10 and TSPP III/3/1.
 2. Sections 2.3.5 and 2.3.6.

2.3 International legal standards

2.3.1 THE NEED FOR INTERNATIONAL LEGAL STANDARDS[3]

Unilateral national measures to control oil pollution are proliferating, and so it is clear that certain governments do not subscribe to the view that pollution law should develop by internationally agreed standards: or, at any rate, that the political value of 'going it alone' is greater than the less immediate advantages of the unification of private law in the field of oil pollution.

It is apparent that the question whether or not to applaud or support unilateral measures is ultimately one of personal preferences, and so those of the author are openly declared now. The development of oil pollution law should be confined to the ratification of international standards for three reasons.

First, enough has already been said to make it clear that marine-based oil pollution is an international problem, and so should be solved by international agreement.

Secondly, unilateral measures can affect fair competition in an open market. For instance, if State A alone enacts that all ships flying her flag shall be fitted with segregated ballast tanks, or oily water separators, or shall comply with other such regulations, such ships will bear economic and operational burdens unknown to ships registered elsewhere.

Thirdly, it is most important to shipowners and to personnel aboard that a different set of regulations do not have to be complied with at each different port visited on a voyage. It makes for simpler and more efficient ship management to know exactly where the ship stands legally at any one moment and in any given situation, and uncertainty or confusion over local law can have serious effects. One example may be taken: if a ship is involved in an accident, the master will have to decide on his best course of action. It may be open to him to head for State A, or State B. If he is leaking oil, he will be worried about criminal and civil liability in both states. He should be able to rely on the law being identical in both, so that his choice of state is uncluttered by legal considerations. Alternatively, if the accident occurs in State A, he may be worried about whether or not he will be criminally liable for failure to report oil spillage, or what will be the legal effect of a decision to jettison oil. The decisions he makes should be unaffected by such considerations, as they would be if oil pollution law was completely unified throughout the world.

It follows that the author places great importance on the comprehensiveness and effectiveness of international legal standards,

---

3. For a review of this question with specific reference to US unilateral action, see S. A. Wallace, 'Why National Control and How Far?', Paper presented at the Nautical Institute's *Conference on Shipping Tomorrow, London, 5–6 January 1977*, 31.

and so these are examined and evaluated below. However, adherence to the above viewpoint does not imply that *all* unilateral national regulations which have some effect on oil pollution are necessarily undesirable: examples are where a state enacts a traffic separation scheme within its territorial sea, or makes pilotage compulsory in certain waters within its jurisdiction.

The question of the enforceability of international standards is dealt with in Chapter 4.

2.3.2 DISCHARGE STANDARDS FOR TANKERS

The International Convention for the Prevention of Pollution of the Sea by Oil, 1954[4], was adopted under the auspices of IMCO and has been amended in 1962[5], 1969[6] and 1971[7]. Until 1973, it was the only international, as opposed to bilateral or regional, convention relating to preventive standards for oil discharges, and it has attracted wide support[8]; but in 1973 the International Convention for the Prevention of Pollution from Ships[9] adopted provisions designed to replace those in the earlier Convention[10].

2.3.2.1 The 1954–62 standards[11]

In 1954 LOT had not been invented, and so the delegates to that conference proceeded on the basis that oil discharges were inevitable. Reception facilities were even scarcer than they are nowadays, and so the approach was to limit tanker discharges to areas outside prohibited zones.

4. UKTS No. 56 of 1958 (Cmnd. 595); 327 UNTS 3. See generally E. D. Brown, *The Legal Regime of Hydrospace*, 1971, London, 130–135.
5. UKTS No. 59 of 1967 (Cmnd. 3354); 600 UNTS 332.
6. IMCO Resolution A175 (VI); UK Misc. No. 7 of 1970 (Cmnd. 4347); 600 UNTS 336; 9 ILM 1. See generally E. D. Brown, *The Legal Regime of Hydrospace*, 1971, London, 135–139.
7. IMCO Resolution A232 (VII), 11 ILM 267. IMCO Resolution A246 (VII), 11 ILM 267; UK Misc. No. 36 of 1972 (Cmnd. 5071).
8. As at 30 August 1977 the following states had become parties to the 1954–62 Convention: Algeria, Argentina, Australia, Austria, Bahamas, Belgium, Bulgaria, Canada, Chile, Democratic Yemen, Denmark, Dominican Republic, Egypt, Fiji, Finland, FGR, Ghana, Greece, Iceland, India, Ireland, Israel, Italy, Ivory Coast, Japan, Jordan, Kenya, Kuwait, Lebanon, Liberia, Libya, Madagascar, Malta, Mexico, Monaco, Morocco, Netherlands, New Zealand, Nigeria, Norway, Panama, Philippines, Poland, Portugal, Saudi Arabia, Senegal, Spain, Surinam, Sweden, Switzerland, Syria, Tunisia, USSR, UK, USA, Uruguay, Venezuela, Yugoslavia. It had been extended to Netherlands Antilles and territories under USA jurisdiction.
9. UK Misc. No. 26 of 1974 (Cmnd. 5748); 12 ILM 1319.
10. Article 9.
11. Entered into force 28 May 1967.

By Article III(a), subject to certain exceptions and defences contained in Articles II, IV and V[12], 'the discharge[13] from a tanker[14] to which the present Convention applies, within any of the prohibited zones referred to in Annex A to the Convention, of oil or oily mixture[15] shall be prohibited'. Since *oil* is defined in Article I(1) as meaning 'crude oil, fuel oil, heavy diesel oil and lubricating oil'[16], it can be seen that the Convention applies only to the discharge of certain *persistent* oils: non-persistent oils such as aviation spirit are not covered. The prohibited zones referred to are (1) all sea areas within 50 miles from the nearest land[17]; (2) certain special areas defined in Annex A of the Convention[18]; (3) any area within 100 miles from the nearest land along the coasts of a state which has declared such a zone. These zones have been chosen because of the density of traffic therein and/or because of their environmental sensitivity.

It can readily be seen that from the environmental point of view this standard is virtually useless, for it allows tankers lawfully to discharge oil over the vast majority of the world's seas. While coasts are given a certain measure of protection, it is of little practical use: oil residues discharged by tankers not operating LOT are quite capable of drifting over 100 miles and of remaining in the sea for long periods. Further, it can be seen from Map 3[18] that there are 'holes' in the Black Sea and Mediterranean Sea, into which lawful discharges may be made. In view of the fact that many tankers voyaging in these seas will be on too short a haul to operate LOT, the existence of the holes is even more serious.

For these and other reasons, the 1962 Conference adopted a completely different standard for new ships of 20,000 tons grt and over. Article III(c) begins as follows: 'The discharge from a ship of 20,000 tons gross tonnage or more to which the present Convention applies and for which the building contract is placed on or after the date on which this provision comes into force, of oil or oily mixture shall be prohibited'.

12. The exceptions and defences contained in Articles II, IV and V, insofar as they concern fuel oil purification sludges and discharges from tanker machinery space bilges, are discussed in section 2.3.3 in connection with discharge standards from other ships. Insofar as they concern other matters they are not discussed here because they do not affect operational oil pollution.
13. Defined in Article I(1) as '. . . any discharge or escape howsoever caused'.
14. Defined in Article I(1) as meaning 'a ship in which the greater part of the cargo space is constructed or adapted for the carriage of liquid cargoes in bulk and which is not, for the time being, carrying a cargo other than oil in that part of its cargo space'. Thus it includes OBOs and Ore/Oil carriers when laden with oil or when empty.
15. Defined in Article I(1) as '. . . a mixture with an oil content of 100 parts or more in 1,000,000 parts of the mixture'.
16. 'Oily' is to be construed accordingly.
17. Defined as 'from the baseline from which the territorial sea of the territory in question is established in accordance with the Geneva Convention on the Territorial Sea and the Contiguous Zone, 1958'.
18. Reproduced in *Charts of Prohibited Zones*, IMCO, 1972; IMCO Sales No. 72.03.

The Article goes on to provide an exception for the situation where the Master is of opinion that special circumstances make it neither reasonable nor practicable to retain the oil on board, but this does not affect the fact that for ships covered by Article III(c) all oil would have to be retained on board in most situations. In 1962 this meant that new ships would have to be fitted with sufficient segregated ballast tankage, or operate to loading ports and repair yards which had adequate reception facilities. Clearly, the result of the amending conference was unsatisfactory in the light of the dearth of reception facilities around the world and the disinclination of governments to ensure that they were provided.

The percentage of the world tanker fleet covered by Article III(c) will increase as older, smaller vessels are scrapped and are replaced by their larger modern counterparts. However, the formulation of this provision does not accord with the operation of LOT, and it was not until 1969 that international law caught up with the practice of the industry.

2.3.2.2 The 1969 standards

The new discharge standard, which entered into force on 20 January 1978[19], looks technical but is in fact quite simple to understand. By the new Article III(b), discharges from tankers[20] are prohibited unless the following conditions are all satisfied:

'(i) the tanker is proceeding en route;
(ii) the instantaneous rate of discharge of oil content[1] does not exceed 60 litres per mile;
(iii) the total quantity of oil discharged on a ballast voyage does not exceed 1/15,000 of the total cargo-carrying capacity;
(iv) the tanker is more than 50 miles from the nearest land.'

This standard is directly tailored to the operation of LOT, and it can only be understood in those terms. When a tanker is operating LOT it will normally be empty of all cargo and will be proceeding en route for a loading port. At two points in the LOT procedure (at least) separated seawater is discharged, and this will contain traces of oil.

19. In accordance with Article XVI (4) the 1969 Amendments entered into force for all contracting states except those which declared before entry into force that they did not accept the Amendments. No such state has made such a declaration. In fact, six states had put the Amendments into force in advance of their entry into force internationally: Canada, Japan, Liberia, Sweden, USSR, and UK.
20. The definitions of discharge and tanker remain unchanged.
1. Defined in the new Article I as 'the rate of discharge of oil in litres per hour at any instant divided by the speed of the ship in knots at the same instant'.

The oil concentration will vary according to where the effluent originates – thus, the bulk of the settled dirty ballast typically contains about 30 p.p.m. of oil, the bulk of the settled slop tank water will usually contain around 150 p.p.m. and the final discharge from the slop tank may have as much as 1,000 p.p.m.[2]. Condition (ii) can therefore always be achieved by adjusting the discharge rate to suit the speed of the ship and the type of effluent being discharged[3]. However, Condition (ii) effectively prohibits the discharge of separated oil (i.e. pure oil), either from the ballast tank or the slop tank. To achieve 60 litres per mile even at 15 knots, pure oil (1 million p.p.m. effluent) could only be discharged at the rate of 0.9 m³/hr.!

Condition (iii) also effectively prohibits the discharge of separated oil by placing a limit on the total quantity of oil discharged on a ballast voyage[4]. Clingage varies from 0·1 to 1·0% of cargo volume: if all this was discharged, the limit would be greatly exceeded. The figure has been set so that if LOT is practised to a reasonable degree of efficiency, the discharge will be lawful[5].

Therefore, for a tanker to comply with the 1969 Amendments it must either operate LOT, or it must retain all its residues on board for eventual disposal ashore. The standard therefore makes life very difficult for the tanker with no segregated ballast tankage which cannot for a legitimate reason operate LOT, for it will usually be wholly[6] dependent on reception facilities for compliance with the law. This point will be further developed in discussing the legal standards relating to reception facilities[7].

The 1969 standard has replaced the old concept of oil discharges

2. Figures from, *Clean Seas Guide for Oil Tankers: The Operation of Load on Top*, Joint OCIMF/ICS publication, 1973, 18.

3. The oil discharge rate in litres per mile equals:

$$\frac{\text{p.p.m. of oil in effluent} \times \text{effluent discharge rate in m}^3/\text{hr.}}{\text{ships speed in knots} \times 1,000.}$$

Thus if the tanker is travelling at 15 knots and the bulk of separated dirty ballast is to be discharged with an expected oil content of 30 p.p.m., a discharge rate of up to 30,000 m³/hr. can be contemplated before condition (ii) is broken. But if bad weather has been encountered and the oil content is expected to be 100 p.p.m., only 9,000 m³/hr. can be discharged. Even this is a good discharge rate, so it is not difficult to keep inside condition (ii).

4. There appears to be a small error in the drafting of condition (iii). If the tanker had only carried a part cargo on her last voyage (a very rare occurrence) she can still discharge 1/15,000 of her total *capacity* – she does not have to keep to 1/15,000 of the cargo which gave rise to the residues aboard.

5. If the clingage is 0·1% of total cargo, then 6·67% of it can be discharged before the limit is exceeded – thus at least 93% (approximately) of clingage must be saved. If the crude is heavier, and the clingage is, say, 0·4% of total cargo, 1·67% of it can be discharged and 98% must be saved. If the clingage is the maximum, 1·0%, then only 0·67% of it can be discharged and 99% must be saved. These figures illustrate the dramatic effect of operating LOT.

6. It could, as a third alternative, designate certain cargo tanks as segregated or clean ballast tanks, but, as has been pointed out (section 2.2.3) this means deadfreighting the ballast capacity – and that is expensive.

7. Section 2.3.4.

being permissible except inside prohibited zones[8], with the new idea that discharges may be made if the oil is sufficiently dispersed on discharge[9]. It will be seen that technically 1/15,000 of all oil transported in tankers may be lawfully discharged to sea – the 1975 figure would have been about 100,000 tons[10] – but this must be done in an environmentally acceptable way. The standard represents a considerable improvement on the 1954 – 62 standards.

2.3.2.3 The 1971 amendments

One of the two sets of Amendments made in 1971 concerns operational pollution; IMCO Resolution A232(VII)[11] redefines the phrase 'nearest land' in Article III so that the Great Barrier Reef is given the extra protection it lost when Annex A was deleted in 1969. As at 30 June 1977 only 20 nations[12] had accepted this Amendment, while 38 were needed for entry into force.

2.3.2.4 The 1973 standards[13]

The opportunity was taken at the 1973 conference to improve the standards relating to operational oil pollution. Two standards are established: one for certain specially protected areas, another for elsewhere. These standards are contained in Annex I (Regulations for the Prevention of Pollution by Oil), and references below are to Regulations contained therein, unless otherwise stated. The other Annexes to the Convention concern matters outside the scope of this work.

a) *Outside special areas*
The standards for areas outside special areas are contained in Regulation 9(1)(a). Oil tankers may only discharge oil if certain conditions are all fulfilled, these being the same as those imposed by the 1969 and 1971 Amendments already mentioned, but with three differences: (1) for 'new tankers'[14] the total quantity of oil discharged

---

8. Annex A of the Convention is therefore deleted.
9. See section 2.2.1.
10. 1/15,000 × 1,508 million tons: *B.P. Statistical Review of the World Oil Industry, 1975.*
11. 11 ILM 267.
12. Algeria, Canada, Finland, France, Greece, Italy, Jordan, Lebanon, Liberia, Malta, New Zealand, Norway, Philippines, Saudi Arabia, Sweden, Switzerland, Syria, Tunisia, USSR, UK.
13. See section 2.3.6 for the status of this Convention.
14. Regulation 1(b) defines 'new ship' but not 'new tanker'; however, it is clear from Regulation 1(4) that an 'oil tanker' is a species of 'ship'. A 'new ship' is defined in terms of the date of its building contract, keel laying, delivery or major conversion. Basically, new ships are those ordered after 31 December 1975 or delivered after 31 December 1979. The 1978 Protocol to this Convention contains a definition of 'new oil tanker' but this is limited in application to Regulation 13, 13A to E and 18(5).

to sea must not exceed 1/30,000 of the total quantity of the particular cargo of which the residue formed a part whereas 'existing tankers'[15] need only keep to the 1/15,000 figure; (2) for the discharge to be lawful, a tanker must have in operation an oil discharge monitoring and control system and a slop tank arrangement as required by Regulation 15; (3) 'oil' is defined by Regulation 1 and Appendix 1 to include non-persistent oils.

The reduction by half of the maximum quantity of oil discharged during LOT means that the system must be operated to a much higher degree of efficiency, which can be achieved largely by improvements in shipboard equipment and design – for instance, by having more than one slop tank (a requirement which Regulation 15 makes compulsory for new oil tankers over 70,000 dwt tons) by operating crude oil washing or recirculatory washing[16], by fitting slop tank heating coils and oil/water separators, and by improving the design and siting of discharge pipe ducts in the slop tank. While this reduction is generally welcome, it will be more difficult for the smaller tanker to achieve than for the VLCC – indeed, most VLCCs already achieve the 1/30,000 limit, because they can use recirculatory or crude oil washing.

The second major change – the requirement of a Regulation 15 discharge monitoring and control system and slop tank arrangement – is of more doubtful utility. The requirements in Regulation 15 can be traced back to *Study III*, which concluded that 'present procedures depend to an undesirable degree upon the efficiency and conscientiousness of those charged with carrying them out and upon human observation and judgement.... The best prospects of further reductions in the amount of oil getting into the sea in the normal operation of ships therefore lies in eliminating as far as possible this reliance on the human element...'[17].

The result was that Regulation 15(3) requires oil tankers of 150 tons grt and above to be provided with a discharge monitoring and control system which 'shall be fitted with a recording device to provide a continuous record of the discharge in litres per nautical mile and total quantity discharged, or the oil content and rate of discharge. This record shall be identifiable as to time and date and shall be kept for at least three years. The oil discharge monitor and control system shall come into operation when there is any discharge of effluent into the sea and shall be such as will ensure that any discharge of oily mixture is

15. Regulation 1(7) defines an 'existing ship' as a ship which is not a new ship.
16. Recirculatory washing is a variant of LOT technique whereby the separated water in the slop tank is used to wash further cargo tanks, rather than being discharged. This technique considerably improves LOT performance, but may only be used where tankers are fitted with an inert gas system. A full description of the technique is contained in *Study III*.
17. *Study III*, 55.

automatically stopped when the instantaneous rate of discharge of oil exceeds that permitted by Regulation 9(1)(a) of this Annex'.

In addition, regulations concerning the size and arrangement of slop tanks are made by Regulation 15(2). These are more easily justified than the control system of paragraph (3) because they are relatively easy to comply with[18]. The control system has not been developed to a sufficient degree of accuracy to enable it to comply with paragraph (3)[19], although doubtless it will one day. The point is that the development will have been costly, and will be reflected in the price of the systems manufactured. The installation cost must be added to this, and then there is the cost of administering the new system of enforcement which the device represents. What has been achieved for such a cost? It is difficult to pinpoint anything at all. A little oil may be saved from the sea by virtue of this automatic cut-off, and a little more by the deterrent effect of discharges being more detectable: the total will be very small, and much of it will represent oil that would anyway have been discharged in a sufficiently dispersed form to enable biodegradation to take place within hours.

The new definition of oil has immense practical implications for the shipping industry, because up to the entry into force of this Convention (perhaps the early 1980s) discharges of non-persistent oils will continue to be unregulated. The preparation of the shipping and oil industries for this aspect of the Convention is under review by IMCO's relevant Committees, but there are serious difficulties involved in the development of retention-on-board techniques for this trade and in the identification of the type and volume of associated reception facilities.

The standards described above concern the problems that an oil tanker has with its cargo. Regulations 16 and 17 concern all ships, and deal with arrangements to cope with the problems associated with fuel oil and bilges. These are considered below, section 2.3.3, in connection with discharge standards from ships other than tankers. Regulation 18 makes certain requirements as to pumping, piping and discharge arrangements for oil tankers, the most important of which is that, with certain minor exceptions concerning segregated ballast, all discharges shall take place above the waterline – so that they can be seen.

b) *Special areas*
A special area is one 'where for recognised technical reasons in relation to its oceanographical and ecological condition and to the particular

18. But OBOs and gas carriers classed for the carriage of naphtha may have difficulties: see MEPC VI/4, page 3.
19. MEPC VI/4 of 30th September 1976: 'Although there are no oil content meters which have yet reached the draft specification, much development work is in progress' – per UK (page 2). The MEPC has drawn up specifications on performance for such devices: MEPC VI/17, Annex II. For further discussion see MEPC VII/19, paras. 58–62.

character of its traffic the adoption of special mandatory methods for the prevention of sea pollution by oil is required'[20]. These areas are listed in Regulation 10 and cover the Mediterranean Sea, the Baltic Sea, the Black Sea, the Red Sea and the Persian Gulf. There are no 'holes' in the Mediterranean Sea and Black Sea, as with the 1954 Convention.

The standard is the highest yet adopted: with a minor exception in favour of ships other than tankers under 400 tons grt[1], no ship may discharge any oil whatsoever while in a special area[2]. The effect is summed up in Regulation 10(2)(b): 'Such ships while in a special area shall retain on board all oil drainage and sludge, dirty ballast and tank washing waters and discharge them only to reception facilities'[3].

This makes the provision of adequate reception facilities in special areas vital[4]. The prohibition of even LOT discharges in these areas is probably justifiable. The quantity of oil saved from these seas, which at present suffer serious pollution, may have a significant effect on their cleanliness, and the initial cost of effecting this improvement will fall largely on governments rather than private companies.

2.3.3 DISCHARGE STANDARDS FOR OTHER SHIPS

We saw in Chapter 1 that operational discharges from ships other than tankers were estimated in *Study VI* to constitute about 11% of the annual loss of oil to sea from ships and offshore installations, with a further 1·4% from tanker bilges. This is nearly double the estimate for tankers operating LOT. What is perhaps more important is that much of this oil may not be discharged in the environmentally acceptable way in which LOT discharges take place. Discharge standards in relation to ships other than tankers and to tanker bilges are therefore important.

The main 1954 Convention standard is contained in Article III(b). For the first three years after the Convention comes into force for the ship's flag state, discharges need only be made, 'as far as practicable from land'. Thereafter, Article III(a) is applied to ships as it is to tankers[5], 'except that the discharge of oil or of oily mixture from such a ship shall not be prohibited when the ship is proceeding to a port not provided with such facilities for ships other than tankers as are referred to in Article VIII' – i.e. reception facilities for residues. As has

20. Regulation 1(10).
 1. Regulation 10(3)(a).
 2. Regulation 10(2)(a).
 3. The last seven words should not be read as denying the alternative of discharging the residues outside a special area in accordance with Regulation 9: see Regulation 10(5).
 4. Standards relating to reception facilities are discussed below, section 2.2.4.
 5. See section 2.3.2.1; Article III(a) prohibits discharges inside prohibited zones.

been seen[6] such facilities are lacking in many ports, so that very often a ship may discharge oil even within the prohibited zones.

These standards apply mainly to discharges of ballast water carried in fuel tanks because discharges of oil originating elsewhere in the ship are provided for separately. Discharges of fuel oil purification sludges are by Article IV(c) exempted from the operation of Article III, 'provided that such discharge is made as far from land as is practicable', and discharges of machinery space oily bilges are exempted by Article V(b) if the effluent contains only lubricating oil drained or leaked from the machinery spaces.

It can therefore be seen that the 1954 standards are environmentally useless, insofar as discharges from ships other than tankers are concerned. The 1962 Conference failed to amend Articles IV(c) and V(b), and made an ineffectual attempt to improve the dirty ballast standard by adopting Article VII(2), which states that 'carrying ballast in oil fuel tanks shall be avoided if possible'. That Conference also adopted Article III(c), which, as we have seen[7], prohibits oil discharge from large new ships except in special circumstances. However, the effect of this provision on the world's dry cargo fleet is minimal, because so few of such vessels, even today, exceed 20,000 tons grt.

The 1962 Conference actually made matters worse in one small respect. Article VII of the Convention adopted in 1954 required ships to be so fitted as to prevent the escape of fuel oils or heavy diesel oil into bilges whose contents were discharged straight to sea; in 1962 this was amended so that such fitting was required only 'so far as reasonable and practical... unless effective means are provided to ensure that the oil in the bilges is not discharged in contravention of this Convention'[8].

The 1969 Amendments greatly improved matters. Article III(a) now provides that, subject to certain exceptions and defences:

'The discharge from a ship to which the present Convention applies, other than a tanker, of oil or oily mixture shall be prohibited except when the following conditions are all satisfied:
   (i) the ship is proceeding en route;
   (ii) the instantaneous rate of discharge of oil content does not exceed 60 litres per mile;
   (iii) the oil content of the discharge is less than 100 parts per 1,000,000 parts of the mixture;
   (iv) the discharge is made as far as practicable from land'[9].

6. Section 2.2.5. The lack of reception facilities for fuel oil purification sludges has prevented ICS publishing a supplement to their Pollution Prevention Code: see MEPC VII/19, para. 31.
7. Section 2.3.2.1.
8. In 1969 this provision was extended to cover all oil, not just fuel oil and heavy diesel oil.
9. The erroneous omission of the word 'nearest' between 'from' and 'land' was corrected by the 1971 Amendment contained in IMCO Resolution 232(VII).

Significantly, the exemptions contained in Articles IV(c) and V(b) were deleted, and the discharge of oil from a tanker's machinery space bilges specifically brought within the new Article III(a) standard[10].

Conditions (ii) and (iii) of the new Article III(a) mean that oil must be discharged in an environmentally acceptable way, and in practice this means that ships must discharge oily bilges, dirty ballast and bunker tank washings through a suitable separator, and must retain on board in sludge tanks the sludges from purification of fuel oils[11]. These Amendments are a long overdue improvement[12].

The 1973 Convention seeks to improve on these standards. Regulation 9(1)(b) of Annex I replaces condition (iv) above with the requirement that the ship be outside a special area and more than 12 nautical miles from the nearest land; and it adds that the ship must have in operation an oil discharge monitoring and control system, oily-water separating equipment, oil filtering system or other installation as required by Regulation 16. The standard for special areas is the same as that for oil tankers within special areas[13], with certain minor exceptions[14].

Regulation 16 requires[15] that any ship of 400 tons grt and above be fitted with oily-water separating or filtering equipment such as will ensure that any oily mixture discharged to sea after passing through it has an oil content not exceeding 100 p.p.m. In addition, ships of 10,000 tons grt and above must be fitted *either* with an oil discharge monitoring and control system almost identical to that required for oil tankers[16] *or* with an oil filtering system which accepts the discharge from the required separating system and reduces the oil content of the effluent from not more than 100 p.p.m. to not more than 15 p.p.m.

As with the standards for oil tankers, these 1973 requirements are environmentally acceptable and superior to previous ones, but the new mandatory equipment requirements of Regulation 16 are probably not cost effective. The alternative of an oil filter which reduces the oil content of the effluent to 15 p.p.m. or less may prove more economic than the discharge monitoring and control system, and so is welcome, but since the legal limit has been set at 100 p.p.m. it is difficult to see the logic behind providing such a strict alternative.

There is an additional requirement for all ships of 400 tons grt and

---

10. New Article III(c)(ii).
11. However, there will be a real problem in relation to these sludges if more reception facilities for the contents of the sludge tanks are not rapidly provided.
12. They did not enter into force until 20 January 1978.
13. Section 2.3.2.4.
14. Regulation 10(3): ships of less than 400 tons grt may discharge effluent with an oil content of 15 p.p.m. or less, or of less than 100 p.p.m. if the ship is proceeding en route and the discharge is at least 12 nautical miles and as far as practicable from the nearest land.
15. Special provisions are made in Regulations 16(3) and (4) for ships under 400 tons grt and for existing ships.
16. See section 2.3.2.4.

above: by Regulation 17 they must be provided with sludge tanks of adequate capacity to accept the residues which cannot be dealt with in accordance with the requirements of Annex I, such as those resulting from the purification of fuel and lubricating oils and some oil leakages in machinery spaces. This important requirement is welcome, for it is the only way to deal with this problem – and in fact most ships already comply[17]. Finally, Regulation 14 requires that new ships of 4,000 gross tonnage and above other than oil tankers, and new oil tankers of 150 gross tonnage and above, shall not carry any ballast water in any oil fuel tank[18]. Hitherto, it will be remembered, this was to have been avoided 'if possible'[19]. To comply with this regulation new ships other than tankers will need to carry segregated ballast tanks, whereas most tankers can comply by using cargo tanks for ballast.

2.3.4 RECEPTION FACILITIES

The approach taken by the 1954 Convention to discharge standards clearly made the provision of adequate reception facilities important to the success of the Convention as a whole. Accordingly, Article VIII provided that governments 'shall ensure' the provision in each main port of facilities adequate for the reception of residues from oily ballast water and tank washings remaining for disposal by ships other than tankers. While the mandatory language was desirable, it was too much for some states, which entered reservations[20]. The provision was, however, deficient in that it required facilities only at main ports, only for ships other than tankers, and only for residues (rather than for sludges or the dirty ballast or washings themselves).

The 1962 Conference tried again, amending Article VIII in a number of ways. First, governments now only had to take 'all appropriate steps to promote the provision of facilities'. This provided the escape route required, so that in practice no government actually had to spend any money. However, the facilities whose provision now had to be promoted expanded to include all ports being used by ships other than tankers, although the volumetric limits remained. In addition, similar provision was made for oil cargo loading terminals and ship repair ports.

This, it can be clearly seen, was not enough, for even today the provision of reception facilities is inadequate[1]. The opportunities

17. The Convention also makes governments provide adequate reception facilities for the contents of such tanks: see section 2.3.4.
18. Except in certain abnormal circumstances: Regulation 14(2). Existing ships shall comply, 'as far as reasonable and practicable'.
19. Article VII(2), 1954–62 Convention.
20. E.g. USA (Cmnd. 1627) and Liberia (Cmnd. 1806).
 1. Section 2.2.5.

of 1969 and 1971 were not taken, and it was left to the 1973 Conference to produce some realistic standards. The failure to make the provision of these facilities mandatory is the failure of the international community of states. Had these facilities been available from 1967, no ship would today have any real excuse for discharging oil into the sea.

The 1973 Convention standards are contained in Regulations 10(7) (special areas) and 12 (other areas) of Annex I. The main provision in Regulation 12 is as follows:

> '(1) Subject to the provisions of Regulation 10 of this Annex, the Government of each Party undertakes to ensure the provision at oil loading terminals, repair ports, and in other ports in which ships have oily residues to discharge, of facilities for the reception of such residues and oily mixtures as remain from oil tankers and other ships adequate to meet the needs of the ships using them without causing undue delay to ships'.

Paragraphs (2) and (3) go on to detail the capacity of facilities and the ports where they are to be provided. Amongst others, four of the problems associated with LOT and which required adequate reception facilities for their solution are given special attention[2]. The capacity must basically be that capable of accepting what cannot be discharged in accordance with the discharge standards of the Convention[3].

Even higher standards are enacted by Regulation 10(7) for special areas, the main difference being that all oil loading terminals and repair ports and all ports handling dry cargo ships must be provided with adequate reception facilities, not just to take residues left after lawful retention-on-board techniques have been operated, but to take all the dirty ballast and tank washing waters. This is a natural complement to the almost absolute prohibition on all discharges within special areas.

These standards are, at last, realistic, and they are greatly welcomed. It is to be hoped that they will be fulfilled within the time limits set[4].

2.3.5 SEGREGATED BALLAST, DEDICATED BALLAST AND CRUDE OIL WASHING

The 1973 Convention provided a legal requirement for segregated ballast tanks for the first time: Regulation 13 of Annex I provided that

2. Short-haul tankers, coastal tankers, pre-maintenance washing and OBOs – see sections 2.2.3.2, 3, 5 and 6 above.
3. See sections 2.3.2 and 2.3.3.
4. Regulations 12(4), 10(7)(a)(i), 10(7)(b)(i) and 10(7)(b)(vii).

every new oil tanker[5] of 70,000 tons dwt and above must be provided with segregated ballast tanks of specified capacity, and that in no case should ballast water be carried in the oil tanks of such a vessel except in weather conditions so severe that, in the opinion of the master, it would be necessary to carry additional ballast water therein for the safety of the ship.

Such provisions were a welcome addition to legal standards, because the extra building cost for such large vessels was reasonable, tanker owners did not have to retrofit existing ships, and the benefits were obvious: there is no doubt that such tankers need to discharge much less oil than their non-segregated sisters. The provisions had the further merit of being limited to oil tankers, so that other vessels not really needing segregated ballast tanks did not have to have them.

However, the 1978 Protocol to the 1973 Convention replaces[6] these provisions with a completely new[7] and greatly extended set of regulations. References in this section and in section 2.3.6 are to the amended texts of the relevant Regulations of Annex I of the 1973 Convention, unless otherwise stated. As explained in section 2.3.6, the provisions of the Protocol form a 'package' which represents a delicate compromise between the two main schools of thought represented at the 1978 Conference. Nevertheless, three clearly discernible principles are followed:

1) the provisions should be more onerous with increasing size of vessel;
2) the provisions should be more onerous for crude oil carriers than for product carriers;
3) the provisions should be more onerous for new vessels than for existing vessels.

Hence, the most onerous provisions are for new crude oil VLCCs.

A blanket application of these principles would, however, have failed to take account of individual cases, and so would have resulted either in undue hardship or completely unnecessary over-regulation, or both. The Conference therefore increased the complexity of the provisions by including a limited number of exceptions. The resulting Regulations are so detailed that only the major provisions can find space here, but it is hoped that this will at least ease the path of those who must have recourse to the text of the Protocol itself.

5. A new oil tanker was defined by Regulations 1(4) and (6) as, broadly speaking, one ordered after 31 December 1975 or delivered after 31 December 1979.
6. It is anticipated that, now that the Protocol has been adopted, states will become party to the Protocol rather than to the 1973 Convention, the Protocol containing in Article I(1) an obligation to give effect to the 1973 Convention as amended. See section 2.3.6 for an explanation of this mechanism.
7. The provisions of the 1973 version of Regulation 13 are in fact re-enacted, but using different wording.

2.3.5.1 Crude oil tankers

a) *New crude oil tankers*

By Regulation 13(1) every[8] new crude oil tanker[9] of 20,000 tons deadweight and above must be provided with segregated ballast tanks of specified capacity, and may not carry ballast water in cargo tanks except where necessitated by very severe weather conditions (and if this does happen, the discharge of such ballast must be made in accordance with the discharge standards of the Convention[10] and the cargo tanks used must have been crude oil washed). Thus, the limit for compulsory segregation of ballast has been reduced by the Protocol from 70,000 to 20,000 tons dwt.

In addition, every new crude oil tanker of 20,000 tons dwt and above must, by Regulation 13(6), be fitted with a cargo tank cleaning system using crude oil washing, which, with limited exceptions to account for practical difficulties, must be operated in accordance with and conform to specifications contained in Regulation 13B and Resolution 15 of the 1978 Conference[11]. These requirements include the fitting of an inert gas system[12].

b) *Existing crude oil tankers*

An essential ingredient in the compromise adopted by the 1978 Conference was that, while segregated ballast tanks and crude oil washing could be made concurrent requirements for new crude oil tankers, such a requirement was financially too onerous if applied to existing tankers, and so they must be alternatives for such vessels. A third alternative, the operation of dedicated ballast tanks ('clean ballast tanks'), was also introduced. These alternatives are qualified, in the case of existing tankers, by special provisions relating to tankers engaged in specific trades and tankers already having special ballast arrangements[13].

Accordingly, by Regulations 13(7) and (8) every existing crude oil tanker[14] (unless exempted pursuant to Regulations 13C and 13D) of 40,000 tons dwt and above must comply with the segregated ballast

8. Regulation 1(5) provides that the vessel's flag state may make separate provision for the segregated ballast in tankers less than 150 metres in length.
9. Regulation 1(29) defines 'crude oil tanker' as an oil tanker engaged in the trade of carrying crude oil. Regulation 1(28) defines 'crude oil'. Regulation 1(26) defines 'new oil tanker' in such a way that those vessels which would have had to have segregated ballast tanks according to the old provisions of Regulation 13 must still have them; the new provisions on segregated ballast and crude oil washing apply, broadly speaking, to vessels ordered after 1 June 1979 or delivered after 1 June 1982.
10. See section 2.3.2.4.
11. The specifications contained in Resolution 15 may be revised by IMCO.
12. See further section 3.1, footnote 11.
13. These provisions are contained in Regulations 13C and 13D. They are not further dealt with in this work. See also Resolution 16 of the 1978 Conference, by which IMCO may develop these exemptions.
14. An 'existing oil tanker' is defined in Regulation 1(27) as an oil tanker which is not a 'new oil tanker'.

tank requirements for new crude oil tankers of 20,000 tons dwt and above (described above) from the date on which the Protocol enters into force[15]; alternatively, every such tanker must comply with the crude oil washing requirements described above. A further alternative is provided by Regulation 13(9) for a limited period varying with the deadweight of the tanker, whereby the vessel may operate with dedicated ballast tanks ('clean ballast tanks') in accordance with specifications contained in Regulation 13A and Resolution 14 of the 1978 Conference[16].

2.3.5.2 Product carriers

There can be little justification for the new provisions on segregated ballast and dedicated ballast introduced for product carriers by the 1978 Protocol to the 1973 Convention. It was seen in section 2.3.2.4 that the discharge standards for white oils introduced for the first time by the 1973 Convention are sufficiently vigorous to ensure that there is no environmental danger from operational discharges by product carriers.

a) *New product carriers*
By Regulation 13(1), every[17] new product carrier[18] of 30,000 tons dwt and above must comply with the same segregated ballast tank requirement as for a new crude oil tanker of 20,000 tons dwt and above (see section 2.3.5.1), although of course there is no requirement that ballast taken into cargo tanks during very severe weather must be taken into a tank which has been crude oil washed; neither is there an additional requirement that a product carrier be fitted for crude oil washing (since by definition[18] product carriers do not carry crude oil).

The old Regulation 13 of the 1973 Convention had applied to product carriers as to crude oil tankers, and so the 1978 Protocol achieves a lowering of the limit from 70,000 to 30,000 tons dwt.

b) *Existing product carriers*
The same principle of alternatives is followed here as for crude oil tankers, but of course the cargo washing alternative is absent. Hence,

---

15. Not expected before 1981. See further section 2.3.6.
16. Resolution 14 may be revised by IMCO.
17. Regulation 1(5) provides that the vessel's flag state may make separate provision for the segregated ballast in tankers less than 150 metres in length.
18. Regulation 1(30) defines 'product carrier' as an oil tanker engaged in the trade of carrying oil, other than crude oil.

Regulation 13(10) provides that from the date of entry into force of the Protocol, every existing product carrier of 40,000 tons dwt and above shall comply with the same segregated ballast tank requirements as for new product carriers (described above), or alternatively operate with dedicated ballast tanks in accordance with Regulation 13A and Resolution 14 of the 1978 Conference. This alternative, unlike that for existing crude oil tankers, is available permanently.

2.3.6 THE INTERNATIONAL CONFERENCE ON TANKER SAFETY AND POLLUTION PREVENTION 1978

The detailed study of the circumstances surrounding the calling of this Conference belongs to books on the politics of pollution control. It is enough here to state that, in response to demands by the United States, made as a result of a series of incidents in November and December 1976, the Conference was held in London from 6 to 17 February 1978[19].

The main work of the Conference was divided into three committees. The work of Committee Two covered enforcement, steering gear and radar and collision avoidance aids, and these matters are dealt with in section 3.4. The work of Committee Three covered the controversial questions of segregated ballast tanks, dedicated ballast tanks, double bottoms and protective layout of segregated ballast tanks, crude oil washing and inert gas systems: the provisions relating to these are mentioned elsewhere in this work[20]. The form of the regulations finally adopted on these matters is the result of a compromise on all of them – no one issue was treated in isolation to the others. This explains the complex and somewhat arbitrary form of the individual provisions.

Committee One discussed the form of the instruments to be adopted and the entry into force requirements. These matters require brief mention here. As to the form of the instruments, the problems faced are well summarised in the Report of the joint MSC/MEPC meeting[1] preceding the Conference. The solution adopted by the Conference was to adopt two Protocols, one to SOLAS 74 and one to the 1973 Convention. These two Protocols are quite different in character, being tailored to the status in 1978 of the Conventions to which they relate. The SOLAS 74 is close to entry into force, and so its Protocol takes the usual form of a quite separate contract which

19. The background to the Conference is recited in MSC/MEPC/10, paras. 6–14.
20. See section 2.3.5 for segregated ballast, dedicated ballast and crude oil washing; section 3.1, footnote 11, for inert gas systems; section 3.4 for double bottoms and protective layout of segregated ballast tanks.
 1. MSC/MEPC/10, paras. 21–44.

only parties to SOLAS 74 are eligible to ratify or accede to. The entry into force provisions of the Protocol are less strict than those of SOLAS 74: the Convention requires ratification or accession by 25 states the combined merchant fleets of which constitute not less than 50% of the gross tonnage of the world's merchant shipping and enters into force twelve months thereafter[2], whereas the Protocol requires the same percentage of world tonnage but needs only 15 ratifications or accessions and enters into force six months thereafter (but not before SOLAS 74 has entered into force)[3]. It is therefore hoped that SOLAS 74 and its Protocol can enter into force at about the same time. Resolution 2 of the Conference recommends that all Governments adopt a target date of June 1979 for the entry into force of both instruments. The chances of even the keenest states being able to pass the necessary legislation in time to enable this target date to be achieved are remote.

The Protocol to the 1973 Convention is in a quite different form, being modelled on the 1975 Montreal Protocol (No. 4) to the 1929 Warsaw Convention for the Unification of Certain Rules relating to International Carriage by Air. At the time of the 1978 Conference, the 1973 Convention had been ratified or acceded to by just three states – Kenya, Jordan and Tunisia. It was a long way off entry into force, having the same requirements as SOLAS 74 (with variations for its Annexes)[4]. The technical difficulties involved in compliance with Annex II (noxious liquid substances)[5], which was a compulsory Annex, prolonged the entry into force of the Convention and Annex I beyond the date which could be achieved if Annex II, like Annexes III to V, was to become optional, or if its entry into force was delayed.

Consequently the Protocol to the 1973 Convention contains two features to try and remedy these problems. The first is that parties to the Protocol undertake to give effect to the provisions of the Protocol and the Convention[6]: hence, a state may become party to both instruments at once, and there is no need to separately ratify or accede to the 1973 Convention. Kenya, Jordan and Tunisia will, it is hoped, now become parties to the Protocol. The second feature is that, by Article II, parties to the Protocol 'agree that they shall not be bound by the provision of Annex II of the Convention for a period of three years from the date of entry into force of the present Protocol or for such longer period as may be decided by a two-thirds majority of the Parties to the present Protocol...'. By Article V, the Protocol will enter into force twelve months after not less than fifteen states, the

2. Article X, SOLAS 74.
3. Article V(1) of the Protocol.
4. Article 15 of the 1973 Convention.
5. The main technical difficulties are summarised by the United Kingdom in MEPC VI/4, and include the provision of adequate port reception facilities for chemical residues and meeting the discharge requirements for effluent containing certain noxious liquid substances.
6. Article I(1) of the Protocol.

combined merchant fleets of which constitute not less than 50% of the gross tonnage of the world's merchant shipping, have become parties to it.

As a result, Resolution 1 of the 1978 Conference sets June 1981 as the target date for the entry into force of the Protocol (and hence of the 1973 Convention as amended by it). As with the target date set for the Protocol to SOLAS 74, this date seems impossibly early, for it gives states just two years to introduce complicated legislation and to solve the technical difficulties of compliance with Annex I of the 1973 Convention (e.g. the development of the oil content meter demanded by Regulation 15 of Annex I[7]).

2.4 Conclusions

It can now be seen that many of the major contributions to the reduction of operational oil pollution have been made by the oil and shipping industries, rather than by the international community of states. LOT, crude oil washing, the ICS Code, were all the result of industry initiative; by contrast, the major contribution which the international community of states could have made – the provision of adequate reception facilities all around the world – has not been achieved even yet. This may be thought by some to be an appropriate state of affairs: after all, it is from the ships that the oil escapes. However, it is clear that everyone has an interest in the transport of oil by sea, in clean seas and in clean beaches, and that it is therefore appropriate that no one section of society bear an undue burden in solving the problem of oil pollution.

It is also clear that legal standards did not properly address the operational oil pollution problem until 1969, and even then there was a marked failure to amend the provisions relating to reception facilities. Of course, part of the problem was that LOT was not invented until after the 1962 Conference, but the fact remains that the 1969 Amendments did not enter into force internationally[8] until 20 January 1978 – fourteen years after LOT had become established. At one level this is due to the large proportion of ratifications required for entry into force of an Amendment under Article XVI(4) of the 1954–62 Convention (two-thirds of the Contracting Governments), but on a more fundamental level it is due to the reluctance of states to deal with the problem. Happily, it seems that there was a change of attitude in 1973. Not only are the standards in that Convention the first

7. See sections 2.3.2.4 and 4.1.
8. Canada, Japan. Liberia, Sweden, USSR, and UK had put them into force municipally by 1 January 1977.

comprehensive set to take a realistic attitude to solving the problem, but the amendment procedure in Article 16 includes the possibility of a streamlined entry into force for certain amendments.

International legal standards have not, therefore, significantly contributed to the eradiction of operational oil pollution so far. This will have changed on 20 January 1978 when the 1969 Amendments entered into force, but then there are still problems for those tankers unable to operate LOT trading to ports not equipped with adequate reception facilities. There is therefore an urgent legal, as well as an environmental, reason why the provision of such reception facilities should be a priority. By contrast, when the 1973 Convention and its 1978 Protocol enter into force, the problem of standards, and of facilities in the states party to the Convention, should be solved, and it will remain only to induce as many countries as possible to ratify.

The adoption of the 1978 Protocol to the 1973 Convention avoided the worst excesses of the United States proposals for mandatory retrofitting of segregated ballast tanks on all new and existing tankers, by limiting such provisions to new tankers and by granting alternatives to existing tankers; but the application of such provisions to product carriers seems to be taking the process rather too far. The danger is from crude oil carriers, not the carriers of refined products (which are non-persistent). The fact that all new tankers of 30,000 tons dwt and above, whether carrying crude oil or products, must have segregated ballast tanks means that from the date on which the Protocol enters into force more ships (burning more valuable bunkers) will be needed to carry the same quantity of cargo. The person who will pay for all this is, ultimately, the consumer: it would be worth it, perhaps, if the seas really were going to be significantly cleaner as a result, but there is little evidence to suggest this, and the same effect as will be achieved could have been achieved more cheaply without such requirements.

The priorities for action to deal with operational oil pollution must therefore be as follows. First, the immediate provision of adequate reception facilities in accordance with the 1973 Convention must be put in hand without waiting for the entry into force of that Convention. The use of redundant tankers should be considered in appropriate cases, because of the advantages this brings – cheapness of installation and flexibility of reaction to demand. The achievement of this objective will deal with the bulk of the problem posed by tankers which cannot operate LOT and with the problem of operational oil pollution from ships other than tankers.

Second, immediate widespread acceptance of the ICS Code should be encouraged. This would deal with the remainder of the problem posed by tankers which cannot operate LOT. In this connection, states should consider removing legal barriers to their nationals joining the scheme.

Third, states should continue, through IMCO, to prepare to bring the 1973 Convention and its 1978 Protocol into force. There are still difficulties in the way of entry into force, but these are not insoluble, given concerted effort by states and industry alike.

When these objectives are achieved, the equipment necessary for the complete eradication of operational oil pollution will exist, there will be the necessary standards to enforce, and so the problem will be largely solved. It will then remain to deal with the problem of accidental oil pollution.

3 Accidental Discharges[1]

3.1 The nature of the problem

Accidental spillage of oil from ships occurs either in association with an operational procedure aboard ship – e.g. while loading or discharging oil cargo, lightening, bunkering, ballasting or deballasting – or in association with an accident to the vessel – e.g. as a result of collision, stranding, foundering or fire.

It is well known by shipowners and in the industry generally that the vast majority of incidents occur in association with operational procedures aboard ship, but that the vast majority of oil spilled occurs as a result of accidents to the vessel. Thus, the preliminary findings of an ongoing study published in 1975 indicate that less than 3% of incidents occurring to tankers of 5,000 tons dwt and above take place at sea[2], but that these incidents include those causing seven-eighths of the larger spills – i.e. those over 5,000 barrels (about 680 tonnes).

From a numerical point of view, oil spills in port are therefore very important, but they tend to be rather small in size. Further, the facilities in port for cleaning up the spillage quickly and efficiently are often available, and if not, can be brought to the scene in a short period of time. Control of this type of spill is clearly a matter for the port state, there being no international jurisdictional problem. For these reasons, in-port spills are not dealt with further.

Results of four worldwide studies are summarised in Table 3.1[3]. It

1. For a general survey of the problem of accidental marine oil pollution, see *Accidental Oil Pollution of the Sea*, Dept. of the Environment, Central Unit on Environmental Pollution, Pollution Paper No. 8, HMSO, 1976.
2. M. J. Garnett and J. Wardley Smith, *Oil Spills from Tankers*, Paper presented to the IMCO Symposium on Prevention of Pollution from Ships, 22–31 March 1976, IMCO Doc. SYMP X/6. The authors state that their figures 'are drawn from such a limited number of spills that they can only illustrate the problem. They must be treated with considerable caution since they are not conclusive and are not presented as such'. The data was selected from information on 1,500 spills occurring worldwide between 1 January 1974 and 30 June 1975.
3. COLUMN 1: V. F. Keith and J. D. Porricelli, 'An Analysis of Oil Outflows Due to Tanker Accidents', *Proceedings of Joint Conference on Prevention and Control of Oil Spills, March 13–15, 1973, Washington D.C.*, 3. A study of 1,416 tanker casualties (100 grt and over) resulting in 269 spills during 1969 and 1970, of which 266 were analysed in detail.

is important to appreciate that these surveys can only be used to draw very broad conclusions, because the data on which they are founded cannot be regarded as very accurate. Particular problems are encountered in estimating the amount of oil actually spilled in an incident, and, when it comes to comparing surveys, in deciding whether any given accident would have been included, and if so, would have been characterised in the same way in each study. Obviously, the wider the survey and the more detailed the data on which it is based, the more reliable will be its results; there is hope that when the results of the study currently under way at TOVALOP headquarters are published[4], the most accurate picture yet will become available. IMCO is also attempting a study[5].

Collision and grounding will be looked at together because they are both often caused by navigational errors: hence, steps taken to reduce the casualty rate due to the one can be expected to have a like effect on the casualty rate due to the other.

Comparison of the figures in the first row enable certain background conclusions to be drawn, namely that the navigational casualties are numerically the most important source of accidents to tankers. Results on the distribution of other causes are insufficiently homogeneous to enable useful conclusions to be drawn, beyond the obvious ones that structural failure and fire and explosion are both significant.

It is clear from the figures in the second row that the proportion of accidents to tankers which actually give rise to spillages is about one fifth. The next row gives details of how that proportion is distributed amongst the various causes, and it is immediately apparent that again the navigational casualties are the most important. However, here there is much more homogeneity in the distribution of the remainder. Structural failure emerges as the second most important cause, with fire and explosion running third. While this provides useful information on the pattern of spillage risks, it must be combined with the information in the last row to give a better idea of the pollution risks.

A number of interesting points emerge from a comparison of the

footnote 3 contd.

COLUMN 2: C. Grimes, 'A Survey of Marine Accidents with Particular Reference to Tankers', *Journal of Navigation*, Vol. 25 (1972), 496. A study of 13,379 tanker accidents (100 grt and over) from 1959 to 1968.

COLUMN 3: Ecocentre, *Accidental Pollution of the Sea by Oil*, IMCO Doc. MP XIII/2(a)/9. A study of 231 major tanker accidents (7,000 dwt and over), excluding fire and explosion of tankers in light condition, from 1960 to 1970, resulting in 75 spills.

COLUMN 4: J. C. Card, P. V. Ponce and W. D. Snider, 'Tankship Accidents and Resulting Oil Outflows, 1969–73', *Proceedings of Joint Conference on Prevention and Control of Oil Spills, March 13–15, 1975, Washington D.C.*, 205. A study of 3,183 tanker involvements (3,000 dwt and over) from 1969 to 1973, of which 452 resulted in spillage.

4. The preliminary findings of this study, and a description of the research being conducted, are published in SYMP X/6 of 14 October 1975.

5. MEPC VII/19, paras. 16–21.

last two rows. First, while navigational casualties retain their eminence when taken together, groundings emerge as a much more dangerous pollution risk than collisions. Second, structural failures are much

TABLE 3.1 Tanker accidents and oil spillage

	1. V. F. Keith 1969–70	*2. C. Grimes* 1959–68	*3. Ecocentre* 1960–70	*4. J. C. Card* 1969–73
1. All accidents to tankers				
Percentage due to:				
Collisions		33·7⎫	39·3⎫	23·4⎫
Groundings		14·1⎭47·8	29·3⎭68·6	24·8⎭48·2
Structural failure		*	12·9	16·1
Fire and explosion		5·2+	18·5	9·5
Other		47·0*	nil	25·2
2. Proportion of all accidents to tankers giving rise to spillage				
Percentage	19·0		32·5	14·4
3. All accidents to tankers causing spillage				
Percentage due to:				
Collisions	30·8⎫		32·0⎫	27·9⎫
Groundings	26·3⎭57·1		48·0⎭80·0	27·2⎭55·5
Structural failure	19·1		17·3	20·8
Fire and explosion	12·8		2·7	10·6
Other	11·0		nil	13·5
4. Oil spilled				
Percentage due to:				
Collisions	8·0⎫		16·3⎫	19·4⎫
Groundings	28·8⎭36·8		62·4⎭78·7	24·2⎭43·6
Structural failure	49·3		18·4	35·6
Fire and explosion	8·9		2·9	10·2
Other	5·0		nil	10·6

* STRUCTURAL FAILURE not distinguished, so included in OTHER.

+ Figure for FIRE only.

Blank spaces indicate that the relevant information was not published.

more important in terms of oil spilled than in terms of numbers of accidents to tankers, from which it may be concluded that, when a structural failure does occur giving rise to a spill, the spill tends to be significant. This stands to reason: even small leaks are difficult to repair quickly, and when a ship breaks in two the oil spillage is likely to be high. Further, if a structural failure leads to a sinking, the entire cargo would be recorded as spilled. Third, fire and explosion occupy much the same position with regard to oil spilled as with regard to the number of tanker accidents causing spillage.

It may be concluded at this stage that the major pollution problems are structural failure and grounding; that collision, followed by fire and explosion, are of secondary importance; and that divers other causes follow these. This pattern must be seen in the context of the information available concerning the location of accidents. It is clear that the majority of casualties take place near coasts: V. F. Keith et al.[6] conclude that 78% of tanker accidents causing spillage whose locations were known took place in harbours, estuaries, entrances or coastal areas, causing 43% of oil spilled; C. Grimes[7] concluded that 85% of tanker accidents in N. W. European waters occurred within five miles of a coast, and J. C. Card et al.[8] concluded that 77·8% of accidents to tankers causing spillage occurred within 50 miles of land. These consistently high figures are explicable on the basis that it is close to land that the highest traffic densities occur, and that water depth is shallowest.

While it does not appear explicitly from information published in three of the four studies, it may be inferred that the vast majority of groundings take place within 50 miles of land, and that the majority of structural failures – largely associated with bad weather – take place out to sea[9]. Consequently, these considerations tend to equate the importance of structural failure and grounding, where Table 3.1 shows the former to be more important.

It follows from the pattern which has emerged that the standards of international law which are most relevant to the problem of accidental oil pollution are those relating to navigation, the design of ships and their condition, and fire safety measures aboard tankers. To this list we must add personnel standards, for it is apparent that good navigation and safety generally are dependent on good personnel. These

6. 'An Analysis of Oil Outflows Due to Tanker Accidents', *Proceedings of Joint Conference on Prevention and Control of Oil Spills, March 13–15, 1973, Washington, D.C.*, 11.

7. 'A Survey of Marine Accidents with Particular Reference to Tankers', *Journal of Navigation*, Vol. 25 (1972), 501.

8. 'Tankship Accidents and Resulting Oil Outflows, 1969–73', *Proceedings of Joint Conference on Prevention and Control of Oil Spills, March 13–15, 1975, Washington, D.C.*, 213.

9. J. C. Card et al., 'Tankship Accidents and Resulting Oil Outflows, 1969–73', *Proceedings of Joint Conference on Prevention and Control of Oil Spills, March 13–15, 1975, Washington, D.C.*, 213, show nil groundings, and 69·5% of the structural failures, resulting in spillage occurring at sea.

standards will be examined in the remainder of this chapter, with the exception of fire safety. This topic is dealt with admirably elsewhere[10], and it suffices here to mention the relevant provisions in a footnote[11]. The international community does have the question of fire and explosion under close scrutiny through IMCO committees.

Two further points may be mentioned before the law is examined. First, all three of the studies which investigated the role of a tanker's age in relation to structural failure found, as might be expected, a marked preponderance of such casualties amongst the older vessels, the breakpoint being about 15 years[12]. This can be accounted for on various assumptions; structural defects can be expected to take some time to become apparent; metal fatigue takes time to develop; older ships do not have the design advantages of more modern ships; and corrosion and erosion take time to develop, although of course they can be combatted by good maintenance.

Second, there is the emotional question of how dangerous are the big tankers. The sheer size of some modern VLCCs has led to the voicing of fears in the popular press that they represent an inordinate threat to the environment. However, all four studies are united in concluding that there is no evidence to suggest that VLCCs are more prone to accidents than smaller vessels, or that they give rise to more oil spillage; indeed, the evidence points to the opposite conclusion, and it seems that it is the smaller vessels which are the most prone to accidents and which give rise to most pollution, not only cumulatively, but in some cases also in relation to the size distribution of the world

10. R. C. Page and A. Ward Gardner, *Petroleum Tankship Safety*, London, 1971; *International Oil Tanker and Terminal Safety Guide*, OCIMF, London, 2nd ed., 1974.
11. Chapter II, Parts D, E and F, SOLAS 60 and Chapter II-2, SOLAS 74 deal with fire protection, detection and extinction, the provisions of the latter Convention being much stricter and more comprehensive than those of the former and including a special part (Part E) on fire safety measures for tankers. Since then the IMCO Assembly has adopted Resolution A.327(IX) and the International Tanker Safety and Pollution Prevention Conference 1978 has adopted a Protocol to SOLAS 74. Regulations 60 and 62 of Chapter II-2 of SOLAS 74 required inert gas systems to be fitted to all new crude oil and product carriers of 100,000 tonnes dwt and above and to all new combination carriers of 50,000 tonnes dwt and above. The Protocol replaces the text of Regulation 60 with a new text and makes other amendments having the following effect (in summary): new crude oil and product carriers of 20,000 tonnes dwt and above must be fitted with inert gas systems complying with Regulation 62 (or an equivalent); existing crude oil tankers of 20,000 tonnes dwt and above, after a date varying with deadweight, must have such equipment (subject to certain exceptions); and existing product carriers of 40,000 tonnes dwt and above, and of 20,000 tonnes dwt and above if fitted with high capacity washing machines, after a date varying with deadweight, must have such equipment. Resolution 5 of the 1978 Conference provides for IMCO to develop international standards for inert gas systems. For preparatory materials on inert gas systems see MSC/MEPC/10, paras. 105–108 and Annex XX; TSPP III/8, paras. 21–23; TSPP II/2, paras. 17–23 and Annex VI.
12. V. F. Keith et al., 'An Analysis of Oil Outflows Due to Tanker Accidents', *Proceedings of Joint Conference on Prevention and Control of Oil Spills, March 13–15, 1973, Washington D.C.*, 9; Ecocentre, *Accidental Pollution of the Sea by Oil*, IMCO Doc. MP XIII/2(a)/9, Vol. II, 98; J. C. Card et al., 'Tankship Accidents and Resulting Oil Outflows, 1969–73', *Proceedings of Joint Conference on Prevention and Control of Oil Spills*, March 13–15, 1975, Washington D.C., 212.

fleet[13]. Calls for a legal limit on the size of vessels consequently seem misplaced; the need for such measures is further obviated by the 1971 Amendments (Tanks) to the 1954 Convention and the 1978 Protocol to the 1973 Convention (both discussed below[14]).

In so far as the relative importance of accidental spillages and operational discharges is concerned, it should be remembered that accidents often cause a large quantity of oil to be discharged at once, whereas operational discharges are characterised by discharges of relatively small quantities at a time – even though, as was seen in Table 1.1, these discharges collectively account for more oil reaching the sea. This means that the contribution to the costs of oil pollution made by accidental spills is proportionately greater than its contribution to the total quantity of oil spilled.

One may conclude therefore, that, from the environmental point of view, accidents should be considered as being much more important than a simple glance at Table 1.1 would indicate. Indeed, there seem to be good grounds for elevating accidents to the status of operational discharges, so far as causing pollution is concerned.

3.2 Navigational standards

3.2.1 INTERNATIONAL CONVENTIONS

There are three current international agreements on safety of life at sea, each of which contains basic navigational standards. The earliest, the International Convention for the Safety of Life at Sea 1948[15], with Collision Regulations attached[16], is still in force as between 36 states, most of which have few, if any, ships. The current instruments are the International Convention for the Safety of Life at Sea 1960[17], and the International Regulations for Preventing Collisions at Sea 1960[18], both designed to replace the 1948 instruments, which accordingly do not merit study here.

13. V. F. Keith et al., 'An Analysis of Oil Outflows Due to Tanker Accidents', *Proceedings of Joint Conference on Prevention and Control of Oil Spills, March 13–15, 1973, Washington D.C.*, 8; C. Grimes, 'A Survey of Marine Accidents with Particular Reference to Tankers', *Journal of Navigation*, Vol. 25 (1972), 504; Ecocentre, *Accidental Pollution of the Sea by Oil*, IMCO, Doc. MP XIII/2(a)/9, Vol. II, 68; J. C. Card et al., 'Tankship Accidents and Resulting Oil Outflows, 1969–73', *Proceedings of Joint Conference on Prevention and Control of Oil Spills*, March 13–15, 1975, Washington D.C., 211 (Fig. 8).
14. Section 3.4.
15. UKTS No. 1 of 1953 (Cmd. 8720); 164 UNTS 113.
16. UKTS No. 4 of 1954 (Cmd. 9050); 191 UNTS 3.
17. UKTS No. 65 of 1965 (Cmnd. 2812); 536 UNTS 27. This Convention entered into force 26 May 1965, and replaces the SOLAS 1948 as between parties thereto. As at 30 December 1976, 96 states had become party to this Convention, including the world's major maritime states.
18. UKTS No. 23 of 1966 (Cmnd. 2956). Entered into force 1 September 1965. As at 30 December 1976, 70 states had agreed to accept and apply the Regulations.

SOLAS 1960 has been amended regularly since its entry into force[19], but as at 30 December 1976 none of these amendments had gained sufficient acceptances to enter into force. Partly with the hope of bringing the provisions of these amendments into force, they were readopted with other changes in the International Convention for the Safety of Life at Sea 1974[20]. The 1960 Regulations were also altered by the Convention on the International Regulations for Preventing Collisions at Sea 1972[1], which entered into force on 15 July 1977.

The 1960 Convention and Regulations between them lay down basal international standards relating to the navigation of all ships on the high seas and, although they have as their prime object the saving of life, it is clear that they are directly relevant to the prevention of collisions and stranding, and so are environmentally important. Almost every aspect of navigation safety is dealt with, including lights and shapes, behaviour in restricted and unrestricted visibility, speed of vessels, equipment to be carried on board[2], manning, danger messages and even the Ice Patrol. By far the most important provisions from the oil pollution point of view are those concerning ships' routeing. Regulation 8 of Chapter V of SOLAS 60 recognises that, 'the practice of following recognised routes across the North Atlantic . . . has contributed to the avoidance of collisions between ships and with icebergs', and so, 'should be recommended to all ships concerned'. The selection of routes and so on is left to the shipping companies, with assistance from contracting governments, but proposed routes must be publicised. Contracting governments undertake to, 'use their influence to induce the owners of all passenger ships crossing the Atlantic to follow the recognised routes, and to do everything in their power to ensure adherence to such routes in the converging areas by all ships, so far as circumstances will permit'.

In 1964 an investigation by the UK Institute of Navigation discovered that between 87% and 100% of mariners (depending on the country from which they came) favoured routeing, specifically in the Dover Strait[3]. The idea having thus received considerable impetus, IMCO began devising traffic separation schemes and incorporating

19. IMCO Resolutions A108 (ES III) of 1966; A122(V) of 1967; A146 (ES IV) of 1968; A174(VI) and A184(VI) of 1969; A205(VII) of 1971; and A263(VIII), A264(VIII) and A265(VIII) of 1973.

20. IMCO Sales No. 75.01. The Convention was not in force as at 30 December 1977.

1. UK Misc. No. 28 of 1973 (Cmnd. 5471). As at 30 December 1976, 33 states had become parties to this Convention.

2. One particular failing of SOLAS 60 was that no radar had to be carried: see Regulation 12 of Chapter V, dealing only with Radio-Direction-Finding Apparatus. This was not amended until 1968 (by IMCO Resolution A146 (ES IV), when it became mandatory for ships of 1,600 tons gross and above. Neither this Amendment, nor the equivalent provision of SOLAS 74, were in force as at 1 January 1977.

3. *The Separation of Traffic at Sea, Report of a Working Group*, Institute of Navigation, London, 1964. A brief history of routeing is contained in L. Oudet, 'The Economics of Traffic Circulation', *Journal of Navigation*, Vol. 25 (1972) 60.

them into Resolutions, of which a large body now exists. They recommend predetermined routes, deep water routes and areas to be avoided in certain parts of the Baltic Sea, Western European Waters including the English Channel, the Mediterranean, the Persian Gulf and the Atlantic and Pacific coasts of North America[4].

In 1971 the IMCO Assembly adopted an amendment to Regulation 8 of Chapter V of SOLAS 60[5] which made significant changes, including the recognition of IMCO as 'the only international body for establishing and adopting measures on an international level concerning routeing', while the selection of routes 'will be primarily the responsibility of the Governments concerned'. Significantly, 'where the Organisation (IMCO) has adopted traffic separation schemes which specify one-way traffic lanes, ships using these lanes *shall proceed in the specified direction* of traffic flow' (author's italics). Aware that all these words are meaningless without some form of sanction, the General Assembly also passed Resolution A228(VII), which recommends that enforcement in such cases shall be executed by Governments making it an offence for ships of their flag to contravene.

The mandatory wording of this amendment was adopted in Rule 10 of the 1972 Collision Regulations as well, so that when they entered into force on 15 July 1977 it became binding on the ships registered in states party to these Regulations to comply with the schemes adopted by IMCO. It is to be hoped that this will have a significant effect on collisions and groundings[6]. Unfortunately, at the 1974 Conference on the Safety of Life at Sea, convened by IMCO to draw up a new Convention, the 1971 Amendment (which formed one of the reference papers upon which the Conference proceeded) was not fully incorporated. While the recognition of IMCO as the only international body for adopting routeing schemes was retained, the old, ambiguous formula was reverted to. Chapter V, Regulation 8 of SOLAS 74 reads as follows: '. . . (d) Contracting Governments will use their influence to secure the appropriate use of adopted routes and will do everything in their power to ensure adherence to the measures adopted by (IMCO) in connection with the routeing of ships.' – which is only better than the 1960 formula in that it omits the words, 'so far as circumstances will permit'.

The oldest scheme is the one operating in the Dover Strait, where traffic has recently been well monitored. Its effect on the collision

4. IMCO Resolutions A284 (VIII) of 20 November 1973, and A338(IX) of 12 November 1975. For maps see *Ships' Routeing*, 3rd ed., IMCO, 1974.
5. Annex VI of Resolution A205(VII) – (not in force as at 1 January 1977).
6. However, the wording and prolixity of the new Regulations have come under attack from mariners: see F. J. Wylie, *Journal of Navigation*, Vol. 27 (1974), 115; Prof. Hugon, *Journal of Navigation*, Vol. 27 (1974), 530. For a history of Collision Regulations see J. F. Kemp, 'Two Hundred Years of the Collision Regulations', *Journal of Navigation*, Vol. 29 (1976), 341. For an analysis of the effect of the Regulations on VLCCs, see F. E. Couper, 'The Deep Draught Vessel and the Proposed International Regulations for Preventing Collisions at Sea, 1972', (1977) *8 J Mar Law & Comm* 295.

rate is summed up by Captain R. K. Emden of H.M. Coastguard's Dover Strait Operations Centre in these words: 'Traffic separation began in the early 60s and the annual statistics for collisions and groundings show a gradual decrease from this date, and particularly since the multiple collision of 1971, and this over a period during which the world-wide figures have been showing a disturbing increase'[7].

On a wider scale, Captain A. N. Cockcroft reported in 1976 that, 'most of the IMCO designated traffic separation areas are located in the areas in which there has been a significant decrease [in the incidence of collisions]. Collisions in the vicinity of what are now designated as traffic separation areas accounted for almost 50 per cent of the total number of sea collisions during the 8-year period 1959–66, and for approximately 40 per cent in the following 8 years. The proportion had decreased to less than 25 per cent for the 4-year period 1971–74'[8].

Evidence of this nature, and formal IMCO recognition of the importance of traffic separation to the reduction of marine pollution[9], suggests that a closer look at the practical considerations involved in the setting up of a scheme would be valuable.

3.2.2 TRAFFIC SEPARATION

Traffic separation schemes are expensive. Even before a recommended route can be adopted, a new hydrographic survey may need to be done to determine exact bottom depths and the direction of natural channels, so that the choice of deep water routes, sea lanes and areas to be avoided can be made on an informal basis. Once the scheme is adopted by IMCO, the routes must be lit and buoyed, and perhaps also dredged and further surveyed. Radar and communications stations must be set up on shore, and permanent staff employed to man these shore installations. Provision must be made for the removal and marking of wrecks, and for the accurate identification of offenders, which may mean arranging for helicopter or fixed wing surveillance,

---

7. 'The Dover Strait Information Service', *Journal of Navigation*, Vol. 28 (1975), 129 at 136. A further article by Captain Emden is, 'The Dover Strait Information Service: Recent Progress', *Journal of Navigation*, Vol. 29 (1976), 263.
8. 'Statistics of Collisions at Sea', *Journal of Navigation*, Vol. 29 (1976), 215 at 220.
9. Resolution A284(VIII) of 19 December 1973:
   '. . .
   RECOGNIZING ALSO that the practice of complying with routeing measures adopted by IMCO for international use would contribute considerably to the avoidance of collisions between ships,
   RECOGNIZING FURTHER that such practice would consequently reduce the risk of pollution of the marine environment and the risk of damage to marine life resulting from collisions or strandings . . .'
   Similar wording is contained in Resolution A338(IX).

and/or patrol craft (naval or civil); all of this entails the permanent or part-time employment of further manpower or existing services[10].

The real problem, of course, is who is to pay for all this? Since ultimately all nations benefit from an internationally adopted scheme, all nations would, in an ideal world, pay. However, few nations would be prepared to contribute to the cost of a scheme in anything more than the proportion which they conceived they benefitted from it: naturally, doing such a sum would be impossible. So in practice it falls to the coastal state or states concerned to do all the work and pay for it. It is difficult to see how this cost can be directly recovered from shipowners except by the imposition of a levy on all shipping entering the ports of such states, but this may be thought unfair because many of the ships using the scheme will not enter such a port, and because many ships which do enter such a port will not use the scheme. In any given case, if the view of one shipowner that 'the shipowners of the world are undoubtedly going to pay directly or indirectly for any traffic regulation schemes which are set up'[11] may not prove to be right, then it will be the taxpayers of the coastal states who will pay[12].

While it is clear that the existence of the schemes up to now, on a mere advisory basis,[13] has had considerable effect, their success ultimately depends on them taking mandatory form in the law of all flag states. A further passage from Captain Emden's 1975 article[14] illustrates this point well: 'It can be said at once that nearly two thirds of all the rogues are trawlers, mostly French, on passage to and from North Sea fishing grounds. The French Authorities are aware of this but, since the French Government has not yet made the IMCO Recommendations legally binding, there is nothing anybody can do – except keep a sharp lookout!' The question of enforcing these schemes and of enforcing navigational standards generally, must therefore be examined.

3.2.3 ENFORCEMENT OF STANDARDS

The main problem with traffic separation schemes is with identification of offenders. While a radar trace can indicate to the shore station that someone is contravening the rules, and this trace can be

10. See generally L. Oudet, 'The Economics of Traffic Circulation', *Journal of Navigation*, Vol. 25 (1972), 60 and the 1975 article by Captain Emden, 'The Dover Strait Information Service', *Journal of Navigation*, Vol. 28 (1975), 129, and C. Warbick, 'The Regulation of Navigation', *New Directions in the Law of the Sea*, Vol. III (editors Churchill, Simmonds and Welch), 137.
11. Per R. B. Adams, 'A Shipowner's View of Traffic Regulation', *Journal of Navigation*, Vol. 25 (1972), 467.
12. As to the financing of such schemes, see further Chapter 7.
13. By 1975 Belgium, Denmark, GDR, Liberia, Norway, Sweden and UK had made the schemes legally binding on vessels of their flag.
14. 'The Dover Strait Information Service', *Journal of Navigation*, Vol. 28 (1975), 129 at 133.

recorded for subsequent production in court[15], it needs a visual identification before the flag state can be ascertained and before there will be sufficient grounds for notifying it. Such identification is next to impossible at night, and is out of the question in fog. Even during good daytime visibility the wrong ship's name and flag may be taken, which is embarrassing for the coastal state.

The other main problem is that unless an even greater amount of money is spent, it is impossible to identify all those vessels which the radar indicates are rogues. The number of rogues in the Dover Strait scheme was on average 33 per day in 1973, 32 per day in 1974[16] and 25 per day in 1975[17]. However, the declining figures and the entry into frce of the 1972 Collision Regulations should improve matters greatly.

All the enforcement work done by the coastal state will be thwarted if the flag state does not take appropriate action upon receiving notification of an observed infringement or if action is taken too slowly – the need for taking prompt action is evident from the fact that the master may have left the employ of the shipowner soon after the offence, and have all but disappeared. Such difficulties are inherent in the concept of flag state jurisdiction, and have perhaps led to the suggestion that tighter methods of control are necessary[18].

It might be thought, for instance, that in order to secure compliance with routeing schemes, and to ensure that ships travel at a safe and sensible speed, all that is required is a system of control akin to that exercised at airports: when a ship arrives in the vicinity of a routeing scheme she must contact a maritime equivalent of Air Traffic Control, and from then on do as she is told. Her position can be carefully monitored from the shore, as can the positions of all other vessels. Just as it is very rare for an aeroplane to proceed out of circuit, so it would be very rare for a ship to proceed out of circuit.

This idea cannot work under the existing regime of the high seas because it would involve either a unilateral claim to jurisdiction by the coastal state, or acquiescence in the jurisdiction of the coastal state by the ship. The former is clearly contrary to international law[19]: the latter is only technically feasible[20]. States are prepared to acquiesce to

15. Emden, in 'The Dover Strait Information Service', *Journal of Navigation*, Vol. 28 (1975), 129 at 133, states that, 'the lapse-time photographic technique is not at present suitable for use in the Courts and instead the graphic plots ... are preserved, photocopied and used in prosecutions'.
16. Record, *Journal of Navigation*, Vol. 28 (1975), 244.
17. Emden, 'The Dover Strait Information Service: Recent Progress', *Journal of Navigation*, Vol. 29 (1976), 263 at 266.
18. E.g. M. M. Sibthorp (editor), *The North Sea: Challenge and Opportunity*, London, 1975, at 220: 'There is a need for international shipping traffic control to be as closely organised as air traffic control is, and it may be that the time has come for the principle of the complete freedom of the high seas, which is basic to the existing arrangements, to be re-examined'.
19. But would not be without precedent, e.g. the Truman Declaration, Proclamation No. 2667, 10 *Fed. Reg.*, 12303 (1945).
20. Needless to say, it would also be highly unpopular with shipowners.

another coastal state's jurisdiction over that state's territorial sea, and, to a certain extent, over its contiguous and exclusive economic zones, but it would be unrealistic at the moment to think that states will be willing to let any other state exercise jurisdiction in this way over the high seas. The only possible alternative would be some kind of marine traffic control operated by the United Nations.

But even if this were to solve the jurisdictional problem, there would remain the problem of how physically to enforce the scheme. A warship could stop a vessel from proceeding according to her own will, but the immense danger of that course cannot be justified on the grounds that a scheme designed to ensure the safety of ships is being enforced. Hence the only method of enforcement would be ex post facto – which brings us back to the existing regime, and if the flag state fails to take any action, there is no enforcement.

The problems associated with the enforcement of navigational equipment standards are not dissimilar: the onus is very much on the flag state. However, Regulation 19 of Chapter I of both SOLAS 60 and SOLAS 74 empowers contracting states to verify whether the Certificate of Safety prescribed by the Convention is on board. If it is, it must be accepted 'unless there are clear grounds for believing that the condition of the ship or of its equipment does not correspond substantially with the particulars of that certificate'. Should this be so, 'the officer carrying out the control shall take such steps as will ensure that the ship shall not sail until it can proceed to sea without danger to the passangers or the crew'. This power does at least give a port state a small measure of control over ships registered in other Contracting States. Recently, IMCO has passed a Resolution, A321 (IX) of 12 November 1975, detailing procedures for the better exercise of this control.

The steps which a flag state can take need not prove too costly, as the recent example of Liberia shows[21]. All flag states can ensure that their ships are properly equipped by inspecting them regularly when they call at the home state or when they call at certain ports abroad. Liberia has taken the latter course, because the nature of the Liberian maritime programme is such that her ships seldom, if ever, call at Monrovia, and it would have been unrealistic to have attracted shipping in the way that she has, and then later on force it to visit Monrovia. Therefore, in 1972 the Marine Inspection Division was set up. At present, it has 119 Nautical Inspectors organised into four areas. Eight of these persons are full-time employees, the rest being independent qualified surveyors vetted for a lack of conflict of interest.

21. Liberia has been chosen because she has the largest tonnage of all the world fleets. As at 1 July 1975, she had 2,520 ships, totalling 65,820,414 tons gross (126,053,631 tons dwt): that is, 3·9% of the world's ships, 19·2% of world grt tonnage (22·8% of world dwt tonnage). Her proportion of the world tanker fleet was 13·4% by number, 27·7% by grt and 29·7% by dwt tonnage. Figures are from *Lloyds Register of Shipping Statistical Tables, 1975*.

By Marine Notice No. 117 of 7 August 1972 (made under the authority of Maritime Regulation 7.191) 'all Liberian vessels are required to undergo a periodic safety inspection once in every twelve months', with certain very minor exceptions. For convenience, owners or masters may request their annual inspection at a port convenient for the ship's purpose, but ships whose inspections are overdue must submit to inspection at the first available date after the inspection was due. The inspectors check the ship's documents (safety certificates etc.), the publications and charts carried, licensing and manning requirements and certificates, possession of and operational condition of navigational aids, and details of oil pollution prevention matters. The inspector's report can lead to an investigation and eventual prosecution for an offence or revocation of licence. In particular, Marine Notice No. 124, paragraph 6 warns: 'Owners and masters are cautioned that violation of manning requirements will result in the application of punitive provisions of the Maritime Law and Regulations, including detention of the ship in port until satisfactory compliance is verified'. The cost of the Marine Inspection Division is contributed to, if not wholly borne, by the ships – each inspection costs $250 (Maritime Regulation 7.191, paragraph 4). Inspection is thus possible, even when the ships of a state's registry hardly ever call at the state itself.

The value to flag states in having an enquiry every time one of their ships is involved in a casualty is great, because it turns up navigational and other offences, and thus helps to ensure that standards are maintained in the future. Again, Liberia has recently updated her procedures in this respect, so that all casualties can be investigated (see generally Chapter IX, Liberian Maritime Regulations). The enquiry is the second major element in the enforcement system open to flag states. Regrettably, a flag state is only required to make such an enquiry by Regulation 21 of Chapter I of SOLAS 60 and 74 'when it judges that such an investigation may assist in determining what changes in the present Regulations might be desirable'. This leaves the question of when to hold an enquiry wholly in the discretion of the flag state. Recently, the IMCO Assembly adopted Resolution A322 (IX) of 12 November 1975, reminding governments of their obligations under this Regulation, limited as they are, and so it is clear that the Regulation is not leading to enough enquiries.

To require states to investigate following every casualty would place upon them an intolerable administrative burden, but clearly it is desirable that the duty to investigate should be wider than in SOLAS 60 and 74. Thus, Article 12 of the International Convention for the Prevention of Pollution from Ships, 1973 is welcome: '(1) Each Administration undertakes to conduct an investigation of any casualty occurring to any of its ships subject to the provision of the Regulations if such casualty has produced a major deleterious effect upon the marine environment'[1]. It remains to individual states to interpret when a casualty falls within this formula, but it is nonetheless a major step in the right direction. It is a pity that in 1974, Regulation 21 of Chapter I of SOLAS 60 was not widened to encompass the same idea within the general safety field, by, say, making an enquiry mandatory when a casualty leads to loss of life.

The enquiry, when made, should be public in as many cases as possible, and, following IMCO Resolution A173 (ES IV) of 28 November 1968, should offer to any state polluted as a result of the casualty the right to participate. However, the suggestion by one author[2] that the documents in private arbitrations following a casualty should be made public has at least one serious disadvantage. An enquiry has as its object the discovery of how the casualty occurred, and what future lessons can be drawn therefrom. It may also include the discovery of breaches of regulations which have some form of penal sanction. The object of an arbitration, however, is quite different. The parties may have agreed to proceed on certain assumptions, and to arbitrate about only one or two points. The whole story will not, therefore, appear from the proceedings. That which does appear will be dictated by the areas on which the parties cannot agree, and the arbitration will ultimately have as its aim the assessment of who pays who, and how much.

A second, less serious disadvantage, is that facts which a shipowner may be prepared to admit for the purposes of a private arbitration he may be unprepared to admit if the proceedings are to be made public. The danger is, then, that the shipowner may prefer to be forced into admission by a court action – in other words, he may take the attitude that if he must make these things public, he will make it as hard as possible for that to happen. Clearly, inducements to such an attitude must be avoided if at all possible.

It nonetheless remains true that there are serious shortcomings in the present situation. In many cases the enquiring state will have no means of compelling a foreign ship to deliver up vital information. For instance, if ship A, registered in State Y, is in collision on the high seas[3] with ship B, registered in State Z, State Y will have no means in the absence of treaty to compel ship B to deliver up vital information – e.g. the ship's log, charts, manning details and, indeed, any other information. This can only be achieved if ship A subsequently institutes legal proceedings against ship B, but then the information may come too late for State Y to use in its enquiry, or it

---

1. The operation of this provision will be greatly facilitated by Article 8 and Protocol I of the 1973 Convention which place on the Master the duty to report spillages. See also IMCO Resolution A147 (ES IV) of 26 November 1968 recommending that states require masters to report casualties giving rise to significant spillages of oil.
2. L. Oudet, 'The Economics of Traffic Circulation', *Journal of Navigation*, Vol. 25 (1972), 60.
3. There would not normally be a jurisdictional problem where the collision takes place within the territorial sea or internal waters of State Y.

may be insufficient for the purposes of the enquiry (rather than for the purposes of the legal action). Further, it may be that certain documents will be protected by rules of evidence in the lex fori.

It therefore seems that further research into the following matters would be worthwhile:

1) How important enquiries are likely to be in the enforcement of navigational, personnel and environmental standards.
2) How changes in the current jurisdictional regime could facilitate the effectiveness of enquiries.
3) Whether, if at all, states should have a duty to conduct enquiries, and if so, when; also, what should be the rights of a coastal state.
4) How best to balance the interests of the public and of the shipowner in an enquiry.

It would then be possible to decide whether a new international instrument should be drawn up to effect any changes which may be suggested by the results of such further research, in collaboration with the IMCO Marine Environment Protection Committee.

It is clear that accidents are largely the result of some form of human error. As Captain R. Maybourn of B.P. Tankers Ltd has said: '...despite the high standards set in many shipping companies, accidents still occur and a high proportion are irrational in the sense that they involve intelligent and competent individuals who fail to observe regulations to carry out practices with which they are quite familiar. The possibility must be considered that the present collision rate is to a large extent a manifestation of human fallibility and the collective management philosophy of shipping companies'[4].

It is therefore to the question of personnel standards that attention is now turned.

3.3 Training and personnel standards

The problem of how to ensure that ships are manned by high quality personnel is deeply involved with matters outside the scope of this study – wages, hours of work, contracts of employment, security of employment, benefits, examinations and qualifications for office, and related matters. It is, however, important to appreciate this fact, for otherwise it becomes easy to suggest that, as a matter of law,

---

4. *Journal of Navigation*, Vol. 29 (1976), 230. J. F. Kemp, 'Behaviour Patterns in Encounters between Ships', *Journal of Navigation*, Vol. 26 (1973), 417, suggests that experienced mariners in some cases may react unpredictably *because* they know the Collision Regulations, and that these Regulations, by their verbosity and mass of detail, appear to cause some indecision and confused interpretation.

shipowners should do this and should do that, without addressing the question of how they are to achieve these things. At all times, therefore, one must bear in mind the practical problems of the shipowner.

The second point is that the law has only a limited role to play in this field. Whereas the law is well equipped to set environmentally acceptable discharge standards, or to distribute economic burdens by attributing liability, it cannot make a man a good and conscientious seafarer. The only thing the law can do is to enshrine certain levels of achievement on the assumption that anyone who has attained them ought normally to be a good seafarer. Hence, the law can say that no man shall be master until he has passed certain prescribed examinations and has had a certain length of sea experience of a prescribed type: it cannot guarantee that in a potential accident situation the man will so act as to avoid the accident. However, the law can help to see that the standards it does set are kept.

Below are summarised some of the legal provisions which the author finds relevant to the pollution issue, and then follows a note on enforcement.

3.3.1 LEGAL STANDARDS

Regulation 13 of Chapter V of SOLAS 60 and SOLAS 74 provides that 'the Contracting Governments undertake, each for its national ships, to maintain, or, if it is necessary, to adopt, measures for the purpose of ensuring that, from the point of view of safety of life at sea, all ships shall be sufficiently and efficiently manned'. It can be seen at once that this is a very minimal and vague standard, but the alternative is to have provisions so detailed and complicated as to require a Convention to itself. In practical terms, little help is offered by this provision, and it is for this reason (amongst others) that further work on manning levels is programmed by IMCO for 1979.

The approach to the problem at IMCO has been mainly to provide advice on specific issues thought to be particularly relevant to safety, whatever the manning levels. Thus, Recommendation 39 of the 1960 SOLAS Conference recommends that Contracting Governments should take all practicable steps to ensure that all personnel are adequately trained in the use of navigational aids and safety equipment. More specifically, Resolution A285 (VIII) of 20 November 1973 adopts certain basic principles to be observed in keeping a navigational watch, and Resolution A337 (IX) of 12 November 1975 makes a similar recommendation on Watches in Port. In 1965, Resolution A89 (IV) had adopted a Document for Guidance on training of all personnel, partly in fulfillment of IMCO's role as defined in Recommendation 39 of the 1960 SOLAS Conference; since then, this document has been regularly updated, the latest version being promulgated in 1975[5].

This work, largely done through the Sub-Committee on Standards of Training and Watchkeeping, has culminated in the preparation of a draft Convention and draft Recommendations on Training and Certification of Seafarers[6], to be considered by a diplomatic Conference in 1978[7]. It contains detailed requirements for masters, deck, engineer and radio officers and radio telephone operators[8].

This draft Convention has been prepared in collaboration with ILO, whose general sphere of interest includes employment, safety and health aboard ships. This UN Agency had addressed itself to the problem of personnel standards aboard ships even before IMCO existed. There are three important Conventions which have been drawn up under its auspices and which are germane to the pollution aspect of safety at sea. First is ILO Convention No. 53 (1936), concerning the Minimum Requirement of Professional Capacity for Masters and Officers on Board Merchant Ships[9]; next is ILO Convention No. 74 (1946) concerning the Certification of Able Seamen[10] which lays down minimum requirements for the issue of certificates of qualification as an Able Seaman, and lastly ILO Convention No. 109 (1958), revising earlier Conventions[11], on Wages, Hours of Work and Manning at Sea. Article 20(1) of this Convention provides that 'Every vessel to which this Convention applies shall be sufficiently and efficiently manned for the purposes of (a) ensuring the safety of life at sea; (b) giving effect to Part III of this Convention [Hours of Work on Board Ship] and (c) preventing excessive strain upon the crew and avoiding or minimising as far as practicable the working of overtime'.

It may therefore be concluded that there is no lack of basal legal standards, nor has there been for many years, in the field of manning and personnel. However, it is equally clear from the continuing loss ratio of the world fleet that either these minima are insufficient, or they are not achieved widely enough in practice, or both. It is beyond the scope of this study to evaluate the intrinsic sufficiency of the standards laid down in these various conventions, particularly as mariners themselves disagree on the subject; but it is to be noted that the question is being actively debated in the appropriate international fora, that a new instrument is in draft form[7], and that therefore those in a position to evaluate these standards are constantly doing just that.

5. MSC/Circ. 212.
6. Draft Convention, STW X/2; Draft Technical Annex, STW X/4/1; Draft Recommendations, STW X/5.
7. See Preface.
8. Resolution 8 of the 1978 Tanker Safety and Pollution Prevention Conference urges the adoption of adequate training and certification of tanker crews.
9. Entry into force: 29 March 1939.   10. Entry into force: 14 July 1951.
11. No. 57 of 1936; No. 76 of 1946 and No. 93 of 1949.

It therefore seems appropriate to turn to the question of enforcement.

3.3.2 ENFORCEMENT OF TRAINING AND PERSONNEL STANDARDS[12]

As noted above in connection with the enforcement of navigational standards, the value of regular inspections of ships by the flag state cannot be over-estimated. This will enable the state to ensure that manning levels are kept up to standard, and that the personnel are properly certificated, even if it will not ensure that the holders of such certificates continue to be good mariners. It must remain for the shipowner himself to see that his management system is capable of discovering when a particular individual should, in the interests of safety, no longer be at sea or no longer hold a particular responsibility.

It may further be seen that an enquiry is well suited to turning up deficiencies in personnel standards, and enabling recommendations for future action to be drawn. Consequently, the enforcement of navigational standards goes hand in glove with that of personnel standards.

3.4 Design standards

Here again, it is beyond the scope of this study to attempt an evaluation of the complicated and highly technical provisions relating to the design of ships. The appropriate standards will be merely mentioned, so that it can be seen roughly what role the law plays in this field.

The major provisions are contained in SOLAS 60 and SOLAS 74, Chapters I, II and V. These deal with subdivision, stability, machinery, electrical installations and fire precautions. Further, IMCO Resolution A324(IX) of 12 November 1975 makes recommendations on collision bulkheads in cargo ships, and the International Convention on Load Lines 1966[13] regulates the assignment to a ship of her various freeboards. These provisions all deal with the design of ships in general, and while they are obviously relevant to pollution prevention, they are more specifically aimed at safety of life at sea and ship safety generally. However, there are certain provisions which, because of their particular effect on pollution prevention, require special mention here.

12. See Preface.
13. 640 UNTS 133. Amended by IMCO Resolutions A172 (ES IV), A231(VII), A319(IX) and A320(IX).

a) *Steering gear*

It is self-evident that if the steering gear of a vessel fails, the vessel immediately becomes in need of salvage assistance. The pollution danger of a tanker whose steering gear has failed has long been appreciated, and was most sadly underlined recently by the largest pollution disaster to date, the stranding on 16 March 1978 off Portsall, France, of the *Amoco Cadiz*, following a failure of her steering gear.

On 12 October 1971 the IMCO Assembly adopted Resolution A210(VII) which recommended the provision of certain steering gear on large ships; the SOLAS did not include such recommendations, enacting in Regulations 29 and 30 of Chapter II-1 relatively modest requirements but referring to Resolution A210(VII). On 12 November 1975 the IMCO Assembly adopted another Resolution, number A325(IX), on improved steering arrangements for new ships of various tonnages, and the International Tanker Safety and Pollution Prevention Conference in 1978 amended the provisions of Regulation 29 of Chapter II-1 of SOLAS 74 by making special extra provisions for tankers, in the Protocol to SOLAS 74 which it adopted. These provisions, contained in Regulation 29(d), now require (inter alia) that new and existing tankers of 10,000 tons gross tonnage and above shall have two remote control systems, each of which shall be separately operable from the bridge, for the control of the steering gear, so that if one system fails the other can be brought into immediate operation. Further, all new tankers of 10,000 tons gross tonnage and above shall have two or more identical power units for the steering gear, of specified capability, so that each shall start automatically on the restoration of power after a power failure, and in addition there must be an emergency power source of specified capacity[14].

These new requirements do not present technical difficulties in the construction of new tankers, and many well designed existing tankers already comply: but of course they will add to the cost of a new tanker and will engender conversion costs for existing tankers not already so fitted. The requirements adopted in the Protocol represent a compromise on the original specifications proposed by the United States[15]. The new provisions are clearly an important and welcome addition to international legal standards on accidental pollution prevention.

b) *Radar and collision avoidance aids*

SOLAS 60 contains no requirement that ships should carry radar, although Regulation 12 of Chapter V does require all ships of 1,600 tons gross tonnage and above to be fitted with a specified direction-finding apparatus quite different from radar. Regulation 12 of Chapter

14. See also Resolution 12 of the 1978 Conference on Improved Steering Gear Standards, and on future extension of the new provisions of the 1978 Protocol.
15. See TSPP III/8, paras. 35–37, and MSC/MEPC/10, paras. 57–61 and Annex VI.

V of SOLAS 74 not only requires this, but requires that all such ships carry radar of a type approved by the ship's flag state, and it also makes provision for the mandatory fitting of gyro-compass, echo-sounder and a radiotelephone distress frequency homing device. Resolution A222(VII) of the IMCO Assembly recommends performance standards for navigational radar equipment.

However, a radar device can always fail. At the instigation of the United States, IMCO's Maritime Safety and Marine Environment Protection Committees agreed prior to the 1978 International Tanker Safety and Pollution Prevention Conference that all ships of 10,000 tons gross tonnage and above should be fitted with two radars capable of operating independently of each other[16], and this therefore found its way into the Protocol to SOLAS 74 adopted by that Conference, in the form of a revised wording of Regulation 12(a) of Chapter V. All radars so fitted shall conform to operational standards not inferior to those adopted by IMCO[17]. These new provisions are already complied with by well run and equipped tankers, and, in view of the relatively modest cost involved in compliance, are welcome.

But the United States did not think that this was enough, and wanted all ships of 10,000 tons gross tonnage and above to carry collision avoidance aids as well. There is considerable controversy in the maritime world as to the value of such aids[18]. Thankfully, a United States proposal to the 1978 Conference that such aids be made mandatory by the Protocol, and that the exact specifications for them be developed between 1978 and the entry into force of the Protocol, was considered by the Conference to be pre-judging the issue, and so the proposal was rejected[19]. However, the Conference did adopt Resolution 13 calling on IMCO to develop performance standards and requirements for the carriage of such aids before 1 July 1979.

c) *Double bottoms and protective layout of segregated ballast tanks*
The United States had wanted the 1978 Conference to make double bottoms mandatory for new oil tankers of 20,000 tons dwt and above[20]. The argument in favour of double bottoms is simply that, if a tanker is involved in a collision or stranding, the outer skin may be pierced but the inner one, inside which is the oil, has a good chance of remaining intact[21]. The arguments against such a proposal[1], again put simply, are

16. MSC/MEPC/10, paras. 62–63.
17. Resolution A222(VII) is due to be revised.
18. See K. Jones, 'Collision Avoidance Systems – the real problems', *Nautical Review*, Jan/Feb 1978, 59.
19. For pre-Conference discussion, see MSC/MEPC/10, paras. 64–69 and Annex VIII.
20. See TSPP II/2, paras. 11–16, 31–34 and Annex VI; TSPP III/8, paras. 14–20, 28–34 and Annex III; MSC/MEPC/10, para. 70 and Annex XI.
21. Detailed and technical argument and analysis is contained in J. C. Card, 'Effectiveness of Double Bottoms in Preventing Oil Outflow from Tanker Bottom Damage Incidents', *Marine Technology*, Vol. 12 (1975), 60.
  1. See TSPP II/2, para. 14 and TSPP III/3/2.

that double bottoms create a high risk of explosion, they cause salvage difficulties because they lead to a loss of buoyancy, and they are difficult to inspect, drain and ventilate. Perhaps the most effective argument against them is that in many cases they still will not be effective to prevent an escape of oil due to the seriousness of the casualty, and hence they are not cost-effective.

An alternative to the double bottom is to place the segregated ballast tanks which a tanker has (whether because such a requirement is mandatory[2] or by choice of the shipowner) protectively around the ship, so that if the hull is breached, the chances of the breach occurring in a tank containing ballast water or nothing at all are greatly increased. After considerable discussion at the 1978 Conference, it was this approach which was adopted.

The 1978 Protocol to the International Convention on the Prevention of Pollution from Ships 1973 adds to Annex I thereof a new Regulation 13E, which requires every new crude oil tanker[3] of 20,000 tons dwt and above and every new product carrier[3] of 30,000 tons dwt and above to have their mandatory segregated ballast tanks arranged in a specified way. This specification is not linked, as the United States had wished, to the oil outflow requirements described below, but in deference to those who supported this approach the Conference adopted Resolution 17 recommending further work to be done by IMCO.

d) *Tank size and construction*

There are two important sets of international design provisions which are specifically pollution oriented. The first set are comprised in the 1971 Amendments to the International Convention for the Prevention of Pollution of the Seas by Oil 1954[4]. They were evolved by the IMCO Sub-Committee on Design and Equipment, and they aim to avoid or limit the escape of oil cargo in the event of stranding or collision.

The basic formula is that tankers ordered after 1972 shall have cargo tanks so constructed and arranged that if certain assumed side or bottom damage is sustained, the 'hypothetical outflow of oil' shall not exceed a figure which varies according to the tanker's deadweight, but which shall not for any tanker, however large, exceed 40,000 cubic metres. In addition the volume of centre and wing cargo tanks is limited.

It seems that although at 31 December 1977, these Amendments

2. As to the legal requirements for segregated ballast, see section 2.3.6.
3. For definition see section 2.3.5.1, footnotes 9 (oil tanker) and 18 (product carrier).
4. IMCO Resolution A246(VII); UK Misc. No. 36 of 1972 (Cmnd. 5071); 11 ILM 267. As at 31 August 1977, the Amendments had not entered into force. The following states had ratified or accepted: Algeria, Bahamas, Canada, Finland, Greece, Italy, Ivory Coast, Jordan, Lebanon, Liberia, Malta, Norway, Philippines, Saudi Arabia, Sweden, Switzerland, Syrian Arab Republic, Tunisia, the USSR, the UK and Yugoslavia.

had not entered into force, most tankers ordered since 1 January 1972 have, following IMCO Resolution A247(VII), been built in accordance therewith[5].

The second set of provisions are contained in the International Convention for the Prevention of Pollution from Ships, 1973[6]. Regulations 22–25 of Annex I retain the basic formula of the 1971 Amendments (size and arrangements of tanks) just described, but make two important additions: (1) when a cargo transfer system interconnects two or more cargo tanks (as is invariably the case) valves for separating the tanks from each other must be provided, and must be kept closed while the tanker is at sea, and similar provisions are made for piping which runs near the side or bottom of the ship (Regulation 24(5) and (6)); (2) tankers must be so constructed as to comply with the subdivision and damage stability criteria specified (Regulation 25), the object here being to stop a damaged tanker flooding too much in the event of the assumed damage.

While both these provisions add to the cost of building new ships, and both present technical difficulties[7], they are to be welcomed.

e) *Enforcement of design and equipment standards*

The enforcement of design and equipment standards does not present the same problems which the enforcement of navigational or operational discharge standards presents[8]. A flag state can ensure by inspection that no ship which fails to comply with the relevant standards is registered in that state, and that no such ship is issued with the appropriate certificate of compliance. A port state can inspect ships of any flag to see if the requisite certificate is on board. SOLAS 60 and SOLAS 74 provide for the survey and certification of ships, and for inspection for certificates by port states[9]; the Load Lines Convention 1966 has similar provisions[10], as does the 1973 Convention[11]. The 1971 Amendments to the 1954 Convention provide for certification[12].

However, the large number of sub-standard ships sailing the high seas is a witness to the fact that much was to be desired concerning inspection and certification[13]. Part of this concerns the will of both flag and port states, but part also relates to the provisions of the International Conventions themselves. Only diplomatic pressure and

5. See Resolution 11 of the 1973 Conference (Cmnd. 5748, 126).
6. UK Misc. No. 26 of 1974 (Cmnd. 5748); 12 ILM 1319.
7. See MEPC VII/6(b) and MEPC VII/19, para. 37.
8. As to which, see section 3.2.3 (*Navigational standards*) and Chapter 4 (*Operational discharge standards*).
9. Chapter I, Regulations 6 to 19.
10. Articles 12 to 21.
11. Article 5, and Regulations 4 to 8 and Appendix II of Annex I.
12. Article VI, para. (2) to (4).
13. Resolution A321(IX) of the IMCO Assembly dated 12 November 1975 sets out procedures for the control of ships in respect of SOLAS 60 and the Load Lines Convention 1966.

public opinion can do much to improve the former; the 1978 Conference adopted modifications to two of the latter – the SOLAS 74 and the 1973 Convention.

The Protocols to those two instruments[14] amend the relevant provisions[15,16], inter alia by introducing mandatory unscheduled inspection by the flag state (or annual scheduled inspections instead), and tightening up the regulations relating to the duration of certificates (so that their life is in fact shortened). As before, ships can be prevented from proceeding to sea if they do not comply with the relevant standards. Significantly, the new Regulation 4(4)(c) of Annex I of the 1973 Convention creates an obligation on the master or owner, whenever an accident occurs to a ship or a defect is discovered which substantially affects the integrity of the ship or the efficiency or completeness of the equipment required by Annex I, to report it to the flag state or person responsible for the issue of the relevant Pollution Prevention Certificate; this will enable inquiries to be initiated to see if a survey is needed. If the ship is in a port of a state party to the Protocol, the appropriate authorities of that state must also be informed. Prior to these provisions, the duty to report had been limited to arising when a spill had occurred or probably occurred[17].

Article II(3) of the Protocol to SOLAS 74 now brings that Convention into line with Article 5(4) of the 1973 Convention by providing that states shall apply the requirements of SOLAS 74 and its Protocol so that no more favourable treatment is given to the ships of non-parties.

These new provisions will increase the administrative burden on states[18], which is no bad thing considering that the overwhelming burden of pollution prevention has always been put upon the shipowner; and they are welcome because they may well help in the reduction of substandard ships. Shipowners operating their fleets to high standards have no fear of these new provisions.

3.5 Conclusions

Accidental pollution of the sea is ineradicable: it is part of the price mankind must pay for the benefits of an industrial society. Man must

14. See also Resolution 10 of the 1978 Conference recommending the development by IMCO of guidelines on unscheduled surveys and the standardisation of the periods of validity of the various certificates.
15. See note 9, above.
16. See note 11, above.
17. Article 8 and Protocol 1 of the 1973 Convention.
18. Resolution 6 of the 1978 Conference invites IMCO to further develop procedures and guidelines for the operation of the enforcement provisions of SOLAS 74 and the 1973 Convention.

therefore learn to live with the problem, but that does not mean that he cannot do things to reduce the casualty rate to an acceptable level. It simply means that panic measures of a draconian nature are not called for. It is extremely important to remember that there is a danger of imposing upon the shipowner so many rules and regulations that he will find it too difficult to operate efficiently and at a profit.

Accidental pollution must be regarded at present as of equal importance to operational oil pollution. However, as operational oil pollution diminishes in accordance with the measures discussed in the last chapter, accidental oil pollution will increase its importance in the context of the general problem. It is likely, therefore, that in future IMCO will pay more and more attention to this source. It is greatly to be hoped that the nations of the world will strike a fair balance between the need for a healthy and efficient shipping industry and the need for cleaner seas.

It is clear that IMCO is already hard at work on the main areas affecting accidental oil pollution: the Maritime Safety Committee is developing routeing schemes and navigational standards generally, and its sub-committees on Standards of Training and Watchkeeping and on Design and Equipment have other most important matters under constant review. The MEPC has been active in the design and equipment field too. These fora are the best means for future development of the law in this area. The 1978 Conference on Tanker Safety and Pollution Prevention went far in improving the relevant standards.

It would seem that the immediate aim of reducing both accidental oil pollution and the general casualty rate can be achieved without giving up the traditional and important freedom of navigation on the high seas, within the structure of flag state jurisdiction. However, improvements within the existing regime undoubtedly are needed, notably in the control which states exercise over their own ships. This need cause no concern to the conscientious majority of shipowners, but it will rightly worry the small proportion of less responsible shipowners. Some states are undoubtedly better than others at controlling their fleets, but it is no longer true to say that flags of convenience are, as a group, all in the lackadaisical category, nor has it ever been true that all other flags are not lackadaisical. It is particularly to be noted that Liberia, with the greatest tonnage in the world, and a longstanding flag of convenience, has within a very short space of time devised a control system (albeit one which is still in need of improvement[19]) which many other states would do well to follow. It is the job of diplomacy to pressurise the lackadaisical states into improving their control.

19. The official Liberian report into the stranding of the tanker *Argo Merchant* in December 1976 shows that some ships do still slip through the net. Since then, Liberia has tightened up its procedures.

While there are elaborate legal standards in existence, they clearly need to enter into force before they can have significant effect, and consequently much can be done by states taking it upon themselves to make the preparations to enable them to ratify the various conventions, and in particular the Amendments to SOLAS 60, the SOLAS 74 and its 1978 Protocol, the 1971 Amendments to the 1954 Oil Pollution Convention, the 1973 Convention on the Prevention of Pollution from Ships and its 1978 Protocol. But further work is not obviated by the existence of these standards, and this should be done through IMCO rather than by individual states legislating unilaterally. In particular, it would seem that there is merit in researching the role of enquiring in the enforcement process, to see whether a new instrument is called for.

All this will take time, so that while the immediate prospect does not show a likelihood of a dramatic drop in the accident rate, there are good long-term prospects of a marked improvement; however, this conclusion does not detract from the fact that these prospects will not be fulfilled without a new commitment on the part of all the nations of the world to putting into effect all the new standards.

If a simple answer is needed to the question as to what is the main priority for solving the world's oil pollution problem, it is this: raise the standard of the world's mariners, for it is the mariner who drives the ship into a collision or grounding, not the other way round.

The question of how to raise the standard of mariners is outside the scope of this study, but it is plain that raising the standards of the qualifications they must possess and the experience they must have had is only part of the solution. The other, more important part, lies in improving the standard of the management of shipping fleets and the quality and conscientiousness of those attracted to a life at sea.

4 Enforcement of Operational Standards

This topic has been reserved for a separate chapter because it forms a discrete part of the general debate about oil pollution, and because its importance merits it. The enforcement of traffic separation schemes and personnel standards has already been dealt with[1].

It is self-evident that unless standards are adhered to they are useless, except, possibly, as goals to aim at, if the extent of contraventions, especially those going undetected or punished, is the relevant consideration. The fact that 80% of the industry adheres to LOT places the enforcement issue in context, and the reasons given in Chapter 2 as to why some tankers cannot operate LOT places the non-compliance of the other 20% in context.

It is impossible to say exactly what number of contraventions of international standards there are each year, or exactly what proportion of the world fleet habitually fails to operate anti-pollution procedures, either properly or at all, so as to contravene international standards, but it can be safely concluded that both figures are, relatively speaking, small. Having said that, it is clearly important that the standards are actively enforced, not only to satisfy the demands of the environment and the feelings of those who care for it and want to use it, but to be fair to the great majority of shipowners who do comply, and who in many cases voluntarily exceed international standards.

4.1 Provisions in International Conventions

The 1954–62 Convention contains two main provisions relating to enforcement, one requiring the completion of oil record books, the other enshrining the traditional doctrine of flag state jurisdiction.

1. Sections 3.2.3 and 3.3.2.

By Article IX every ship which uses fuel oil and every tanker to which the Convention applies shall be provided with an oil record book (the form of which is specified in Annex B), and the book must be completed on specified occasions and signed by the master and one other officer. Basically, such occasions are whenever any act is performed on board which means that water will or may come into contact with oil: hence ballasting and cleaning of tanks, all discharges of water or oil from tanks, and so on. The idea is that by inspecting a ship's oil record book, it should be possible to tell whether or not an unlawful discharge of oil has been made.

The competent authorities of any contracting party may inspect a foreign ship's book while in port, and a true copy made of this 'shall be made admissible in any judicial proceedings as evidence of the facts stated in the entry', so that the defence of hearsay shall not avail (Article IX(5)). However, no proceedings may be taken by the port state: by Article X(1), all it may do is to furnish the flag state with particulars in writing of evidence that any provision of the Convention has been contravened by a ship.

By Article X(2), upon receipt of such particulars the flag state 'shall investigate the matter' and if it is satisfied that sufficient evidence is available in the form required by its law to enable proceedings to be taken against the owner or master[2] of the ship, it shall cause such proceedings to be taken as soon as possible. Article VI demands that contravention of Articles III and IX shall be an offence punishable under the law of the flag state, and that the penalties 'shall be adequate in severity to discourage such unlawful discharge' and shall not be less than those imposed in respect of the same infringements within the flag state's territorial sea.

Several points must be made about this system. First, unless the oil record book by itself betrays an unlawful discharge, its value for enforcement purposes will be much reduced. Avoidance of the use of the oil record book is relatively easy if those responsible for signing it are so minded. For instance, a small difference in the recorded position of the ship at the time of discharge is simple to make; and it is of course quite possible to round off figures to hide all but the most blatant breaches. Hence, the effectiveness of the oil record book depends largely on the integrity of the master and officers – and the master or officer who would make an unlawful discharge in the first place can hardly be expected to 'own up' to it in the oil record book. There is also the most serious defect that the officials of the port state can inspect the oil record book, but not the contents of the slop tank.

2. In *Federal Steam Navigation Co Ltd v Department of Trade and Industry* [1974] 2 All ER 97, [1974] 1 WLR 505 the House of Lords by a majority of 3 to 2 held that, in the Oil in Navigable Waters Act 1955, s.1(1), the word 'or' in this phrase is to be construed conjunctively and not disjunctively, so that both owner and master can be convicted of an offence arising from a single unlawful discharge. See also [1974] CLJ 181 (L. Collins).

Therefore, their first and strongest method of checking the accuracy of what is read in the oil record book is not, under international law, available to them. Of course, states are free to legislate to give them this power, but to do this would be contrary to the spirit of the development of the law in this field – uniformity of municipal laws and international law.

Secondly, unless oil record books are inspected regularly, their use will be greatly diminished. It is the inspection by officials at the loading port which is most important. As a matter of practice, oil record books are inspected very rarely in the world's primary loading area, the Middle East. There is a further, somewhat extraordinary circumstance which must be mentioned here: while in most countries which have ratified this Convention the penalties for making an unlawful discharge are severe (of the order of £50,000 or more), the penalties for not filling in the oil record book at all are usually small (of the order of £500). Since in most cases the oil record book will be a valuable source of evidence if filled in correctly and honestly, all that has to be done by a vessel intending to make an unlawful discharge is not to fill in the book at all!

Thirdly, the enforcement system is at the mercy of states exercising little or no control over their vessels – e.g. some flags of convenience[3].

Fourthly, the system is grossly inefficient. Before 1978 the necessary evidence was difficult to collect[4], and in many cases there would be a long gap between detection and prosecution, because the tanker would be far from her flag state. Any good evidence of the offence (e.g. a photograph) will normally have to be made available – if it is admissible – and this involves cost, which is further increased if the form of evidence has to conform to a particular type demanded by the flag state's court system (e.g. affidavit, signed statement and so on). There has been one case reported in which the prosecution was brought two years after the discharge; this meant that the case could not be handled summarily, but had to proceed on indictment[5].

The 1969 Amendments undoubtedly make proof of an offence less difficult by virtue of the fact that the sighting of a ship discharging oil is much more likely to be evidence of a contravention of the standards. The oil record book will still be an important element in the evidence, but whereas up till now it has been the prosecution who have had need of it, after the 1969 Amendments are in force it will primarily be the

3. See below, section 4.3.
4. As seen in section 2.3.2.1 above, the 1954–62 Convention distinguished between a discharge of 'oil' and of 'oily mixture' – the latter being defined as 100 ppm or more. The difficulty of proving a breach of this proportion in court could normally be overcome only be adducing both a photograph and a bottle of the actual liquid. The reports of the Convention show a depressingly high percentage of cases where there was insufficient evidence to bring proceedings: see e.g. MEPC VI/16/2 and MEPC VI/16/2/Add. 1.
5. *R v Federal Steam Navigation Co Ltd, R v Moran* [1973] 3 All ER 849 at 850, CA; affd. sub nom. *Federal Steam Navigation Co Ltd v Department of Trade and Industry* [1974] 2 All ER 97, [1974] 1 WLR 505, HL.

defendant who will want to use it. This is because the 1969 Amendments make all discharges prima facie unlawful; it is for the defence to show that the discharge was within the lawful exceptions, and the only way this can be done is to plead the operation of LOT – as evidenced by the oil record book.

While the oil record book is improved in form by the 1969 Amendments, there is still no right in the port state to inspect the ship's slop tank. Hence, while prosecutions are easier, there is still much room for improving the system, especially by providing for port state inspection of slop tanks[6].

It is the 1973 Convention which really comes to grips with the enforcement question. Most of the machinery is familiar: by Article 1, parties undertake to give effect to the provisions of the Convention, and, by Article 4, flag state jurisdiction is provided for. By Regulation 20 and Appendix III of Annex I, the oil record book provisions are re-enacted with minor changes[7].

There are three innovations. The first is a set of provisions relating to International Oil Pollution Prevention Certificates. By Regulation 4, all vessels (bar the smallest) shall be subject to regular and complete surveys to ensure that the structure, equipment, fittings, arrangements and materials fully comply with the Convention. A ship which does comply must then be issued with a certificate (Regulations 5 and 6) but, significantly, no certificate shall be issued to a ship entitled to fly the flag of a non-party (Regulation 6(4)). The amendments to Regulation 4 of Annex I effected by the 1978 Protocol have already been discussed in section 3.4.

The effect of the certificate is defined in Article 5. It must be accepted by other parties as having the same validity as one issued by themselves (paragraph (1)); a ship required to hold a certificate is subject to inspection by the officers of a party in its ports or offshore terminals for the purpose of verifying that there is on board a valid certificate, and if there are "clear grounds" for believing that the condition of the ship or its equipment does not correspond substantially with the particulars of the certificate, the inspecting party 'shall take such steps as will ensure that the ship shall not sail until it can proceed to sea without presenting an unreasonable threat of harm to the marine environment' (paragraph (2)). By paragraph (4), parties shall apply the Convention so that ships of non-parties get no more favourable treatment.

6. The UK has submitted to IMCO's Marine Environment Protection Committee procedures for improving the control of ships within the the confines of Article X: see MEPC V/11, discussed MEPC V/19, paras. 68–71; MEPC VI/10, discussed MEPC VI/17, paras. 71–75; and MEPC VII/INF. 5, discussed MEPC VII/19, para. 24. The UK recommends the inspection of slop tanks in accordance with the procedure agreed to by ICS and OCIMF in their pamphlet 'Monitoring of Load-on-Top': MP/CONF/INF. 15/6.

7. The 1978 Protocol adds Supplements to the Oil Record Book made necessary by its other provisions.

It remains to be seen how states will interpret the phrase 'clear grounds', but it is least arguable that 'unreasonable threat of harm' should be interpreted to mean that a ship must come very close to qualifying for the certificate it lacks (or which it has, but did not at the time of detention substantially correspond with), before it is allowed to sail.

The second innovation concerns inspection and co-operation. The fact that a ship has a certificate, while indicating that it has the ability to comply with the Convention, does not mean that the discharge standards will actually be complied with. As long as there remains some motive for non-adherence, the need for policing the high seas remains. Recognising this, Article 6 places a duty on parties to co-operate in the detection of violations, and Regulations 9(3) and 10(6) declare that whenever visible traces of oil are observed on or below the water surface in the immediate vicinity of a ship or its wake, governments should 'to the extent that they are reasonably able to do so', promptly investigate the situation, and in particular investigate the wind and sea conditions, the track and speed of the ship, other possible sources of the visible traces in the vicinity, and any relevant oil discharge records.

In addition to the power to inspect for the possession of a certificate and for perusal of the oil record books, Article 6(2) declares that the officers of a port state may inspect a ship 'for the purpose of verifying whether the ship has discharged any harmful substances in violation of the provisions of the Regulations', but flag state jurisdiction is still retained for prosecutions in relation to discharges on the high seas (Articles 6(3) to 6(5)). Thus at last the most important element so far lacking in the enforcement provisions of the international conventions is provided.

The third innovation is that ships must carry an oil discharge monitoring and control system, fitted with a recording device to provide a continuous record of the discharge in litres per nautical mile and total quantity discharged (or the oil content and rate of discharge): see Regulation 15 (tankers)[8] and Regulation 16 (other ships)[9] of Annex I. It has already been suggested[8,9] that this innovation probably goes further than was necessary, but there is little doubt that, when in force, it will considerably strengthen evidence of violations.

The 1973 Convention does, therefore, provide important new machinery which will considerably strengthen the hands of the enforcement agencies. There are, however, three areas in which developments could, in the opinion of some, improve matters even further. The first concerns detection of oil spills and identification of their source, the second relates to the so-called flags of convenience, the third to the introduction of jurisdictional changes.

8. See above, section 2.3.2.4.
9. See above, section 2.3.3.

4.2 Oil slick detection and identification

If whenever a ship discharged oil to sea its flag state came to know of it, it is quite likely that there would be no unlawful operational discharges; but, until the 1973 Convention comes into force worldwide, and the 'black box' described in section 4.1 above is fitted to every ship, this aim is unlikely to be achieved. The science of detecting the existence of oil on the sea, and then of identifying its source, is therefore of considerable importance for the time being, but even after the 1973 Convention does come into force, detection and identification will continue to be important elements in the establishment of a coastal state's capacity to fight oil pollution.

A great deal of work has been done in recent years – largely in the United States – into methods of detecting the existence of oil on the sea. The development of an effective coastal detection capability is an important step which coastal states can take to protect their shores from marine-based oil pollution: the earlier clean-up can be initiated, the better. The major development has been the production of remote sensing systems suitable for fitting into specially adapted aircraft[10]. This enables large areas of coastal waters to be kept under surveillance, and is not limited to the detection of spills visible to the naked eye. However, as one author points out, remote sensing is not continuous and is expensive[11]. This technique can be supported by siting sensors at fixed, strategic points, either on land or on buoys, and by establishing a series of local receiving centres for information from commercial shipping and aviation.

Once an oil slick has been detected, clean-up can be initiated, but the task of identifying the vessel which discharged the oil remains. It may well be that the discharge was made unlawfully, although this is not a foregone conclusion. At present, means of identifying the discharging vessel by characterisation of the type of oil is limited to what has been termed 'passive tagging' – i.e. taking samples of the oil slick and identifying the type of oil from its natural characteristics. An alternative proposal for the future is 'active tagging', whereby a special substance is added to the tanks of a vessel at the unloading port, and then this substance is looked for in the slick.

Passive tagging can be done by a variety of methods, e.g. infra-red and fluorescent spectroscopy, gas chromatography and thin-layer chromatography[12]. The results which can be achieved are not without

10. See J. F. Fantasia and H. C. Ingrao, 'The Development of an Experimental Airborne Laser Oil Spill Remote Sensing System', *Proceedings of Joint Conference on Prevention and Control of Oil Spills, 13–15 March 1973, Washington DC*, 101; and R. W. Ard, 'Coast Guard's Response to Spilled Oil' (1976) *10 Environmental Science and Technology*, 239.
11. R. W. Ard, 'Coast Guard's Response to Spilled Oil' (1976) *10 Environmental Science and Technology*. 239.
12. For a review of modern developments, see M. Gruenfield, 'Identification of Oil Pollutants: a Review of Some Recent Methods', *Proceedings of Joint Conference on Prevention and Control of Oil Spills, 13–15 March 1973, Washington DC*, 179.

error, and so it is unlikely that, alone, such evidence could found a successful prosecution (certainly in a jurisdiction where the burden of proof is beyond reasonable doubt). However, the real value of such identification techniques is that it can tell the coastal enforcement agency that a particular oil (say Unrefined Southern California Heavy Crude of API Gravity 12.8) is the one found. Combined with an estimate of the time it has been at sea, and of the place or area of discharge (calculated by application of wind and tide information), a fairly good idea of which vessels might have discharged the oil can be gained. It is then a question of informing the relevant authorities and asking them to search the appropriate oil record books and interview the masters. If any one of the vessels calls again at the local jurisdiction, the investigating agency can itself carry out such enquiries. It is the results of these enquiries which could found a prosecution; and, even if there is insufficient evidence for this, the process may have frightened the offender enough to induce compliance in the future.

The alternative means of identification is 'active tagging'. Here, it is not the natural fingerprint of the oil which counts (although this can be used as well) but the identification of an added substance. It seems that the idea originated in Sweden[13], to deal with the pollution problem in the Baltic. If put into operation, a ship calling at a state to unload oil would be required to have added to its residues a quantity of microparticles whose composition is known very accurately – say 80% copper, 10% tin, 10% nickel, or some other combination, each combination being used just for one ship. If oil is subsequently found at sea to contain this substance, it must have come from that particular ship.

There are considerable limitations to this system which make it more suitable for use in coastal tankers than deep-sea vessels; however, the coastal trade can probably be more effectively controlled by introducing adequate reception facilities and/or by requiring adequate segregated ballast tanks in new ships. Active tagging does not present viable prospects for use worldwide: the problems of devising enough distinct combinations, and of introducing them into every tank emptied of oil, are impossible of solution at reasonable cost.

4.3 Flags of convenience

'Flag of convenience' is a phrase well known to the layman, but little understood. Here is not the place for a comprehensive account of this

13. See P. O. Agnedal, 'Tagging Oil Residues in Tankers with Microparticles', *Proceedings of Joint Conference on Prevention and Control of Oil Spills, 13–15 March 1973, Washington DC,* 87.

subject: all that will be done is to mention how these flags fit into the pollution picture. The general issues are dealt with elsewhere[14].

A wide definition of a flag of convenience produced by B. A. Boczek in 1962 still holds good today: '...a 'flag of convenience' can be defined as the flag of any country allowing the registration of foreign-owned and foreign-controlled vessels under conditions which, for whatever reasons, are convenient and opportune for the persons who are registering the vessels'[15]. This definition is still valid only because it is so general. In the past, Liberia, Panama, Honduras, Costa Rica, Lebanon, Cyprus, Somalia, Morocco, Singapore, San Marino, Haiti, Malta and Sierra Leone have all at some time or other qualified as flags of convenience, but now only Liberia, Panama, Cyprus, Somalia and Singapore would qualify, even on a wide definition like Boczek's.

In 1970, the Committee of Inquiry into Shipping produced a more detailed definition which included the following characteristic: '... (vi) The country of registry has neither the power nor the administrative machinery effectively to impose any government or international regulations, nor has the country the wish or the power to control the companies themselves'[16]. The account given above[17] of recent advances by Liberia, which is still undoubtedly a flag of convenience, shows that the inclusion of this characteristic in a detailed definition will no longer do. Yet it is this characteristic which is the important one from the pollution point of view, and which has lead to attacks on flags of convenience from environmentalists[18].

While it is still true that 'shipowners whose vessels bear flags-of-convenience continue to escape prosecution for pollution in international waters'[19], this is equally true of some other flags; and it is now also far less true of Liberia. We may therefore conclude that the importance of flags of convenience, as a group, to the problem of enforcing operational pollution standards is now greatly diminished. This is underlined by the proportion of the world oil tanker fleet registered in Panama, Cyprus, Singapore and Somalia as at 1 July 1975: 5·7% by number, 5·1% by gross tonnage and 4·9% by deadweight[20]. Of course, if Liberia were added, these figures would

14. See B. A. Boczek, *Flags of Convenience: An International Legal Study* (Harv UP, 1962); 'OECD Study on Flags of Convenience' (1972) *4 J Mar L & Comm*, 231. The classic work on the nationality of ships is R. Rienow, *The Test of the Nationality of a Merchant Vessel* (Columbia UP, 1937). A more recent general work is H. Meyers, *The Nationality of Ships* (Martinus Nijhoff, The Hague, 1967).

15. *Flags of Convenience: An International Legal Study* (Harv UP, 1962) 2. Another definition along these lines and equally general is contained in the *Review of Maritime Transport 1972* (UNCTAD) para. 37.

16. *Report of the Committee of Inquiry into Shipping* (Chairman: Lord Rochdale) HMSO, 1970, 51.

17. Section 3.2.3.

18. E.g. D. E. Milsten, 'Enforcing International Law: US Agencies and the Regulation of Oil Pollution in American Waters' (1975) *6 J Mar L & Comm*, 273.

19. D. E. Milsten, 'Enforcing International Law: US Agencies and the Regulation of Oil Pollution in American Waters' (1975) *6 J Mar L & Comm*, 283.

20. Calculated from *Lloyds Register of Shipping Statistical Tables* (1975).

rise to 19·1, 32·8 and 34·6% respectively, but there is no longer any reason to class Liberia as a state which does not enforce operational pollution control standards.

What, if anything, can be done to encourage those states (whether or not they are flags of convenience) which do not exercise the requisite degree of control to put their house in order? The only practical thing is to use diplomatic pressure. Other forms of pressure, such as denying entry to ships registered in such a state, are discriminatory, inefficient (in that the vessels can still trade elsewhere) and unfair to the many first rate shipowners who happen to have their vessels registered in the state.

4.4 Jurisdictional changes

4.4.1 ZONAL CONTROL

By Article 1(1) of the Geneva Convention on the Territorial Sea and Contiguous Zone 1958[1], 'the sovereignty of a State extends, beyond its land territory and its internal water, to a belt of sea adjacent to its coast described as the territorial sea'. However, by Article 1(2) 'this sovereignty is exercised subject to the provisions of these Articles and to other rules of international law', the most important of which may be considered to be the right of innocent passage. This right does not include complete immunity from the coastal state's laws. Article 17 provides that 'foreign ships exercising the right of innocent passage shall comply with the laws and regulations enacted by the coastal state in conformity with these Articles and other rules of international law and, in particular, with such laws and regulations relating to transport and navigation'. Such laws clearly include pollution laws, and so it seems clear that under this Convention, the territorial sea may be regarded as a zone in which the sovereignty of the coastal state extends to pollution control: in short, the territorial sea may be viewed by environmentalists as a pollution control zone.

The question of whether the contiguous zone may also be so regarded is open to doubt. The crucial provision is Article 24(1): 'In a zone of the high seas contiguous to its territorial sea, the coastal state may exercise the control necessary to: (a) Prevent infringement to its customs, fiscal, immigration or sanitary regulations within its territory or territorial sea; (b) Punish infringement of the above regulations committed within its territory or territorial sea'. What do the words 'sanitary regulations' mean here? Unfortunately it is not possible to

1. UKTS No. 3 of 1965 (Cmnd. 2511); 516 UNTS 205. Entered into force 10 September 1964.

say with any confidence either that they include preventive anti-pollution measures, or that they exclude them[2]. In view of the fact that Article 24 describes the contiguous zone as 'high seas', and that the Geneva Convention on the High Seas 1958[3], in codifying international law, enshrined flag state jurisdiction as the general rule, it appears that there is insufficient evidence to rebut the presumption that coastal states do not have preventive pollution control jurisdiction in their contiguous zone. Even if this conclusion is wrong, it must be noted that the pollution control granted by Article 24(1) is strictly limited, so that it is doubtful that the coastal state could regulate a ship passing through the contiguous zone *en route* from a place outside it to another place outside it.

International law is developed by the practice of states, and in the pollution field we have seen recently the enactment of national legislation which could provide the basis for a zonal theory of pollution control in international law – an approach which has been seriously championed at the Third U.N. Law of the Sea Conference[4]. Examples are the Canadian Arctic Waters Pollution Prevention Act 1970[5] (extending jurisdiction over arctic waters 100 miles from Canadian land) and the Iranian Act Concerning Protection of the Sea and Frontier Rivers against Pollution by Oil, of 3 February 1976 (14th Bahman 1354), (extending jurisdiction to the outer limit of the waters above Iran's continental shelf in the Persian Gulf, until treaties are concluded with other coastal states of the Persian Gulf and Oman Sea on pollution prevention). The practice of considering such legislation is growing: for instance, a bill introduced into the United States

---

2. E. D. Brown, *The Legal Regime of Hydrospace* (1971) 146, suggests that action taken after an accidental spill (i.e. curative action) would be within the phrase. N. A. Wulf, 'Contiguous Zones for Pollution Control' (1971) *Univ. of Miami Sea Grant Program*, 133–155, points out that from the deliberations of the International Law Commission, 'sanitary' was intended to be limited to disease, and that the Conference cannot be taken (from the official records) to have altered such intention. The same author, in 'Contiguous Zones for Pollution Control' (1972) *3 J Mar L & Comm*, 587, suggests that because there is a necessity to accommodate other users of the contiguous zone who have an interest in navigation, the rights of the coastal state in that zone are 'limited to that which is reasonable to protect coastal state interests' (p. 539). R. H. Neuman, 'Oil on Troubled Waters: the International Control of Marine Pollution' (1971) *2 J Mar L & Comm*, 349 at 354 thinks the phrase does provide a basis for pollution control, but states no reasons.

3. UKTS No. 60 of 1963 (Cmnd. 1929); 450 UNTS 82; entered into force 30 September 1962.

4. See Draft Articles on Zonal Approach to the Preservation of the Marine Environment, UN Doc. A/C.3/L.6 of 31 July 1974; the Informal Single Negotiating Text UN Doc. A/CONF.62/WP.8/Part II, Article 45(1)(d) and Part III, Article 25(c); and the Revised Single Negotiating Text, UN Doc. A/CONF.62/WP.8/REV.1, Articles 21 and 30; and the Informal Composite Negotiating Text, UN Doc. A/CONF.62/WP.10, Articles 212 and 219. Developments at the Law of the Sea Conference up to the end of its Sixth Session (May to July 1977) are summarised by G. J. Timagenis, *Marine Pollution and the Third United Nations Conference on the Law of the Sea: the Emerging Regime of Marine Pollution* (Lloyds of London Press Ltd, London, 1977).

5. 1969–70. c. 47; 1976 Revised Statutes c. 2; reprinted 9 ILM 543. See R. B. Bilder, *69 Michigan Law Review*, 1; D. Pharand, *The Law of the Sea of the Arctic with Special Reference to Canada* (Univ. of Ottawa Press, 1973).

Senate in January 1977[6] by Sen. Edward Kennedy would extend jurisdiction to the waters superadjacent to the continental shelf of the United States (ss. 502(3) and 503(a)(1)).

These developments suggest that there are many who feel that wider zones of pollution control than at present exist are needed. However, wider pollution-control zones are even more difficult to police than the territorial sea; they can really only be enforced ex post facto; and they weaken the uniform-law approach to the solution of the problem. One seriously wonders quite how effective such zonal claims can be, and suspects that they are made largely for political reasons[7]. There seems no environmental justification for encroaching upon the traditional freedoms of the seas in this way, especially when other methods offer equal prospects of achieving the requisite degree of pollution control: see the enforcement provisions of the 1973 Convention[8] and proposals on the establishment of port state jurisdiction[9].

4.4.2 PORT STATE JURISDICTION

The existing regime of flag state jurisdiction demands that a state other than that of the ship's registry cannot prosecute the ship for any offence committed on the high seas. This creates the enforcement difficulty that if the state of the ship's registry is disinclined to prosecute, the ship can effectively escape control. Additionally, all states encounter difficulties in getting the necessary evidence to bring a prosecution, and there are problems of time and expense. There is, above all, the inherent bias against the coastal state which comes from reliance on flag state jurisdiction. Even after the 1973 Convention comes into force, a ship which has discharged oil off the coast of a particular state at a time when it was on the high seas cannot be prosecuted by that state, even though the coast has suffered quite considerable damage. It has been suggested that port state jurisdiction will at least partially, if not wholly, solve these problems[10].

6. The Federal Tanker Safety and Marine Anti-Pollution Bill, 1977, Bill No. S 182.
7. The Canadian Arctic Waters Act conveniently provides an example of federal, as opposed to provincial, state competency over the area; further, the environmental lobby in Canada is electorally important. In the US environmental measures are increasingly popular electorally, and it is noticeable that Bill No. S 182 of 1977 and others were introduced soon after a number of serious incidents had taken place off various parts of the USA at a time when emotions were running high.
8. Section 4.1.
9. Section 4.4.2.
10. E.g. OCIMF, *UN Law of the Sea Conference, 1974*, 11: '...it is OCIMF's considered view that a system of Port State jurisdiction would be the most suitable means of realistically enforcing operational discharge standards for international shipping'.

What, then, is meant by port state jurisdiction?[11] At its simplest, it is that a state at whose port a ship calls shall in certain circumstances be allowed to prosecute it for an offence committed by it on the high seas. Such jurisdiction is to be concurrent with that of the flag state, rather than being exclusive, although clearly provision must be made for the avoidance of double jeopardy. This concurrent jurisdiction is still vital to provide regulation of anti-pollution measures aboard ship (e.g. design and equipment regulations).

The concurrent jurisdiction implied in this proposal raises difficulties for some. How should priority of jurisdiction be allocated between the port state and the flag state? Should the port state's jurisdiction be limited by distance or time, say, by giving it power to prosecute only those offences committed an agreed distance from the port or an agreed time before entry into the port? Should the limits be defined by a combination of the two, for example, since the ship was last in port? Quite apart from the difficulty of establishing the place or the time of the alleged offence, if the jurisdiction of the port state were limited in any of these ways part of the objective would be defeated. Such limitation seems both undesirable and unnecessary. What is needed is a safeguard against double jeopardy, and this can be achieved by an efficient administrative system. As long as penalties are uniform (and that is an important principle), the flag state having priority does not seem to have any particular value.

How would this 'administrative system' work? The main difficulty here is to ensure that the bureaucratic problems encountered under the existing system of intergovernmental communications are not simply replaced by a new set of bureaucratic problems. The answer may be to leave the onus of ensuring that the ship is not prosecuted twice on the ship itself. Thus, instead of placing duties on a state to inquire whether proceedings are being considered or instituted elsewhere, both flag state and port state are at liberty to institute a prosecution without reference to the other. If the ship finds itself prosecuted in both, it can ask for a temporary stay of proceedings in the state which instituted them later, pending trial in the former, which stay the court must grant. If the proceedings in the former state come to trial, the ship can produce a certificate to that effect to the court which granted a temporary stay, in which case those proceedings must be dropped altogether. If the former proceedings do not come to trial, the temporary stay will lapse and the latter proceedings can continue. In this way, the double jeopardy problem is dealt with without any intergovernmental communication at all. Courts in

11. Detailed proposals on port state jurisdiction made at the UN Law of the Sea Conference are summarised in the Informal Single Negotiating Text, UN Doc. A/CONF.62/WP.8/Part III, Articles 27–40; the Revised Single Negotiating Text, UN Doc. A/CONF.62/WP.8/REV.1/ Part III, Articles 28 to 30; the Informal Composite Negotiating Text, UN Doc. A/CONF. 62/WP.10, Articles 219 and 220.

countries with a developed system of law are familiar with applications to stay proceedings, especially in connection with maritime law. The responsibility is laid upon the defendant, who will in nearly all cases be a tanker-owning company with experience in international communications and which, by virtue of its business experience and the position in which it finds itself, is not tied with the thongs of bureaucracy. Further, it will normally be insured against fines by a reputable P & I Club, which will very often handle the case in practice, and whose international communications are excellent.

In addition to these principles, it is agreed on all sides that any Convention setting up port state jurisdiction should make provision to ensure that ships are not unduly delayed by a prosecution. The right of the ship to leave port on the production of a bond equal to the maximum fine it can incur seems to be the best method. The P & I Clubs insurance system already seems well adapted to this idea, and the Clubs insure 90% of all tankers. Of course there is always the problem of abuse: if a port state has jurisdiction over high seas pollution offences, and an excuse is needed to detain or harass the ship for political reasons, what better method than to bring a spurious prosecution? There is nothing a Convention setting up port state jurisdiction could do about this – but then one wonders if there is not already plenty of scope for that sort of thing. One desirable safeguard would, however, be the inclusion of a provision granting a right to damages for undue delay; another would be that sentences of imprisonment should not be passed.

In one sense, port state jurisdiction departs radically from the traditional doctrine of international law that only flag states may prosecute a ship for an offence committed on the high seas. However, one ingenious suggestion to overcome the conflict is that the offence with which the ship is actually charged by the port state is drafted so that the offence is constituted by arrival within the jurisdiction with insufficient excuse for having no slops, or too few slops[12]. The offence would thus only be committed within the jurisdiction of the state itself, and there would be no conflict with traditional doctrines.

It is doubtful whether a device of this nature would be much use in practice. If it were used unilaterally, other states might justly complain that, although the wording is strictly speaking inoffensive, in practice what is happening is that foreign ships are being prosecuted for an occurrence which took place on the high seas. If the device were incorporated in a multilateral Convention, it would not necessarily be of much use: the states prepared to come together to adopt such a Convention ought to be prepared for their ships to be prosecuted abroad for discharges taking place on the high seas, so why not word

12. *The Concept of Port State Jurisdiction*, Paper presented by the British Branch Committee on the Law of the Sea (Chairwoman J. A. C. Gutteridge) to the International Law Association New Delhi Conference, 1974.

the Convention to acknowledge the reality? There is a further point: any such Convention should be closely linked to the 1973 Convention (a Protocol thereto would be best), which, as we have seen[13], provides that ships must be fitted with a 'black box' to monitor and record oil discharges. There is no reason why this record should not alone form the necessary evidence on which to base a port state prosecution.

4.5 Conclusions

The 1973 Convention provides machinery which will enable adequate enforcement of pollution standards to be achieved within the confines of traditional doctrines, but it suffers from certain inevitable drawbacks. These can be remedied by the introduction of a Convention which would enable the port state to prosecute violations, although important safeguards must be built into it as well. It is impossible to say at this stage what will be the outcome of the UN Law of the Sea Conference, but it is greatly to be hoped that the development of wider zones of pollution control, beyond the territorial sea, will be resoundingly rejected.

13. Section 2.3.2.4.

5 Intervention by a Coastal State

5.1 Introduction

Ever since the *Torrey Canyon* grounded on Seven Stones reef on 18 March 1967, states have regarded as important the question of whether or not a coastal state threatened with oil pollution damage may take control of the situation, even against the will of other interested states or persons (who may include the shipowner, charterer, cargo owner, insurers, salvors and the state of registry). Discussion of the question has been complicated by related issues, such as whether there is a right to intervene in international law, or whether there is merely an immunity for what is an unlawful intervention; whether these rights (or immunities) extend to taking action inside the territorial sea of another state, or whether they merely extend to action taken on the high seas; and the extent to which the sovereignty of a state exists over its own territorial sea.

These questions have been examined by others[1] in considerable detail, so there is little to be added here, apart from a brief summary of the relevant customary international law, to enable the international conventions to be understood in context. Furthermore, where they do not apply the only relevant law is customary international law, but treaties generally regulate most situations which arise. Moreover there is now less likelihood that a state will need to exercise control against the wishes of the private interests involved. In a modern case, the coastal state may direct clean-up on the high seas or in its territorial sea without interference with others' interests; it is only when it wishes to exercise control over the stricken ship itself that a problem arises.

Nowadays, almost invariably, experts employed by or acting on behalf of the private interests (notably hull and P & I insurers and

---

1. See e.g. E. D. Brown, *The Legal Regime of Hydrospace* (Stevens, London, 1971) 139–146; L. C. Caflisch, 'International Law and Ocean Pollution' [1972] *Revue Belgique de Droit Internationale* 7; L. C. Caflisch, 'Some Aspects of Oil Pollution from Merchant Ships' [1973] *4 Annales D'Etudes Internationales*, 213. All three contain copious references to earlier work.

salvors) will be involved from the earliest stage. Since 1967, techniques of tanker salvage and the capabilities of petroleum-safe pumps have developed considerably, so that wherever possible the vessel will be emptied of her cargo (or such part of it at risk of leaking) into a relief tanker, and this can normally be arranged as well (if not better) by the private interests as by the coastal state. Familiarity with the ship herself is always important, and it must be remembered that this is an advantage enjoyed by the private interests over the civil servants of the coastal state. Only in very unusual cases will the operation be beyond the resources of the private interests, and so unless a particular incident is within that class, or unless physical conditions preclude salvage, the role of the coastal state is best confined to controlling the clean-up effort.

The power of intervention is, of course, open to abuse, or to well-intentioned misuse. Its extent is therefore a matter of concern to shipowners and their insurers, and there is a need for certainty. The exercise of such a power on the high seas is prima facie an interference with the freedom of navigation, and so it requires justification. This may be accorded by treaty or by a doctrine of customary international law.

5.2 The Geneva Convention on the Territorial Sea and Contiguous Zone 1958

Prior to 1969 the only multilateral treaty under which such justification might have been sought was the Geneva Convention on the Territorial Sea and Contiguous Zone, 1958[2], Article 24(1) of which provides as follows: 'In a zone of the high seas contiguous to its territorial sea, the coastal state may exercise the control necessary to: (a) Prevent infringement of its customs, fiscal, immigration or sanitary regulations within its territory or territorial sea; (b) Punish infringement of the above regulations committed within its territory or territorial sea'. It might be thought that, even if this is taken to cover oil pollution, the restriction of the breadth of the contiguous zone by Article 24(2) to 12 miles renders it of little use, but this is not so: most collisions and strandings take place close to the shore[3]. The question, then, is simply whether oil pollution is a matter within 'sanitary regulations'. This has been considered above[4], where it was concluded that although no definite answer can be found, the better view is that oil pollution is not a matter within 'sanitary regulations'.

2. UKTS No. 3 of 1965 (Cmnd. 2511); 516 UNTS 205. Entered into force 10 September 1964.
3. See section 3.1.
4. Section 4.4.1.

5.3 Customary international law

Under customary international law, there are two doctrines which might form the basis of a justification of intervention by the coastal state: self-defence and necessity. These two have been distinguished by one author[5] as follows: 'The essence of self-defence is a wrong done, a breach of a legal duty owed to the state acting in self-defence.... The breach of duty violates a substantive right, for example the right of territorial integrity, and gives rise to the right of self-defence. It is this precondition of delictual conduct which distinguishes self-defence from the 'right' of necessity[5,6].

It is doubtful whether a shipowner owes a legal duty to a coastal state to take reasonable care to prevent oil pollution of its shores, still less the state of the ship's registry, and it is further doubtful whether the injury suffered by the coastal state constitutes violation of a sufficiently substantive right to justify self-defence[7]. On the other hand, there may be some grounds for thinking that the doctrine of necessity could justify intervention in an oil pollution case, if the degree of necessity is evaluated by balancing the interests of the coastal state with those of the ship's state of registry[8]. The stringent conditions which must be met are well exemplified by one learned writer in this way: 'If an imminent violation...can be prevented and redressed otherwise than by a violation of another state on the part of the endangered state, this latter violation is not necessary, and therefore not excused and justified. When, to give an example, a state is informed that a body of armed men is being organised on neighbouring territory for the purpose of a raid into its territory, and when the danger can be removed through an appeal to the authorities of the neighbouring country, no case of necessity has arisen. But if such an appeal is fruitless or not possible, or if there is danger in delay, a case of necessity arises, and the threatened state is justified in invading the neighbouring country and disarming the intending raiders'[9]. The same learned writer was further of opinion that necessity applied to dangers threatened by the work of nature[10]. Thus if the doctrine is to excuse an intervention, it would appear likely that

5. D. W. Bowett, *Self-Defence in International Law* (Manchester UP, 1958) 9.
6. See further R. Y. Jennings, 'The *Caroline* and McLeod Cases' (1938) *32 AJIL* 82 at 91 for the distinction between self-defence and self-preservation.
7. L. C. Caflisch, 'International Law and Ocean Pollution' [1972] *Revue Belgique de Droit International*, 7 at 20 concludes that only an armed attack can justify self-defence, and so the doctrine cannot justify intervention in an oil pollution case.
8. This argument is adopted by E. D. Brown, *The Legal Regime of Hydrospace* (London, 1971) 144–5, following Professor B. Cheng and the authority of three arbitral awards: the *Neptune* case (1797), J. B. Moore, *4 International Adjudications Modern Series*, 372; the *Russian Indemnity* case (1912), J. B. Scott, (1916) *1 Hague Court Reports*, 532; and the *Oscar Chinn* case (1934) PCIJ Series A/B No. 63.
9. L. Oppenheim, *International Law* (8th ed. (ed. H. Lauterpacht) London, 1955) 298.
10. L. Oppenheim, *International Law* (8th ed. (ed. H. Lauterpacht) London, 1955) 298, note 3.

the danger must be imminent, the rights or interests threatened substantial, the sole remedy the act sought to be justified and, inherent in the concept of necessity, the measures taken proportionate to the importance of the threatened rights.

5.4 The Intervention Convention 1969

The position in 1967 was unsatisfactory because the doctrine was incapable of formulation with the kind of precision and certainty which shipowners and the traditional maritime states were entitled to expect as a matter of commercial expediency. Accordingly, after a request to IMCO by the United Kingdom, a draft convention was prepared. The International Convention Relating to Intervention on the High Seas in Cases of Oil Pollution Casualties[11] was adopted on 28 November 1969. The Preamble indicates that the basis of the Convention is necessity: 'The States Parties to the present Convention, CONSCIOUS of the *need* to protect the interests of their peoples against the grave consequences of a maritime casualty resulting in danger of oil pollution of sea and coastlines, CONVINCED that under these circumstances measures of an exceptional character to protect such interests might be *necessary* on the high seas and that these measures do not affect the principle of freedom of the high seas....' (emphasis supplied).

The core of the Convention is contained in Article I: '(1) Parties to the present Convention may take such measures on the high seas as may be necessary to prevent, mitigate or eliminate grave and imminent danger to their coastline or related interests from pollution or threat of pollution of the sea by oil, following upon a maritime casualty or acts related to such a casualty, which may reasonably be expected to result in major harmful consequences.' It may be immediately seen that this provision is very close to the doctrine of necessity, although of course formulated with much greater precision. The most important feature is that no power to intervene arises unless there is grave and imminent danger. Thus where the tanker grounds a long way offshore, the danger will rarely be grave and imminent (although it may become so after a while). The interest threatened is expressed widely by virtue of the definition of 'related interests' in Article II(4) – they include

11. UKTS No. 77 of 1975 (Cmnd. 6056); 9 ILM 25. The Convention entered into force on 6 May 1975. As at 31 August 1977 the following states had become parties: Bahamas, Belgium, Cuba, Denmark, Dominican Republic, Ecuador, Fiji, Finland, France, FGR, Japan, Lebanon, Liberia, Mexico, Monaco, Morocco, Netherlands, New Zealand, Norway, Panama, Poland, Senegal, Spain, Surinam, Sweden, Syrian Arab Republic, Tunisia, USSR, UK, USA and Yugoslavia. It had been extended to: Hong Kong, Puerto Rico, Guam, Canal Zone, US Virgin Is., American Samoa, US Trust Territories of the Pacific Is., Netherlands Antilles.

fishing activities, tourism and 'the well-being of living marine resources and of wildlife', although these interests must be 'directly affected or threatened by the maritime casualty'. Hence there is a power to intervene based on purely environmental grounds, in contrast to the position regarding civil liability at common law, where a proprietary or pecuniary interest must be injured before there can be a right to compensation[12].

The operation of the Convention is limited to cases where a maritime casualty has occurred. This phrase is defined in Article II(1) to mean an incident of navigation limited to ships, and by Article II(2), 'ship' excludes an installation or device engaged in the exploration and exploitation of the resources of the sea-bed and the ocean floor and the subsoil thereof. By Article I(2), warships and ships owned or operated by a state and used, for the time being, only on government non-commercial service are also excluded. However, there is nothing in the definition of ship to limit the Convention to tankers: apart from the noted exceptions, it applies to any sea-going vessel of any type whatsoever and any floating craft.

One of the most important limitations of the Convention is that it only applies to measures taken on the high seas. The question of whether or not an extension to cover the territorial sea of parties should be made was one which occupied considerable time at the Conference[13]. Those who opposed such an extension, led by Canada, argued that it would erode the sovereignty which under international law the coastal state enjoyed over its territorial sea, and that this would reduce the support which nations gave the Convention. Those who supported the extension, one of the most vehement being the United Kingdom, argued that it was illogical to have two separate regimes, one on the high seas where powers of intervention were to be limited, the other on the territorial sea where a state's power to intervene was virtually unhampered. Unfortunately, the proposal that the Convention extend to a foreign ship using its right of innocent passage through a party's territorial sea[14] was heavily defeated in Committee on a roll-call vote by 24 votes to 8, with five abstentions, and there was no attempt in plenary session to reverse that decision[15].

The illogicality remains, but whether states will take advantage of it by prescribing different sets of regulations for measures taken inside the territorial sea and those taken on the high seas is not a foregone conclusion. At the Conference the concern of those opposing the extension to the territorial sea did not appear to be so much with the

12. See sections 9.8.1 and 10.2.1.
13. See LDG/CONF/3, *OR* 190 (Canada), 191 (Norway), 192 (UK) and LEG/CONF/3/Add. 1, *OR* 240 (Liberia); and LEG/CONF/C.1/SR. 3 and 4, *OR* 285 to 296, and LEG/CONF/C.1/SR. 19, *OR* 408 to 410.
14. LEG/CONF/C.1/WP.2, *OR* 249.
15. LEG/CONF/SR.5, *OR* 93, where Article I was adopted by 41 votes to none with 4 abstentions.

practicalities of control in a real situation as with the preservation of what they saw as a cornerstone of international law, which preservation would provide them with an advantageous position in other fora (e.g. the current United Nations Third Law of the Sea Conference) and in other situations (e.g. in justifying ex post facto excessive action taken in a particular case within the territorial sea). It is interesting to note that the United Kingdom does have two sets of criteria for intervention[16], but that they would in practice probably amount to the same thing. If any ship inside UK territorial waters or any British ship outside thereof[17] suffers an accident the Secretary of State may give directions, or if that is inadequate, take action himself, where in his opinion 'oil from the ship will or may cause pollution on a large scale'[18] in the United Kingdom or her territorial waters; whereas these powers may only be exercised in respect of a foreign ship outside UK territorial waters 'in any case in which the Secretary of State is satisfied that there is a need to protect the coast of the United Kingdom or the waters in or adjacent to the United Kingdom up to the seaward limits of territorial waters against grave and imminent danger of oil pollution'[19].

A more marked distinction is provided by Spain. She has enacted the Convention verbatim into her municipal law[20], so that the high seas test is whether there is a grave and imminent danger. Her pre-existing law, The Law of Ports 1928, only applied to the territorial sea, and so it remains unamended by the ratifying Law of 26 February 1976. The powers granted to the Comandante de Marina are very wide, and exist when a vessel is considered to be a pollution risk. The distinction between the regimes on the high seas and the territorial sea could be inadvertantly created by a state adopting the Convention verbatim without considering amendment of existing law (although there is no evidence that this is the case in Spain).

The final important limitation on the operation of the Convention is that it applies only to pollution (or a threat of pollution) 'by oil': oil is defined by Article II(3) as 'crude oil, fuel oil, diesel oil and lubricating oil'. In the original draft Convention before the Conference, the words 'by oil' were in square brackets[1] and it was an open question whether the Convention should apply to all pollution. It was the first issue to be discussed in Committee[2], and opposition to covering substances other than oil was forthcoming on a number of grounds, e.g. that it was more realistic and practical to limit the Convention to oil, that this

16. Prevention of Oil Pollution Act 1971, ss. 12–16; and the Oil in Navigable Waters (Shipping Casualties) Order 1971, S.I. 1971 No. 1736.
17. Prevention of Oil Pollution Act 1971, s. 16(3).
18. Prevention of Oil Pollution Act 1971, s. 12(1)(b).
19. Oil in Navigable Waters (Shipping Casualties) Order 1971, art. 2.
20. Law of 28 February 1976.
 1. LEG/CONF/3, *OR* 195.
 2. LEG/CONF/C.1/SR.1 to 3, *OR* 275 to 289.

would assist wide acceptance, that insufficient data on the effect of substances other than oil was available and that drawing up a list (or an exhaustive list) of such substances was impossible. As a compromise, it was agreed to limit the Convention to oil but to investigate the possibility of an additional Protocol on other substances[3]. A Working Group produced such an instrument (but called it an Additional Act) and a draft Resolution[4], but after a debate only the latter was adopted[5]. The Resolution on International Co-operation Concerning Pollutants Other than Oil[6] recommended that IMCO intensify its work on substances other than oil, and this led to the eventual adoption of a Protocol to the Convention at the 1973 Conference[7].

The decision of the Conference to confine the Convention to oil called for a definition of oil, and this, proposed by Sweden[8], was adopted in Committee[9]. Sweden had deliberately omitted the word 'persistent' because it was believed that non-persistent oils might cause considerable damage during the time needed to remove them[10], and for much the same reason the qualification of 'heavy' for 'diesel oil' was also omitted[11]. However, crude oil, fuel oil, diesel oil and lubricating oil are all normally regarded as persistent, and so the wording chosen seems to have defeated the intent to include non-persistent oils (such as gasolene)[12].

While Article I describes when the right of intervention arises, Articles III and V describe how that right shall be lawfully exercised. Article III provides that the measures taken shall be predicted by due consultation with states or persons whose interests are affected, except in cases of extreme urgency. This is an important safeguard against abuse[13]. Article III also provides, as a partial safeguard against misuse of the powers, that states 'may' consult with independent experts chosen from a list maintained by IMCO under Article IV (this list is

3. LEG/CONF/C.1/SR.3, *OR* voting on LEG/CONF/C.1/WP.1, *OR* 248.
4. LEG/CONF/C.1/WP.8, *OR* 252.
5. LEG/CONF/C.1/SR.18 to 19, *OR* 401 to 407.
6. *OR* 184.
7. Adopted on 2 November 1973. UK Misc. No. 26 of 1974 (Cmnd.) 5748; 12 ILM 1319. As at 31 December 1976 only Sweden and Tunisia had ratified the Protocol. By Article VI(1), 15 States parties are needed for entry into force. The Protocol extends the Convention to 'substances other than oil', defined in Article I(2) as '(a) those substances enumerated in a list which shall be established by an appropriate body designated by [IMCO] and which shall be annexed to the present Protocol, and (b) those other substances which are liable to create hazards to human health, to harm living resources and marine life, to damage amenities or to interfere with other legitimate uses of the sea'.
8. LEG/CONF/C.1/WP.5, *OR* 250.
9. LEG/CONF/C.1/SR.8, *OR* 324–5 (debate); LEG/CONF/C.1/SR.19, *OR* 407–8 (vote).
10. LEG/CONF/C.1/SR.8, *OR* 324.
11. LEG/CONF/C.1/SR.19, *OR* 408.
12. As to the meaning of persistent, see section 10.1.1.1.
13. The value of negotiations by the coastal state is illustrated by the *Wafra* case in February 1971 off South Africa; see W. K. Bissell, 'Intervention on the High Seas' (1976) 7 *J Mar L & Comm*, 718 at 727.

now in existence). What use will be made of this list remains to be seen, but its existence is at least encouraging. More significantly, Article V provides for the degree of the measures taken. By Article V(1), they shall be 'proportionate to the damage actual or threatened' – the so-called proportionality principle. Hence, by Article V(2), the measures 'shall not go beyond what is reasonably necessary to achieve the end mentioned in Article I[14] and shall cease as soon as that end has been achieved; they shall not unnecessarily interfere with the rights and interests of the flag state, third states and of any persons, physical or corporate, concerned'. Although this principle is inherent in the customary doctrine of necessity, the Convention improves considerably thereon by enumerating (in Article V(3)) the considerations to be taken into account when deciding what measures are proportionate to the damage threatened or suffered: '(a) the extent and probability of imminent damage if those measures are not taken; and (b) the likelihood of those measures being effective; and (c) the extent of the damage which may be caused by such measures'.

Article VI makes important provision for compensation where the measures taken are in contravention of the Convention. This element too is probably present in the concept of necessity in customary international law[15] and so it is not surprising to see it included in the Convention. However, it had a lengthy consideration at the Conference and aroused considerable disagreement[16]. An attempt by Canada[17] to link the Civil Liability Convention and this one rightly failed on a roll call vote[18] by 24 votes to 10 with 4 abstentions, but unfortunately a more sensible proposal by Canada[19] that compensation be recovered by direct action in the courts rather than by inter-party conciliation and arbitration was also rejected. The result is that the Convention contains a lengthy Annex on conciliation and arbitration, and the only way for a private party who seeks compensation under Article VI to succeed is if the State of which he is a national takes up the case under Article VIII (unless, of course, the coastal state voluntarily agrees to negotiate and settle direct with such a claimant).

The Convention has only these few shortcomings, and is much to be preferred to the customary international law it codifies[20] simply

14. I.e. the prevention, mitigation or elimination of the danger.
15. 'It is a fact that in certain cases violations committed in self-preservation are not prohibited by the Law of Nations. But, nevertheless, they remain violations, may therefore be repelled, and indemnities may be demanded for damage done' per L. Oppenheim, *International Law*, (8th ed. (ed. H. Lauterpacht), London, 1955) 298.
16. LEG/CONF/C.1/SR.11 to 12, *OR* 347 to 358; LEG/CONF/C.1/SR.16 to 18, *OR* 380 to 401.
17. LEG/CONF/3, *OR* 212–4.
18. LEG/CONF/C.1/SR.17, *OR* 394.
19. Introduced at LEG/CONF/C.1/SR.18, *OR* 401, and rejected by 29 votes to 4 with 5 abstentions.
20. See L. F. E. Goldie, 'International Principles of Responsibility for Pollution' (1970) 9 *Columbia J of Transnational L*, 283 at 301–3, concurring that the Convention effects a codification.

because it puts matters on a more certain footing: shipowners and governments alike need to know where they stand, specially when a serious casualty requires urgent measures. It is therefore to be hoped that more states enjoying long and exposed coastlines will ratify or accede to it.

6 International Co-operation

The degree of a state's preparedness for an oil pollution incident will clearly affect the efficiency and success of the clean-up operation – if the sort of equipment, and the people with the right skill to operate it, are not readily available, the oil is more likely to reach the shorelines and is more likely to stay there longer and so perhaps inflict more damage. Hence it is vital that an accident involving the escape of oil (or the possibility thereof), or the existence of a slick of unknown origin be known about as soon as possible by those states likely to be affected by it.

The General Assembly of IMCO, evidencing the generally increased awareness of this fact after the *Torrey Canyon* disaster in March 1967, passed a number of resolutions in 1968 and 1969 recommending various forms of action on the part of governments, covering the reporting of accidents involving significant spillages of oil[1], national arrangements for dealing with them[2], regional co-operation[3] and exchange of information concerning pollution incidents[4]. Five[5] significant steps have been taken on the international front since then – (i) the Bonn Agreement for Co-operation in dealing with Pollution of the North Sea by Oil 1969, (ii) the Copenhagen Agreement on Co-operation in taking measures against Pollution of the Sea by Oil 1971, (iii) parts of the International Convention for the Prevention of Pollution by Ships 1973, (iv) parts of the Convention on the Protection of the Marine Environment of the Baltic Sea 1974, and (v) the Protocol on Co-operation to the Convention for the Protection of the Marine Environment Against Pollution in the Mediterranean 1976.

1. Resolution A147 (ES. IV).
2. Resolution A148 (ES. IV).
3. Resolution A149 (ES. IV).
4. Resolution A189 (VI).
5. See Preface for a brief account of a sixth development, the Kuwait Regional Convention of 1978.

6.1 The 1969 Bonn Agreement[6]

The parties to the Bonn Agreement for co-operation in dealing with Pollution of the North Sea by Oil 1969, which came into force on 9 August 1969, are all the North Sea coastline states, and the area of sea covered is the whole of the North Sea and the English Channel. By Article I the Agreement applies 'whenever the presence or the prospective presence of oil polluting the sea...presents a grave and imminent danger to the coast or related interests of one or more Contracting Parties'. Thus it does not apply to small slicks or spills or the prospect thereof, for these would not present a 'grave' danger to the coasts or other interests; but it seems that fishing grounds and offshore installations would be within 'related interests', and so serious danger to them is covered. The limitation to larger slicks can be justified on the grounds of *de minimis*.

A party undertakes to inform any other contracting party whenever it becomes 'aware of a casualty or the presence of oil slicks' to which the Agreement applies (Article 5). Although by Article 5(2) there is a duty on parties to request[7] masters of their flag ships and registered aircraft to report to them all casualties causing or likely to cause marine oil pollution, and the presence, nature and extent of all slicks to which the Agreement applies, there is no duty on them to make this obligatory, nor is there a duty on them to undertake any systematic patrols. The reason for the first omission is probably the impossibility of enforcing a mandatory rule; for the second, expense.

Once a pollution situation, or a potential one, is discovered, Articles 6(1) to (4) apply to regulate the initial responsibility for assessment and observation. The division of the North Sea and English Channel into zones of responsibility is an excellent innovation, for it avoids duplication of effort and provides the initial framework for a single command structure to be set up. In addition, once the situation is discovered, the state in whose zone the danger lies comes under a duty to keep it under observation: the words 'shall keep....' in Article 6(3) are clearly mandatory.

By Article 7 a party requiring assistance in disposal of oil floating on the surface of the sea or polluting its coast may call on the other contracting parties for help, starting with those which also seem likely to be affected, and parties so requested 'shall use their best endeavours' to bring such assistance as is within their power. This could be very considerable, and in a disaster situation (or even in the case of a lesser spill) could mean the difference between failure and success. The right of request and duty to respond exist, it seems,

---

6. UKTS No. 78 of 1969 (Cmnd. 4205); 9 ILM 359.
7. C.f. IMCO resolution 147 (ES IV): '...Recommends to governments that they (a) require masters of all ships to report....'

irrespective of whether the other machinery of the Agreement has been used or needed.

The Agreement is silent on the question of who pays for the assistance rendered, but it can be safely assumed that this will fall upon the requesting state. Any other alternative is bound to provide such a disincentive to comply with an Article 7 request that it might be rendered inoperative.

6.2 The 1971 Copenhagen Agreement[8]

The Copenhagen Agreement on Co-operation in taking measures against Pollution of the Sea by Oil 1971, replacing an earlier Agreement on the same subject of 8 December 1967, is made between Norway, Denmark, Finland and Sweden, and is clearly inspired by the 1969 Bonn Agreement, because its Preamble recites that it takes that Agreement into account. It came into force on 16 October, 1971.

Like the 1969 Bonn Agreement, the parties undertake to inform each other of the sighting of any significant oil slick which may drift towards a party's territory (Article 1), and a threatened state may request help from another, who 'shall do what is possible to render such assistance' (Article 3). But no area of sea is divided into zones as in the 1969 Bonn Agreement, probably because the parties do not enclose an area of sea. This omission is not, however, a serious or even very important one, partly because it does not decrease the efficacy of the Agreement, partly because the 1974 Convention on the Baltic Sea Environment does divide the Baltic into surveillance zones.

In addition to providing for the exchange of information on various topics (Article 8) and for planning co-operation (Article 9), the Agreement places a duty on parties to maintain stocks of slick-fighting equipment (Article 4). This is an improvement on the 1969 Bonn Agreement, which contains no such provision. Another important difference is that Article 7 of this Agreement provides for co-operation in enforcing international regulations in the following terms: 'The Contracting States shall render assistance to each other in the investigation of offences against the regulations concerning pollution by oil which are presumed to have been commited within the territorial or adjacent waters of the Contracting States. Such assistance may include inspection of the oil record book, the ship's official log-book and the engine-room log, the taking of oil samples and so on'. This power to take oil samples (presumably limited to ships registered in a contracting state), is interesting because it provides an important element lacking in the enforcement of preventive standards at the

8. NDLS Volume II, 637.

present time[9], and is to be welcomed in the areas covered by the states parties to this agreement.

6.3 The 1973 Convention

The 1973 International Convention for the Prevention of Pollution by Ships[10] is not yet in force, although responsible nations will wish to act within its spirit. Article 6(1) contains a duty to co-operate drafted in the widest possible terms, and so is really of little practical importance. However, Article 8 and Protocol 1 lay down a realistic set of duties. Notable differences from the Bonn Agreement are that the parties undertake to issue 'instructions' to their maritime inspection vessels and aircraft and to other appropriate services to report pollution incidents (Article 8(4)), and masters of ships 'shall' report the particulars of such incidents in accordance with Protocol 1. While elaborate details of the nature of the report to be made are given in the Protocol, the duty on states to co-operate with each other is limited to notifying the ship's flag state, and 'any other State which may be affected' (Article 8(3)). The duty to report can be regarded as a slight improvement on the Bonn Agreement, but in practice is unlikely to lead to any greater speed or efficiency. Despite certain defects in drafting[11], Article 8 can be regarded as a desirable adjunct to the international regime.

6.4 The 1974 Baltic Convention[12]

Annex VI of the Convention on the Protection of the Marine Environment of the Baltic Sea Area 1974 contains provisions binding as between the parties (all the Baltic Sea coastal states) which are almost completely identical to the combined provisions of the Bonn Agreement and the above mentioned parts of the 1973 Convention. However, one important difference must be noted: in the Baltic Sea Convention the parties have, it seems, undertaken to conduct regular

9. See section 4.1.
10. UK Misc. No. 26 of 1974 (Cmnd. 5748); 12 ILM 1319.
11. For example, it is not made absolutely clear to which contracting state a master must make his report. Article 1(2) of the Protocol does not specify which of the named persons–owner, charterer, manager, operator or their agents– shall execute the master's duty in the event of an abandonment: are all of them to be charged with the duty?
12. 13 ILM 544. As at 30 October 1976, only Finland and Sweden had ratified the Convention. It will enter into force two months after the deposit of the seventh instrument of ratification.

surveillance patrols – see Regulation 3. In this respect, the Convention is superior to the other two. It is perhaps because of the very special danger that the Baltic Sea is in that the parties have decided to undertake this extra burden.

6.5 The 1976 Protocol on Co-operation to the Mediterranean Sea Convention[13]

This Protocol, like the Bonn Agreement, applies only in cases of 'grave and imminent danger' to a Party's coast or 'related interests', but it goes further in that it also applies if the danger is to 'the marine environment' (Article 1). This implies that if a slick does not look likely to threaten the coastal areas, it may still attract the provisions of the Protocol, although if a party disperses it, it will be unable to call for assistance in so doing unless the coast is threatened. The Protocol is also interesting in that it defines 'related interests' to include 'Activities in coastal water, in ports or estuaries, including fishing activities; the touristic and historical appeal of the area in question; the health of the coastal populations; [and] the preservation of living resources'.

The Convention and Protocol deal with the whole Mediterranean Sea, the largest area yet to be covered by an agreement of this type. So, in addition to making general undertakings to maintain and promote combat facilities and to develop and apply monitoring activities, the parties agree to establish regional centres, through which all information is to be disseminated (Article 6). Calls for assistance may be channelled through these centres, and in certain circumstances a centre may co-ordinate an operation (Article 11).

Article 10 provides that a party faced with a grave and imminent danger described in Article 1 shall, inter alia, 'take every practicable measure to avoid or reduce the effects of pollution'. By Article 11, it may call for assistance if its coast is threatened, and Parties shall use their best endeavours to render the assistance so requested.

6.6 Conclusion

Regional co-operation agreements are an important part of the battle against oil pollution, and are to be encouraged. The proposed[14] Kuwait Convention on the Protection of the Marine Environment is

13. 16 ILM 290.
14. See Preface.

greatly to be welcomed as it will cover one of the most important areas of the world currently lacking a regional agreement. In view of the fact that exploration for oil is going on in the Celtic Sea, and more particularly in view of the large number of tankers entering Milford Haven in Pembrokeshire, or passing through the Channel, an agreement between the United Kingdom and Ireland would seem worth consideration. Doubtless an analysis of tanker routes would reveal still further areas where an agreement would be worthwhile.

Wherever possible, it is desirable that states undertake surveillance. The great problem here is the cost, but there is no reason why means of combining existing military training and oil pollution surveillance should not be investigated – already RAF aircraft on military duties perform oil slick surveillance, and it may be that this idea can be adopted in other areas too. If surveillance proves too costly, then there should at least be a commitment by parties to maintain adequate stocks of dispersant and other oil pollution combat equipment, in addition to the basic mutual co-operation provisions. The means of assessing what defences are likely to be needed are available and have recently formed the basis of a published re-appraisal by the United Kingdom[15].

15. Dept. of the Environment, Central Unit of Environmental Pollution, *Accidental Oil Pollution of the Sea* (HMSO, 1876 (DOE Pollution Paper No. 8)).

7 Financing a National Anti-pollution Programme

The point has been demonstrated several times already that the cost to a shipowner of complying with anti-pollution standards can be considerable, but it is also true that the cost of running an adequate and efficient national pollution defence programme is considerable; it is this fact which probably accounts for the absence of some countries from the lists of parties to international conventions, and for the very long time it took the community of nations to agree that they should provide adequate reception facilities. This cost falls not only upon a coastal state wishing to guard itself from oil pollution from ships, but also upon a maritime state wishing to exercise effective anti-pollution control over its fleet. Some inquiry into how anti-pollution measures may be financed is, therefore, an important element in trying to establish how best to solve the world's oil pollution problem.

As we shall see in Part II, the fundamental principle adopted with regard to civil liability for oil pollution is that the polluter pays, although this has been extended to include those with an interest in the pollutant itself. Of course, this principle can only be fulfilled partially, because the polluter merely insures against the risk and passes on the cost thereof to the rest of society in the price he charges for the services (or goods) he provides. Nonetheless, the imposition of legal duties on the polluter is what dictates the pattern of insurance, and the need to be competitive gives the potential polluter a considerable impetus to keep his premiums down by not causing any pollution. This principle has been adopted by some countries not only in respect of compensation of victims but also in respect of the cost of maintaining stocks of dispersant, pollution surveillance teams, research into pollution abatement, and all other elements which go to make up an efficient national anti-pollution programme.

The means of finance often adopted has been the levy, although it must be said that many of the funds to which these levies contribute are in fact available purely or substantially for compensating victims or for paying the costs of clean-up operations, rather than for financing a complete national anti-pollution programme. This does not, however, mean that levies are not equally well adapted for financing purely preventive measures.

The alternatives to a levy of some kind are unattractive to many governments. Basically, there are just two: central (or local) government taxation, or the charging of fees for anti-pollution services rendered. The first alternative may, of course, be the best solution in a country which can actually afford to increase its public expenditure; the second alternative is of limited practical use. If it is a question merely of installing reception facilities, then there is little doubt that their capital and running costs can be recovered by charging a realistic fee for their use (even if their use is compulsory), but if it is a question of doing not only this, but of strengthening (or instituting) a coast guard service, of stockpiling dispersant and other equipment and of training personnel in their use, there is no way in which a fee-charging system can pay for the entire programme.

The levy, then, must feature strongly in the list of alternatives being considered by any government keen to ensure that the nation is adequately defended against oil pollution risk. There are two major alternatives when it comes to considering the object of the levy – ships, and oil – and further alternatives may be developed by adding other sources of income such as pollution fines, interest from bonds and guarantees against pollution offences, or by levying some other entity who will pass the cost directly to shipowning or oilowning interests such as the licensee or operator of a port, terminal or refinery. All these alternatives are actually in operation in various parts of the world at present.

The most popular object of levy is oil. This kind of levy is currently in operation in Norway, Finland, Canada, New York State and Alaska, and is proposed for the United States Federal law. The Norwegian, Finnish and New York systems are particularly relevant to the present discussion, in that their funds exist to provide the means to protect against oil pollution damage and not merely for the compensation of claims[1]. The Finnish fund has a 4 million Marks maximum, and is levied on those who import oil at the rate of 1/10 of one Mark per ton[2]. In Canada, the levy is on oil imported or exported, at the rate of

1. The Norwegian fund is purely to provide the means of protection, for under s. 10 of the Act Concerning Protective Measures against Damage from Oil Pollution of 6 March 1970,
'...No one suffering damage as a result of discharge or escape of oil or oily mixture can claim reimbursement from the fund.' For the New York Fund see Navigation Law Amendments Act 1977.
2. Act No. 668 of 1972.

Can. $0.15 per ton, but the fund is limited to compensating victims in cases where pollution has been caused by an unidentified slick[3].

The fund set up by U.S. Federal Statute and drawing its finance from oil loaded at the trans-Alaska pipeline terminal (at a rate of US $0.05 per barrel) is also for compensating victims, but the system exhibits the novelty that the fund is generally only available to compensate in cases where the victim has suffered pollution from oil which has borne the levy[4]. Under a Federal Bill introduced into the Senate in January 1977, the same levy on oil transferred between a vessel and an offshore facility, or between two offshore facilities or between a vessel and a deepwater port would provide money for clean-up costs in cases where no other compensation was available, and for research into methods of preventing, containing and removing of oil[5].

The only problem of principle involved with a levy on oil is that there is no guarantee that the oil involved in a particular incident will be owned by a person actually contributing to the levy, so that one group can effectively pay for the response to an incident caused wholly by another group (or individual). This problem no doubt dictated the form of the Trans-Alaska Pipeline Act provisions just mentioned, but such a solution is not suitable where the fund is to be used for paying for a nation's entire anti-pollution programme. Ships carrying oil through such a state's territorial sea, or even further offshore, can pose a threat calling for the establishment of a national anti-pollution programme, but there is no means of levying the oil that such ships carry. This is an inevitable imperfection in an oil-levy system.

The second fundamental system is to levy ships, as Australia has done. Under the Pollution of the Sea by Oil (Shipping Levy) Act 1972, ships over 100 tons which are at any time during a quarter in an Australian port and which, while in such port, have on board at least 10 tons of oil, pay 8/10 of one cent per ton (of the ship) per quarter. This money goes into a fund which pays for stocks of dispersant and for clean-up costs where action against the polluter is impossible. This system too is discriminatory, but as with the oil levy the imperfection is inevitable. One advantage it has over the oil levy is that dry cargo vessels, which as we have seen make a not insignificant contribution to the world's oil pollution problem[6], contribute to the fund as well as tankers. This is not to say that the rating system is not capable of further refinement.

Other systems in operation use a number of other sources of finance. Under Argentine legislation[7] a fund was to have been

3. Sections 737–751 and 756, Canada Shipping Act, Part XX (Ch. 27, 1971) and the Maritime Pollution Claims Fund Regulations, P.C. 1973–2699.
4. Section 204(c) of the Trans-Alaska Pipeline Act, 1973, 87 Stat. s. 87.
5. Sections 506 and 507 of the Federal Tanker Safety and Marine Anti-Pollution Bill, 1977 No. S182.
6. Sections 1.1 (Table 1.1), 2.1.2 and 2.3.3.
7. Decree Law No. 20.481 and Integral Regulations.

financed[8] by the fines imposed on those guilty of pollution, and under Greek law fines are devoted to detection of offences[9]. This system is bound to be inadequate unless fines for pollution are made really heavy[10], but at least it has the attraction of being a highly relevant use of fine-money, and it is less discriminatory than ship or oil levies. The problem is that a punishment should fit the crime, and so there is a practical limit to which a civilised society can go in imposing fines. In addition, as the world shipping industry becomes more effective at preventing accidental spills in port, the number of offences will decrease, but the threat of accidental offshore casualties will still be present and will still require a response at a time when fine-revenue is falling. This system, then, is impractical as the sole source of revenue for a national anti-pollution programme, but is clearly of value as an element in a wider scheme, as is the case of New York.

In Maine the revenue for the Coastal Protection Fund is raised by the fees charged for oil terminal facility licences[11]; this is a wider variation on the oil and ship levies in another guise, for this fee will be passed on to the users of such facilities by their owners. New York has a similar system. However, it has the administrative advantage of strictly limiting the number of those taxed, and of eliminating problems of identifying the owner of oil (as in Alaska for instance). In South Africa, the Oil Pollution Prevention Fund obtains its revenue from a number of mixed sources: guarantees and deposits required by legislation, fines, and the proceeds of claims for clean-up costs incurred by the Minister[12]. It seems likely that deficiencies would arise here and would need to be supplied out of central government funds.

This short survey of systems already in operation leads to some positive conclusions. The ideal system would discriminate as little as possible, it would ensure a constant revenue not falling below a specified amount, and it would be simple to administrate (so that the revenue is spent on pollution prevention and not on administration). These principles dictate mixed sources of revenue, which should include the proceeds of fines, and they favour the system in operation in Maine over that in operation in Australia or Canada; in Maine, by taxing the terminal itself, the cost will have an opportunity to be passed directly to both shipowner and oilowner. However, no specific

---

8. It appears that the legislation was suspended by Resolution No. 171/74 of 19 April 1974.
9. Articles 3(5), L.D. No. 4529 of 25 July/10 August 1966.
10. In 1975 the total of all oil pollution fines imposed in Australia was A.$ 56,115 (see MEPC VI/16/2) and in the United Kingdom £78,350 (MEPC VI/16/2/Add.1). The size of fine varied with the seriousness of offence, the largest being £26,000 imposed upon the *Hemitroches* (British flag) for an offence on 13 June 1975 in Lyme Bay. Unfortunately other countries have seen no reason to relate the size of fine to the seriousness of offence, and have imposed fines as high as $100,000 for the spillage of a tiny quantity of oil.
11. Section 551 of the Maine Oil Discharge Prevention and Pollution Control Act (Me. Rev. Stat. Ann. title 38, Ch. 3).
12. Section 9 of the Prevention and Combating of Pollution of the Sea by Oil Act, 1971 (as amended in 1972 and 1973).

preference for any system currently operating can be expressed here because each system should be tailored to the individual trading position of each nation. The existence of the schemes described is valuable evidence that pollution defence can in practice be funded by means other than central government expenditure.

To establish a levy of some kind is not inconsistent with becoming a party to any of the international conventions examined in this book. Whatever system of funding is adopted, it is better that states elaborate an adequate anti-pollution programme, and that the community pays for it, than that no such measures are taken. Prevention, with respect to oil pollution, is always better than cure. Indeed, there is a clear advantage in both having a levy and becoming party to international civil liability conventions, in that the latter obviates the need for the fund created by the former to remiburse the victims of oil pollution damage (except perhaps in cases where the culprit cannot be identified), and so reduces the demands on the fund.

9 Cases Not Covered by the International Convention on Civil Liability for Oil Pollution Damage 1969 (CLC)

9.1 Sphere of application

The common law principles discussed in this chapter are important for two reasons: they illustrate the position prior to CLC, and they govern the position today, not only in common law countries where the government has not become a party to CLC, but also in such countries where the government has become party to CLC but where CLC does not apply to a particular case. It is now very likely that if the government of a common law country has not become party to CLC, it will have passed its own municipal legislation on civil liability for oil pollution – examples are the USA[1], Canada[2] and Australia[3] – but even here, if such legislation does not apply to a particular case then it is to common law that a plaintiff must have recourse.

There is a surprisingly large variety of situations to which CLC does not apply, so that even in a country like the United Kingdom which has become a party, the common law principles of liability are of considerable importance. As will appear below[4], there are six main areas not covered by CLC, and these are as follows:

1) Oil escaping from river and lake vessels, offshore installations, land installations and pipelines[5].
2) Oil escaping from dry cargo ships and tankers not carrying oil in bulk as cargo.
3) Damage caused by non-persistent oils.
4) Damage suffered by installations outside the territory or

---

1. Federal Water Pollution Control Act 1970, s. 311, as amended by the Federal Water Pollution Control Act Amendments 1972, and the Clean Water Act 1977.
2. Canada Shipping Act, Part XX (1971, Ch. 27, 2nd Supp.).
3. Navigation (No. 2) Act 1970, s. 329 J and K.
4. Sections 10.1.3 and 10.2.1.
5. In the UK, s. 30 of the Petroleum and Submarine Pipelines Act 1975, and s. 11 of the Mineral Workings (Offshore Installations) Act 1971 give special actions in respect of breach of statutory duty, but they apply only to personal injury. Oil pollution rarely causes personal injury.

territorial sea of a party to CLC and all damage suffered on the
territory or territorial sea of a non-party to CLC.
5) Claims against salvors and bareboat charterers[6].
6) Damage caused by oil spilling onto the sea and then catching
fire.

Turning to an examination of the principles of liability at common
law, it is as well to remember that oil pollution not covered by the
Convention can occur in a variety of different ways – for instance, it
may occur as a result of a deliberate act such as the discharge of slops,
oily bilges or cargo tank washings, or accidentally, as a result of
collision, stranding, or leaks in bunker tanks or hoses. It might also
occur if a bunker filling operation is negligently carried out, or during
the transfer of crude oil at a single buoy mooring. In addition,
pipelines may leak or burst for various reasons, and of course there
will be other serious circumstances such as a blow-out from an
offshore well.

9.2 The Southport Corporation case[7]

This case is undoubtedly the most important authority on oil
pollution, and there will be constant cause to refer to it; consequently
a brief review of its facts will now be given.

In December 1950 a small oil tanker of 680 tons gross, the
Inverpool, was on a voyage from Liverpool to Preston. At the entrance
to the Ribble estuary she encountered some very heavy seas, and for
some unexplained reason her steering thereafter became erratic. The
master decided to continue on course for Preston, although this
involved the navigation of a narrow and shallow channel. She ran
aground in this channel on a revetment wall. She was lying in a
dangerous position, and was in danger of breaking her back. The
safety of the ship and her crew were in peril. The propellor was found
to be striking some object, and so the engines could not be used to get
her off. The master decided to discharge about 400 tons of oil to
lighten the ship, and this was carried by the wind and tide to the
plaintiff's beach, which occasioned them considerable expense in the
clearing-up.

The subsequent action was heard at first instance by Devlin J

---

6. Under UK and certain other municipal law, salvors, bareboat charterers and others may be
   completely immune against proceedings for oil pollution damage claims – see below, section
   10.1.1.2.
7. *Esso Petroleum Co Ltd v Southport Corpn* [1956] AC 218 at 222 (Devlin J); revsd. [1954] 2
   QB 182, CA; restored [1956] AC 218, HL.

(assisted after the hearing by one of the Elder Brethren), in the Court of Appeal by Singleton, Denning and Morris LJJ, and in the House of Lords by Earl Jowett LC and Lords Normand, Morton, Radcliffe and Tucker. In the course of the litigation, causes of action in trespass, public nuisance, private nuisance and negligence were all discussed. We shall consider the first three causes of action in turn.

9.3 Trespass

9.3.1 DIRECT AND CONSEQUENTIAL INJURY

Trespass to land has been defined as 'unjustifiable interference with the possession of land'[8]. Even the slightest interference will suffice to ground an action[9], but it seems to be agreed by writers[10] that the interference must be direct – if it is consequential, the appropriate remedy is nuisance. The distinction arises from the ancient forms of action: trespass lay only for direct injury, case for consequential injury.

The distinction between direct and consequential interference is extremely difficult to perceive, and could be called a disgrace to our jurisprudence. Thus, it has been held that the roots of a tree on a defendant's land encroaching on a plaintiff's land is consequential, not direct[11], but to throw stones upon a neighbour's land is direct injury[12]. Counsel for the defendants in the *Southport Corporation* case submitted that the interference by the oil was consequential, and not direct, and that therefore trespass would not lie[13]. Devlin J, while declining to go into the matter, thought that the injury probably was direct[14], and at one point Morris LJ seemed to agree[15]; but Denning LJ was firmly of opinion that the distinction between direct and consequential injury mattered[16], and that this was a clear case of the latter. He cited two ancient cases[17] and Viscount Simonds in *Read v J.*

8. *Winfield and Jolowicz on Tort* (10th ed.) 299.
9. E.g. *Westripp v Baldock* [1938] 2 All ER 779 (sand resting against the plaintiff's wall); *Gregory v Piper* (1829) 9 B & C 591 (a stone rolling down from a pile onto the plaintiff's wall).
10. *Winfield and Jolowicz on Tort* (10th ed.), 304; *Salmond on the Law of Torts* (16th ed.) 42; Harry Street, *The Law of Torts* (6th ed.) 63; J. G. Fleming, *The Law of Torts* (4th ed.) 16–17.
11. *Davey v Harrow Corpn* [1958] 1 QB 60, [1957] 2 All ER 305.
12. *Mann v Saulnier* (1959) 19 DLR (2d) 130, per West JA, at 132 approving a passage from *Salmond on the Law of Torts*.
13. [1956] AC 218 at 224.
14. [1956] AC 218 at 225.
15. [1954] 2 QB 182 at 204.
16. [1954] 2 QB 182 at 195.
17. *The Prior of Southwark's case* (1498) YB Trin 13 Hen 7, f. 26, pl. 4; and *Reynolds v Clarke* (1725) 2 Ld Raym 1399.

Lyons & Co[18] in support. Lord Radcliffe was hesitant: he was 'not prepared to say that...the appellants' action did constitute a trespass'[19] while Lord Tucker expressly agreed with Denning LJ[20]. None of the other judges offered an opinion on the point. The weight of opinion[1] and authority[2] is in favour of the distinction still being of importance, and of the view that even where oil is deliberately discharged onto the sea, the injury will be insufficiently direct[3], on the basis that rarely will there be sufficient certainty that the spillage or discharge of the oil onto the sea will lead to the shore being contaminated – even in these days the wind and tide are not wholly predictable. However, a situation where the injury might be sufficiently direct is where the discharge takes place in harbour or at a terminal, and the harbour or terminal is affected. At any rate, it is quite clear that if oil spills onto the water and then catches fire, resulting damage would be consequential.

Does it make any difference if the vessel has accidentally spilled oil? Suppose, for instance, that there was an accidental spillage in circumstances such that the injury was direct – would trespass still lie?

There are two cases concerning trespass to the person which seem relevant. The first is *Fowler v Lanning*[4]. The plaintiff pleaded in his statement of claim that 'the defendant shot the plaintiff'. Diplock J held that trespass to the person did not lie if the plaintiff's injury was caused unintentionally and without negligence on the defendant's part. He relied heavily on the 'traffic' cases discussed below in section 9.3.2, and on two obiter dicta by Blackburn J (also discussed below).

The second case is *Letang v Cooper*[5], in which the plaintiff sued the defendant in trespass and negligence, for running over her legs with his motor car while she was sunbathing in the grass car park of a hotel. It was clear that her action for negligence was time-barred, and the question was whether her action in trespass was also. The Court of

---

18. [1947] AC 156 at 166.
19. [1956] AC 218 at 242.
20. [1956] AC 218 at 244.
 1. See F. H. Newark, 'The Boundaries of Nuisance' (1949) *65 LQR*, 480; R. W. M. Dias and B. S. Markesines, *The English Law of Torts* (Brussels, 1976) 95–96. Mr. Dias has suggested in a private communication that some forms of interference which *look* to be direct but which are held consequential (e.g. encroaching tree-roots) are so held because the action is invariably being brought in respect of the interference with use and enjoyment consequent on the encroachment.
 2. *Gregory v Piper* (1829) 9 B & C 591 is an authority that to deliberately put matter where natural forces would take it onto the plaintiff's land is a trespass – and the need for a high probability in the effect of the natural forces was stressed. The interference relied on there was, per Bayley J, 'a necessary or natural consequence' of the act. Per Parke J 'the defendant must be taken to have contemplated all the probable consequences of the act...the defendant [is responsible] for the necessary or natural consequences of his own act...'
 3. C. J. Hamson takes a contrary view, [1954] CLJ 172, but he cites no authority and gives no supporting argument.
 4. [1959] 1 QB 426, [1959] 1 All ER 290.
 5. [1965] 1 QB 232, [1964] 2 All ER 929.

Appeal held that it was, and in so doing Lord Denning MR and Dankwerts LJ held that when the injury to a plaintiff is caused by the defendant's intended act, the cause of action is trespass; when unintended, negligence[6]. Diplock LJ thought that no procedural consequences flowed from the choice by the pleader of describing a factual situation as either trespass or negligence[7]. Lord Denning MR, in a passage which seems to totally contradict what he said in the *Southport Corporation* case, said:

'The truth is that the distinction between trespass and case is obsolete. We have a different sub-division altogether. Instead of dividing actions for personal injuries into trespass (direct damage) or case (consequential damage), we divide the causes of action now according as the defendant did the injury intentionally or unintentionally. If one man intentionally applies force directly to another, the plaintiff has a cause of action...in trespass to the person.... If he does not inflict injury intentionally, but only unintentionally, the plaintiff has no cause of action today in trespass. His only cause of action is negligence....

The modern law of this subject was well expounded by Diplock J in *Fowler v Lanning*, with which I fully agree. But I would go this one step further: when the injury is not inflicted intentionally, but negligently, I would say that the only cause of action is negligence not trespass....'[8]

Does this apply to trespass to land, even though both cases are expressly on trespass to the person? The arguments in the cases rely in part on trespass to land cases, and those parts directed towards the distinction between case and trespass are equally relevant to trespass to land. Professor Street's opinion is that while *Letang v Cooper* illustrates the current judicial tendency to avoid overlap of trespass and negligence, 'it is too soon to conclude that trespass has no relevance when negligent conduct is relied on'[9]. Perhaps a stronger conclusion is possible: that it is unlikely that trespass will be allowed when the oil spillage has been accidental.

It may therefore be concluded that trespass will not normally lie in oil pollution cases, either because the injury suffered will be held to be consequential, not direct, or because, in cases where the discharge was unintentional, the court is not likely to allow any other action than one in negligence.

These conclusions make consideration of possible defences to an action in trespass somewhat redundant, but since two special defences

6. [1965] 1 QB 232 at 240, per Lord Denning MR, and at 242 per Dankwert LJ.
7. [1965] 1 QB 232 at 243.
8. [1965] 1 QB 232 at 239–40.
9. H. Street, *The Law of Torts* (6th ed.) 16.

were argued in the *Southport Corporation* case, and since they are also relevant to the case in nuisance, they will be mentioned here.

9.3.2 THE SO–CALLED 'TRAFFIC' RULE

Devlin J at first instance regarded it as 'well established that persons whose property adjoins the highway cannot complain of damage done by persons using the highway unless it is done negligently: *Goodwyn v Cheveley*[10], *Tillett v Ward*[11], and *Gayler and Pope Ltd v B. Davies & Son Ltd*[12,13]. He then relied on two well-known dicta of Lord Blackburn[14] which indicate that the rule applies as much to navigable waterways as to highways on land. Morris LJ agreed with him[15], as did Lord Tucker[16], the other judges not expressing an opinion on the point. That the rule is established for highways on land is undoubted: the question is, is it really established in relation to the owners of land abutting navigable waterways?

Despite the concurrence of three judges in the *Southport Corporation* case, there is considerable doubt that it is. The authority for the extension of the rule from land to sea rests on two obiter dicta; the judicial endorsement thereof in the *Southport Corporation* case is weakened by the fact that Lord Tucker's remarks on the point were also obiter – he felt that there was no cause of action in trespass anyway. Devlin J gave no policy reason for such an extension being desirable, and Morris LJ's concept of the basis for the rule seems off the mark: he thought (with Lord Blackburn in *Fletcher v Rylands*) that 'the circumstances were such as to show that the plaintiff had taken that risk upon himself', whereas it is plain from reading the traffic cases themselves that the basis is quite different. Martin B in *Goodwyn v Chevely*[17] said: 'if a man . . . will not [fence his land] it seems to me he must put up with some of the inconveniences consequent upon it'. In *Tillett v Ward*[18] Stephen J said it is 'an exception which is absolutely necessary for the common affairs of life'. The cases themselves concern straying cattle and bolting horses, against which eventuality it is at least technically possible to guard one's premises: it is impossible to guard one's coastline in such a direct way against oil

10. (1859) 28 LJ Ex 298.
11. (1882) 10 QBD 17.
12. [1924] 2 KB 75.
13. [1956] AC 218 at 226.
14. *Fletcher v Rylands* (1866) LR 1 Exch 265 at 286; *River Wear Comrs v Adamson* (1877) 2 App Cas 743 at 767.
15. [1954] 2 QB 182 at 203–204.
16. [1956] AC 218 at 244–5.
17. (1859) 28 LJ Ex 298 at 302.
18. (1882) 10 QBD 17 at 21.

pollution. It is further difficult to see how allowing the rule in oil pollution cases is absolutely necessary for the common affairs of life.

It is not absolutely clear from the report whether the traffic cases were cited by the defence at first instance in *The Wagon Mound (No. 2)*[19], but they probably were because Walsh J expressly rejected Devlin J's reasoning in the *Southport Corporation* case: '. . . it cannot here be said that the spillage came about from the ordinary use of the harbour waters by the *Wagon Mound* and not from any unreasonable or excessive user, or that this was a risk which other users of the harbour must be regarded as having taken upon themselves. . . .'[20] On appeal to the Privy Council, counsel for the defendants cited the argument[1], but the Board did not deal with it specifically in its advice.

For these reasons it seems wrong in law to apply the rule to oil pollution cases[2]. The trouble is that the only judicial authority positively against such an extension of the rule is Walsh J, cited above; and these things tend to be self-perpetuating. It would, therefore, be wrong to conclude that courts would not in the future continue to apply the rule to oil pollution cases: for the sake of principle, one can only hope they would not.

9.3.3 NECESSITY

The defence of necessity was argued in the *Southport Corporation* case, but is unlikely to be of much practical significance nowadays because it is only likely to apply where cargo is emptied onto the sea to save the ship. Such an occurrence is extremely unlikely these days: salvors and owners alike would always prefer to transfer the cargo to another tanker or a barge if this is at all possible. If it is not, it must be decided whether greater loss will be caused in oil pollution damage than will be suffered if the oil stays in the ship.

The plea also raises the issue of negligence: it was agreed by all the judges in the *Southport Corporation* case that the defence would not apply if the situation in which the vessel found herself was caused by her own negligence[3].

19. [1963] 1 Lloyd's Rep 402.
20. [1963] 1 Lloyd's Rep 402 at 429.
1. [1967] AC 617 at 621–622.
2. F. H. Newark, 17 MLR 579 at 580, submits that the rule 'is restricted to purely involuntary trespass,' but gives no reasons for such a submission. However, the idea is in accordance with the principle that trespass is an *intentional* tort. If the act were involuntary, there would be no trespass, and P would have to show negligence.
3. Although Walsh J, obiter, in *The Wagon Mound (No. 2)* [1963] 1 Lloyd's Rep 402 thought the defence could be raised in an oil pollution case, this is in doubt, as is the question of whether compensation would be payable: see H. Street, *The Law of Torts* (6th ed.) 83; J. G. Fleming, *The Law of Torts* (4th ed.) 91–95; F. N. Newark, 17 MLR 580 at 581: 'We may approve an act done to save life, but there is no more justice in charging up to a stranger the cost of saving your life than there is in requiring him to foot the bill for your daily keep'.

For these reasons, the defence of necessity does not merit further consideration here.

9.3.4 CONCLUSION ON TRESPASS

Trespass will not normally lie where oil has been deliberately discharged to sea because the injury will rarely be sufficiently direct: in those rare cases, such as discharges in harbours or terminals, the spillage is in practice hardly ever deliberate. Where oil has been accidentally discharging to sea, trespass may well not lie on the grounds that the tort is only committed when the injury is intentional. Even if trespass does lie, there is some authority to show that a plaintiff adjoining a navigable waterway must prove negligence if he is to have a remedy. In practice, the defence of necessity will rarely apply, and when it does, the issue of negligence is raised anyway.

9.4 Public nuisance

9.4.1 THE TRADITIONAL TEST OF PUBLIC NUISANCE

In *Attorney-General v PYA Quarries Ltd*[4], Romer LJ produced the following definition of public nuisance, after a comprehensive review of the authorities: 'It is ... clear, in my opinion, that any nuisance is "public" which materially affects the reasonable comfort and convenience of life of a class of Her Majesty's subjects. The sphere of the nuisance may be described generally as "the neighbourhood"[5]; but the question whether the local community within that sphere comprises a sufficient number of persons to constitute a class of the public is a question of fact in every case.'[6] There is always a danger in treating judicial definitions as statutory, but this particular definition has found such favour that it can be safely replied upon[7].

It is immediately apparent that there is no problem here, as there is with trespass, of injury having to be 'direct': it is sufficient if it is

4. [1957] 2 QB 169, CA.
5. See *A-G v Stone* (1895) 60 JP 168; *A-G v Cole & Son* [1901] 1 Ch 205; *A-G v Corke* [1933] Ch 89; all cited by Romer LJ.
6. [1957] 2 QB 169 at 184, closely echoing the words of Joyce J in *A-G v Keymer Brick and Title Co Ltd* (1903) 67 JP 434, which he quoted.
7. *Winfield and Jolowicz on Tort* (11th ed.) 316; *Salmond on Torts* (16th ed.) 50; *Clerk & Lindsell on Torts* (13th ed.) para. 1392. Approved by Brown J in *A-G of British Columbia ex rel. Eaton v Haney Speedways and District of Naple Ridge Ltd* (1963) 39 DLR (2d) 48 at 54, where he held that 7 families were sufficient to constitute a class.

consequential (although, as will be seen in section 9.4.3, it must be foreseeable). It is also clear that if the area affected is too small, there can be no public nuisance; thus, as Denning LJ said in the case, 'when the nuisance is so concentrated that only two or three property owners are affected by it . . . then they ought to take proceedings on their own account to stop it and not expect the community to do it for them'[8]. In the *Southport Corporation* case the oil was deposited with small breaks for a distance of $7\frac{1}{2}$ miles, it was 1 to 3 inches thick and varied in width from 3 to 20 feet, and doubtless this was in the same learned judge's mind when he held that there was a public nuisance in that case[9]. Unfortunately, his judgment on that point was not well reasoned; in the *Southport Corporation* case Lord Radcliffe simply conceded that it may 'possibly' have been a public nuisance[10], and Devlin J seemed to think it was, but his remarks are not explicit[11]. It must always remain a possibility that the neighbourhood affected in a particular oil pollution incident is too small for the incident to constitute a public nuisance.

In addition, it must be possible that in a particular case, notwithstanding the fact that a neighbourhood has been affected, an insufficiently large number of persons to constitute a class of Her Majesty's subjects will have been affected. It might be different if there was always a public right of way over the foreshore[12], in that interference with such rights will always affect a class[13]; but, although in particular cases there may be such a right, there is no public general right of passage or bathing[14]. If the owner of the foreshore (usually but not always[15], the Crown) or of the land above high-water mark habitually allows the public access to the areas which have been polluted, then it seems that the test will have been fulfilled, even though no rights have thereby been granted, for the question is whether or not a sufficiently large class has been affected, and not necessarily whether their rights have been affected. However, where the oil has interfered with the public right of fishing[16], it would appear that the requirement that a class be affected will be satisfied.

8. [1957] 2 QB 169 at 191, citing *R v Lloyd* (1802) 4 Esp 200.
9. [1954] 2 QB 182 at 196–197; citing *R v Mutters* (1864) Le & Ca 491 and *Scott v Shepherd* (1773) 2 W Bl 892.
10. [1956] AC 218 at 242.
11. [1956] AC 218 at 225.
12. The shore between the high and low water marks of ordinary tides.
13. Per Denning LJ in *A-G v PYA Quarries* [1957] 2 QB 169 at 191: 'Take the blocking up of a public highway or the non-repair of it. It may be a footpath very little used except by one or two householders. Nevertheless, the obstruction affects everyone indiscriminately who may wish to walk along it . . .'. It was accepted in *The Wagon Mound (No. 2)* [1967] AC 617, [1966] 2 All ER 709, that the spillage of oil onto the waters of Sydney harbour was an interference with a public navigable waterway, and so a public nuisance.
14. *Blundell v Catterall* (1821) 5B & Ald 268, followed by the Court of Appeal in *Brinckman v Matley* [1904] 2 Ch 313.
15. E.g. the plaintiffs in *Blundell v Catterall* and *Brinckman v Matley* were private owners.
16. See below, section 9.8.1.3.

It may therefore be concluded that in by no means all cases will oil pollution constitute a public nuisance. If even quite a large stretch of coastline (say two or three miles) owned by one person, and not habitually used for recreation by more than a few members of the public, were to be polluted, it is doubtful whether there would be a public nuisance. But where such a stretch is so used – for instance, harbours, public beaches, marinas – there probably will be a public nuisance. In such cases, the question of whether or not a plaintiff can recover damages will rest on whether he can show 'special damage'.

9.4.2 SPECIAL DAMAGE

It is established law that a plaintiff can only recover damages in an action for public nuisance if he can show some damage peculiar or special to himself, which is in some way appreciably different from the annoyance and inconvenience suffered by the general public[17]. It is quite clear in oil pollution cases that the owner of land suffers special damage, for the cost of clear-up[18] and damage to oyster or shellfish beds[19], and indeed just the contamination of the land itself[20], is clearly different in nature and extent to that suffered by the general public, but the fisherman is in a different position[1]. The only judge in the *Southport Corporation* case to specifically mention special damage was Denning LJ, and he seems to have thought it beyond doubt that the plaintiffs there had suffered it[2]. One writer has suggested, however, that where the damaged shoreline is owned by the public, special damage cannot be shown because all members of the public have suffered alike[3]. Unfortunately this argument was not discussed in the case, but to lift the corporate veil here could lead to absurdity. Suppose, for instance, that a defendant causes a nuisance by emitting noise, vibrations and stenches from his premises. Along the nearby high street there are various private traders and a trading office of a nationalised industry, all of whom suffer trading loss as a result of the nuisance. To suggest that a private trader cannot sue for damages for

17. *Iveson v Moore* (1699) 1 Ld Raym 486 (where colliery owner recovered for loss of profit occasioned by obstruction of the highway); *Rose v Miles* (1815) 4 M & S 101 (where a carrier recovered for the expense of having to unload his barges and transport their cargo by land due to defendant's obstruction of creek); *Ricket v Metropolitan Rly Co* (1865) 5 B & S 156 (where a publican failed to recover loss of profit but where the principle was accepted); *Winterbottom v Lord Derby* (1867) LR 2 Exch 316 (passer-by failed to recover for obstruction of public way because no damage beyond delay and diversion, which was common to all).
18. Now recoverable under UK law by virtue of the Merchant Shipping (Oil Pollution) Act 1971, s. 15: see section 9.8.1.1.
19. See below, section 9.8.1.1.
20. See below, section 9.8.1.2.
 1. See below, section 9.8.1.3.
 2. [1954] 2 QB at 197.
 3. 104 LJ 507 (J.B.M.).

public nuisance because the public, through the nationalised industry, have also suffered such a loss, is ludicrous. Again, if the owners of the *Corrimal* in *The Wagon Mound (No. 2)* case had not been private, but a state-owned trading company, to adopt the argument would be to deny the right of recovery in nuisance. The answer seems to be to treat the juridical person suffering loss as one juridical person.

9.4.3 FORESEEABILITY OF SPECIAL DAMAGE

The Privy Council held in *The Wagon Mound (No. 2)*[4] that for a plaintiff to recover in public nuisance, his damage must be of a foreseeable kind. As a decision of the Privy Council, strictly speaking it does not bind United Kingdom courts; but despite this fact and the somewhat doubtful grounds for the decision (Lord Reid, in delivering he advice of the Board, admitted that the authorities were inconclusive[5]), the case is likely to be followed in future[6]. It is noticeable that Parliament, while making preventive measures specifically recoverable in certain cases of non-CLC liability[7] (and thus exceeding the United Kingdom's obligations under the Convention), refrained from specifically making damage by fire subsequent to the spillage automatically recoverable, thus retaining the *Wagon Mound (No. 2)* rule that it will be so only if it is foreseeable.

9.4.4 HAS THE TRADITIONAL TEST BEEN CHANGED?

In the *Wagon Mound (No. 2)* there was a great deal of discussion about the overlap of nuisance and negligence, and whether the latter must be shown to found an action in the former. This issue is discussed below, section 9.6.1, after private nuisance has been mentioned.

9.4.5 IS DAMAGE BY FIRE FORESEEABLE?

This question is also relevant to an action in private nuisance, for as we shall see, foreseeability of damage is a condition of recovery there too.

It will be seen that damage caused by fire and explosion is

4. [1967] AC 617, [1966] 2 All ER 709.
5. At 638.
6. *Winfield and Jolowicz on Tort* (10th ed.) 320–322; H. Street, *The Law of Torts* (6th ed.) 241. R. W. M. Dias, 'Trouble on Oiled Waters' [1967] *CLJ* 62 at 65, note 12. The principle has been applied in *Heaven v Mortimore* (1967) 117 LJo 326. (Karminski J).
7. Merchant Shipping (Oil Pollution) Act 1971, s. 15; see below, section 9.8.1.3.

specifically exempted from the Convention[8], and so even if oil is discharged from a tanker carrying oil in bulk as cargo, the question of whether or not it is recoverable is governed by common law.

In *The Wagon Mound*[9] the Privy Council held that on the facts of the case, fire damage was *not* foreseeable[10]; in *The Wagon Mound (No. 2)* the same court[11], in an action arising from the same incident, held that it was. Lord Reid, in giving the advice of the Board, purported to reach this opposite conclusion on the basis that the evidence before that court was 'substantially different'[12] than the evidence before the earlier court. Regrettably, his subsequent explanation remains unconvincing.

Lord Reid's remarks on the subject indicate that the question of what damage, or of what kind of damage is foreseeable, depends upon the facts of each case before the court; this is supported by subsequent cases[13]. It is not, therefore, possible to say that in future damage by fire or explosion as a result of oil spilling onto water and subsequently igniting will always be held to have been foreseeable. However, such a finding must now be regarded as a serious possibility.

9.5 Private nuisance

9.5.1 MUST THE DEFENDANT OWN OR USE LAND?

In the *Southport Corporation* case, Denning LJ said: 'In order to support an action on the case for a private nuisance the defendant must have used his own land or some other land in such a way as injuriously to affect the enjoyment of the plaintiff's land'[14], and he cited Lord Wright in support[15]. Lord Radcliffe in the House of Lords agreed with him[16]. But Devlin J at first instance had thought that there was no principle that the nuisance must emanate from the defendant's close[17], and Morris LJ seemed to agree[18].

8. Section 10.2.1.1.
9. [1961] AC 388, [1961] 1 All ER 404.
10. This conclusion was also reached by Walsh J in *The Wagon Mound (No. 2)* [1963] 1 Lloyds Rep 402.
11. [1967] 1 AC 617, [1966] 2 All ER 709; Lords Reid and Morris both sat in both cases!
12. [1967] 1 AC 617 at 640 E.
13. E.g. *Bradford v Robinson Rentals Ltd* [1967] 1 WLR 337 (per Rees J at 345: '... what were the facts known to the defendants ... which would reasonably lead them to foresee injury to the health of the plaintiff...?'); *Cook v Swinfen* [1967] 1 WLR 457, CA, especially at 461–462, per Lord Denning MR; *Lamond v Glasgow Corpn* 1968 SLT 291 especially at 292–293, per Lord Thomson; *Tremain v Pike* [1969] 3 All ER 1303, [1969] 1 WLR 1556.
14. [1954] 2 QB 182 at 196.
15. In *Sedleigh-Denfield v O'Callaghan* [1940] AC 880 at 903.
16. [1956] AC 218 at 242.
17. [1956] AC 218 at 224, 225.
18. [1954] 2 QB 182 at 204.

Even if in 1953 there was ground for doubt on the matter, there is none now: for there is a line of cases which clearly establishes that a defendant can be liable for nuisance even though it did not emanate from his land, or from another's[19], and Devlin J.'s approach has been expressly approved[20]. The weight of opinion is also in favour of this rule[1].

9.5.2 THE TRADITIONAL TEST OF PRIVATE NUISANCE

Private nuisance has been described as the unlawful interference with a person's use or enjoyment of land, or some right over or in connection with it[2]. Both Devlin J[3] and Denning LJ[4] in the *Southport Corporation* case agreed that for the plaintiff to succeed, he must have a proprietary interest in land which has been interfered with. This explains why the plaintiffs in the *Wagon Mound (No. 2)* could not sue in private nuisance[5] – their injury was to their ships – but the plaintiffs in *The Wagon Mound (No. 1)*[6], whose wharf suffered damage, did.

Proof of the nuisance shifts the burden of proof that the interference is justifiable (i.e. reasonable) on to the defendant. It is this aspect of the tort which has given it its traditional advantage over negligence, where the plaintiff must prove that the defendant's conduct was below that of the reasonable man. As one learned writer has said 'the distinguishing aspect of nuisance, as compared with other heads of liability like negligence, is that it looks to the harmful result rather than to the kind of conduct causing it'[7]. Prove your nuisance, and liability is established unless the defendant can exculpate himself. No defendant will be able to show that oil pollution is reasonable – it is simply not that kind of interference.

19. *Smith v Great Western Rly and Anglo-American Oil Co* (1926) 135 LT 112 (oil company liable in nuisance for leakage of oil from a railway tank on another's premises); *Hall v Beckenham Corpn* [1949] 1 KB 716 at 728, per Finemoore J, obiter (saying that a member of public flying model aeroplanes in a park could be liable in nuisance); *Newman v Conair Aviation Ltd* (1972) 33 DLR (3d) 474 (aviation company spraying crops held liable in nuisance); *Gertsen v Municipality of Metropolitan Toronto* (1973) 41 DLR (3d) 646 (corporation whose refuse lay on another's land and caused pollution by escaping methane gas held liable).
20. Per Wilson CJSC in *Newman v Conair Aviation Ltd* (1972) 33 DLR (3d) 474 at 479–480; per Lerner J in *Gertsen v Municipality of Metropolitan Toronto* (1973) 41 DLR (3d) 646 at 682–683. Perhaps also per Veale J in *Halsey v Esso Petroleum Co Ltd* [1961] 1 WLR 683 at 700.
1. [1954] CLJ 172 at 173 (C. J. Hamson); *Winfield and Jolowicz on Tort* (10th ed.) 335; *Salmond on Torts* (16th ed.) 69.
2. Per the late Professor Winfield; the description has been judicially adopted – see the references in *Winfield and Jolowicz on Tort* (10th ed.) 318.
3. [1956] AC 218 at 224.
4. [1954] 2 QB 182 at 196.
5. Walsh J rejected the plaintiff's claim in private nuisance – [1963] 1 Lloyds Rep 402 at 427.
6. [1961] AC 388, [1961] 1 All ER 404. The question of liability for nuisance was remitted to the Supreme Court of NSW for determination, but the action was dropped.
7. J. G. Fleming, *The Law of Torts* (4th ed.) 338.

9.5.3 FORESEEABILITY OF DAMAGE

Although the *Wagon Mound (No. 2)* was a case in public nuisance, what it had to say about foreseeability of damage seems to apply equally to private nuisance, and there are dicta in the case to that effect[8].

9.6 Proof of a case in nuisance[9]

9.6.1 HAVE THE TRADITIONAL TESTS OF NUISANCE BEEN CHANGED?

In the *Southport Corporation* case, all the judges except Denning LJ were agreed that the question of liability ultimately depended on whether or not the defendants had been negligent – but this was because they held that either the traffic cases[10] applied, or the question was raised by the defence of necessity[11]. Ironically, the question of whether or not negligence need be proved arose also in the *Wagon Mound (No. 2)* – and the hornet's nest it stirred up has been of considerable proportions. If the boundaries of nuisance were not exactly clear before 1966[12], they are considerably less clear now[13]. The problem has arisen because Lord Reid, in the course of his judgment, had some unfortunate things to say about when negligence need be proved in nuisance cases. It is important to see why he said them.

Walsh J, in the Supreme Court of New South Wales, had held[14] that the fire damage to the plaintiff's vessels was not reasonably foreseeable by those for whose acts the defendants were responsible, but that this did not affect the defendants' liability in nuisance, because foreseeability of damage was not, in his view of the law, a pre-requisite to recovery in that tort; however it was in negligence, and so he held that the defendants were not liable in negligence.

Now Lord Reid, delivering the advice of the Board, addressed himself to the question of whether or not foreseeability of damage was a prerequisite to recovery in nuisance[15]. After his own review of the cases[16], he concluded: 'In their Lordships' judgment the cases point

---

8. [1967] AC 617 at 636G–637A, 638E, and 638F–640D, per Lord Reid.
9. See also section 9.7.
10. Above, section 9.3.2.
11. Above, section 9.3.3.
12. P. H. Winfield, 'Nuisance as a Tort' [1931] *CLJ* 189; F. H. Newark, 'The Boundaries of Nuisance' (1949) 65 *LQR* 480.
13. R. W. M. Dias, 'Trouble on Oiled Waters' [1967] *CLJ* 62 at 66.
14. [1963] 1 Lloyd's Rep 402.
15. [1967] 1 AC 617 at 633G–634E.
16. [1967] 1 AC 617 at 634E–638D.

strongly to there being no difference as to the measure of damages between nuisance and negligence *but they are not conclusive*[17] (my emphasis). So it was desirable to consider the question in principle, and it was in the course of so doing that the trouble began. It is important to realise that at this stage Lord Reid is still addressing himself to the question of foreseeability of damage. This question concerns not whether the plaintiff has to prove something about the actual quality of a defendant's conduct to succeed in nuisance, but whether, given the events which did take place, the damage actually suffered by the plaintiff ought to have been contemplated by a reasonable man.

Lord Reid said:

'Comparing nuisance with negligence the main argument for the respondent was that in negligence foreseeability is an essential element in determining liability and therefore it is logical that foreseeability should also be an essential element in determining the amount of damages: but negligence is not an essential element in determining liability for nuisance and therefore it is illogical to bring in foreseeability when determining the amount of damages. It is quite true that negligence is not an essential element in nuisance. Nuisance is a term used to cover a wide variety of tortious acts or omissions and in many negligence in the narrow sense is not essential. An occupier may incur liability for the emission of noxious fumes or noise although he has used the utmost care in building and using his premises. The amount of fumes or noise which he can lawfully emit is a question of degree and he or his advisers may have miscalculated what can be justified. Or he may deliberately obstruct the highway adjoining his premises to a greater degree than is permissible, hoping that no one will object. On the other hand the emission of fumes or noise or the obstruction of the adjoining highway may often be the result of pure negligence on his part: there are many cases (e.g. *Dollman v A. and S. Hillman Ltd*[18]) where precisely the same facts will establish liability both in nuisance and in negligence. And although negligence may not be necessary, fault of some kind is almost always necessary and fault generally involves foreseeability, e.g., in cases like *Sedleigh-Denfield v O'Callaghan*[19] the fault is in failing to abate the nuisance of the existence of which the defender is or ought to be aware as likely to cause damage to his neighbour. (Their Lordships express no opinion about cases like *Wringe v Cohen*[20], on which neither counsel relied.) The

17. [1967] 1 AC 617 at 638E.
18. [1941] 1 All ER 355, CA.
19. [1940] AC 880, [1940] 3 All ER 349.
20. [1940] 1 KB 229, [1939] 4 All ER 241, CA.

present case is one of creating a danger to persons or property in
navigable waters (equivalent to a highway) and there it is
admitted that fault is essential – in this case the negligent
discharge of the oil.

> "But how are we to determine whether a state of affairs in
> or near a highway is a danger? This depends, I think, on
> whether injury may reasonably be foreseen. If you take all
> the cases in the books, you will find that if the state of affairs
> is such that injury may reasonably be anticipated to persons
> using the highway it is a public nuisance" (per Lord Denning
> MR in *Morton v Wheeler*[1]).

So in the class of nuisance which includes this case foreseeability
is an essential element in determining liability.

> It could not be right to discriminate between different cases of
> nuisance so as to make foreseeability a necessary element in
> determining damages in those cases where it is a necessary
> element in determining liability, but not in others. So the choice
> is between it being a necessary element in all cases of nuisance or
> in none. In their Lordships' judgment the similarities between
> nuisance and other forms of tort to which *The Wagon Mound
> (No. 1)* applies far outweigh any differences, and they must
> therefore hold that the judgment appealed from is wrong on this
> branch of the case. It is not sufficient that the injury suffered by
> the respondents' vessels was the direct result of the nuisance if
> that injury was in the relevant sense unforeseeable.'

In his consideration of principle, Lord Reid was seeking to find
common ground between nuisance and negligence, so that he could
conclude that, as foreseeability of damage was a prerequisite to
recovery in the latter (see *The Wagon Mound (No. 1)*[2]), it ought to be
in the former. He found the common ground in that 'fault' is required
to establish liability in each[3]: '... although negligence may not be
necessary, fault of some kind is almost always necessary'. Having done
so, he completed his object by continuing '... and fault generally
involves foreseeability'.

It is perfectly clear that Lord Reid understood that not all fault is
negligent fault: the sentence just quoted proves that, as does his
previous statement that 'it is quite true that negligence is not an
essential element in nuisance'[4]. The person who commits a nuisance

1. (1956) 31st January (unreported), CA (No. 33 of 1956).
2. [1961] 1 AC 388.
3. [1967] 1 AC 617 at 639F.
4. [1967] 1 AC 617 at 639C.

may be legitimately described as being at fault, even though he has not been negligent – and indeed the traditional concept is that if he has committed a nuisance, proof that he has taken all reasonable care will not avail him, because his task is to show that the nuisance itself, the state of affairs complained of, is reasonable. Lord Reid simply raised the level of generality at which he chose to look at negligent fault in the tort of negligence, so that he could find common ground between that tort and nuisance.

It seems therefore that, so far as any of the comments in that passage might look as if they are referring to when a plaintiff must prove negligence and when not, they conflict with other of his comments (notably 'negligence is not an essential element in determining *liability* for nuisance'[5] (my emphasis)); and that they are obiter, because they are made in connection with an exposition of the law relating to foreseeability of damage.

If that argument does not convince, the following passage may still be thought to present problems: 'Nuisance is a term used to cover a wide variety of tortious acts or omissions and in many negligence in the narrow sense is not essential'[6]. This seems to suggest that in some cases, at least, negligence is essential to liability in nuisance (and that in such cases the two torts are identical). But his example given to illustrate this sentence clearly shows that he is thinking of cases where negligence can in fact be proved: '... emission of fumes or noise or the obstruction of the adjoining highway may often be the result of pure negligence on his part: there are many cases (e.g. *Dollman v Hillman* [1941] All ER 355) where precisely the same facts will establish liability both in nuisance and in negligence'[7].

If this is correct, then Lord Reid has left the law described above in sections 9.4 and 9.5 unscathed. If it is not correct, then we must answer the question, when will proof of negligence in the narrow sense be a prerequisite to success in a nuisance action? The authors of one leading text-book have submitted that the answer lies in the nature of the defendant's conduct. 'If he was or ought to have been aware that it was an inevitable or likely consequence of his activity that damage would be caused to the plaintiff's interest then, providing the injury or interference is sufficiently substantial, there is a prima facie case in nuisance and it is for the defendant to exculpate himself. Otherwise the plaintiff must himself prove that the defendant was negligent in the manner in which he prosecuted his activity or in failing to abate the nuisance[8].' In other words, if he was deliberate or reckless as to the damage to be caused, it is nuisance; if negligent, negligence. I respectfully agree that if there are cases where negligence is a

5. [1967] 1 AC 617 at 639C.
6. [1967] 1 AC 617 at 639C.
7. [1967] 1 AC 617 at 639E.
8. *Winfield and Jolowicz on Tort* (10th ed.) 324.

prerequisite to success in nuisance, they are to be ascertained on this test, if only because it is extremely difficult to think of a rational alternative.

9.6.2 CONCLUSION ON PUBLIC AND PRIVATE NUISANCE

There is no binding precedent to suggest that the traditional basis of nuisance has been changed; the remarks of Lord Reid in *Wagon Mound (No. 2)* are obiter, and should be confined to the purpose with which they were made, namely, to help establish a foreseeability of damage rule in nuisance. Only time will tell whether the courts will clarify the boundary between nuisance and negligence, or whether they will further obscure it. If it became established law that, for a plaintiff to succeed in nuisance 'proper' without proof of negligence, he must show that the defendant was or ought to have been aware that damage to the plaintiff's interest was an inevitable or likely consequence of the defendant's activity, the tort of nuisance would rarely be of use to a plaintiff in oil pollution cases. The reason is that, although some ships do deliberately discharge oil (largely tank washings or oil bilges) near enough to coasts inevitably to affect a plaintiff's interests, the number is very small indeed, and the chances of finding the culprit are extremely slim[9]. Where the discharge has not been deliberate, as where there has been a stranding due to a navigational error, to show that oil pollution damage was an inevitable or likely consequence of that error would, in many cases, be as difficult to prove as negligence itself.

It is reasonable to conclude that the traditional law has a good chance of survival after *The Wagon Mound (No. 2)*, so that serious oil pollution incidents, including those which are in fact accidental, will be capable of founding actions for damages in public nuisance, without proof of negligence. Oil pollution incidents interfering with an interest in land appear capable of founding an action in private nuisance. However, it must remain possible that a court will follow the 'traffic' cases (section 9.3.2) and consequently hold in some cases that the plaintiff must prove negligence.

The barriers to a plaintiff trying to recover without proof of negligence are therefore considerable. Trespass to land is probably not

---

9. It may be noted here that in *Eastern Asia Navigation Co Ltd v Fremantle Harbour Trust Comrs and Commonwealth of Australia* (1951) 83 CLR 353, where P's vessel had suffered fire damage due to oil floating in Fremantle harbour, their claim failed because, inter alia, they could not show that any defendant had been responsible for the spillages of oil causing the fire, or were in control of all the areas where spillages likely to have contributed to the oil in the harbour were made.

available (section 9.3.4). In nuisance, he must fight arguments that the 'traffic cases' apply, or that he must show that the defendant knew, or ought to have known that what he did was likely to cause the plaintiff actionable damage – or resort to negligence if he cannot.

9.7 Negligence

9.7.1 SOME DIFFICULTIES IN PROVING NEGLIGENCE

In this section, for ease of exposition, it will be assumed that there has been a stranding leading to an oil pollution incident, unless otherwise stated.

The first difficulty a plaintiff might find is the argument that the oil pollution damage has resulted not from the stranding (which may be denied to have been negligent), but from the subsequent failure to keep the oil from reaching the place where it caused damage; and that there has been no negligence involved in that failure. The kind of situation in which this argument is likely to be of use to a defendant is where the shipowner has had the resources to mount a speedy and impressive lightening and clean-up operation following a casualty[10], although it is also less likely that such a defendant would wish to adopt such an argument.

It can be seen at once that this argument raises the whole question of what is the cause of an event, a question which has exercised the minds of lawyers over the centuries, and on which no single consensus has yet emerged. It is, however, now plain that in law an event can have more than one cause[11], and so the attractiveness which this argument may have had in the past for judges who adhere to the sole or monistic theory of causation[12] can no longer be relied upon. No attempt will be made here to assess the chances which the argument might have in an action today, for, as one writer has put it, 'the whole approach to the concept of causation is unfettered and permits infinite variation with freedom to choose one or more causes out of a selection of factors which contributed towards the actual happening of the event'[13]. It is sufficient to point out that, should a modern bench be

10. A fairly common occurrence, especially where the shipowner is a subsidiary of a large multi-national oil company.
11. See e.g. the majority decision in the House of Lords in *Stapley v Gypsum Mines Ltd* [1953] AC 663, [1953] 2 All ER 478, and the unanimous decision of the House of Lords in *Baker v Willoughby* [1970] AC 467, [1969] 3 All ER 1528.
12. Notably Lord Wright: see 'Notes on Causation and Responsibility in English Law', [1955] *CLJ* 163, emphasising the importance of this theory.
13. *Charlesworth on Negligence* (5th ed. (ed. R. A. Percy)) para. 77.

inclined to take the view urged by the argument, there are precedents to support such a view[14].

A second argument which invites a similar view of the events but which is quite opposite in its approach, is that the pollution was the result, not of the failure to keep the oil in, but of the stranding; and that, while the failure to keep the oil in may or may not be admittedly negligent, the stranding itself was not negligent. This argument will be particularly attractive to the defendant where the ship has gone aground as a result of the negligence of another vessel, as may be the case when, for instance, the stranding has resulted from a course alteration made to avoid another ship proceeding in the wrong direction down a traffic separation scheme[15].

Another argument may be stated in this way: that the casualty and the spillage must be regarded as a single, continuing event, and that, because all reasonable efforts were made after the spillage to contain the oil, there has been no breach of the duty of care. This argument impliedly formulates the duty of care for breach of which the plaintiff must sue as being a duty to take reasonable care to stop any spilled oil reaching a place where it affects a plaintiff, rather than being a duty to take care that oil does not spill at all.

Naturally, the chances of any one of these arguments succeeding in any given case will depend heavily on the individual circumstances which pertain, but they do illustrate some of the legal difficulties which may be encountered in proving negligence in an oil pollution case.

9.7.2 BREACH OF NAVIGATION REGULATIONS

Revised International Collision Regulations, agreed at the International Conference on the Safety of Life at Sea 1960[16] came into force for United Kingdom law[17] by virtue of the Collision Regulations (Ships and Seaplanes on the Water) and Signals of Distress (Ships) Order 1965[18], and some traffic separation schemes recommended by IMCO are added thereto as collision regulations by the Collision

---

14. E.g. *Radley v London and North Western Rly* (1876) 1 App Cas 754, HL; *British Columbia Electric Rly Co v Loach* [1916] 1 AC 719, PC; *Swadling v Cooper* [1931] AC 1, HL; *Quinn v Burch Bros (Builders) Ltd* [1966] 2 QB 370, [1966] 2 All ER 283, CA; *Norris v W. Moss & Sons Ltd* [1954] 1 All ER 324, [1954] 1 WLR 346 (Vaisey J).

15. This is thought to have been the cause of the collision between *H.M.S. Achilles* and the *Olympic Alliance* in the Dover Strait on 12 November 1975. See *The Times*, 13/11/75, p. 1; *The Guardian*, 13/11/75, p. 1; *The Times*, 19/2/76, p. 4.

16. See above, section 3.2.1.

17. As extended to the Isle of Man and Channel Islands. For the effect of the Regulations on foreign ships, see sections 418(2) and 424 of the Merchant Shipping Act 1894.

18. S.I. 1965 No. 1525.

Regulations (Traffic Separation Schemes) Order 1972[19]. Further revised regulations are expected now that the 1972 International Convention which revised the 1960 Convention has come into force internationally, and more will follow when the 1974 International Convention on the Safety of Life at Sea does so[20].

Before 1911, the rule was that a breach of the Regulations raised a presumption of causative fault; section 419(4) of the Merchant Shipping Act 1894 enacted that 'where, in a case of collision, it is proved to the court before which the case is tried that any of the collision regulations have been infringed, the ship by which the regulation has been infringed shall be deemed to be in fault, unless it is shown to the satisfaction of the court that the circumstances of the case made departure from the regulation necessary'. This rule has now been abolished by section 4 of the Maritime Conventions Act 1911, and so the question nowadays is, did the failure to obey the regulations contribute to the damage suffered?[1] If not, the failure will not affect the question of civil liability; if so, the question will be whether the failure was negligent[2]. Hence, the issue of negligence must be met at common law without the assistance of presumptions, and a plaintiff will be unable to avail himself of the fact that in almost every casualty some breach of the regulations (albeit usually a minor one) can be shown.

9.7.3 EVIDENCE: THE MARINE INQUIRY

It often happens that, following a marine casualty, an inquiry is held and a report made. One important question in relation to the burden of proof in negligence is whether the findings of such an inquiry are admissible in subsequent civil proceedings as evidence of the truth of the matters referred to therein. It is not only a plaintiff who may wish to adduce the report: there may be findings of fact, or evidence of witnesses, favouring the defence.

The rules under which such inquiries take place naturally vary widely from jurisdiction to jurisdiction. The provisions currently governing such inquiries in the United Kingdom are contained in Part VI of the Merchant Shipping Act 1894, but much of this has been prospectively repealed by s. 100(3) of, and Sch. 5 to, the Merchant Shipping Act 1970, as from a day yet to be appointed[3], and replaced

19. S.I. 1972 No. 809, as amended by the Collision Regulations (Traffic Separation Schemes) (Amendment) Order 1974, S.I. 1974 No. 1890 and by S.I. 1972 No. 1267 (which postponed until 1 December 1972 the commencement of one of the schemes).
20. See above, section 3.2.1.
 1. See *Marsden's The Law of Collisions at Sea* (11th ed. by K. C. McGuffie) Chapters 1 and 23.
 2. See e.g. *The Karen Toft* [1955] 2 Lloyd's Rep 120.
 3. As at 21 September 1976 no day had been appointed and no regulation under the 1970 Act promulgated.

with new provisions contained in sections 52 to 61 of that Act. Under the 1894 Act, the person conducting the formal inquiry will be a public officer acting under a duty, the inquiry will normally be in open court and a report must be made. It is likely that these elements of the rules[4] will be reproduced when new regulations under the 1970 Act are made. One may note with interest that not every likely oil pollution casualty could give rise to an inquiry: for instance, the *Torrey Canyon* casualty was not inquired into under the Merchant Shipping Act because, not being a British ship, nor being stranded 'on or near the coasts of the United Kingdom'[5], there was no jurisdiction for such an inquiry. The inquiry which was made was quite different[6].

The findings of a court of inquiry expressed in documentary form, or the oral testimony at subsequent civil proceedings of the officer who conducted the inquiry, would be regarded at common law as opinion evidence or hearsay or both. A finding that ship X failed to alter course to starboard would be opinion evidence, as would a finding that this constituted negligence; the recorded evidence of an eye-witness to the effect that ship X failed to alter course to starboard would be hearsay at the subsequent civil proceedings.

Many of the more valuable parts of the report are, therefore, likely to be opinion evidence in subsequent civil proceedings, and as such are excluded at common law unless (a) the evidence concerns matters which call for the special skill or knowledge of an expert and the witness is an expert on such matters, or (b) the facts upon which that opinion is based cannot be stated without reference to the opinion in a manner equally conducive to the ascertainment of the truth[7]. This latter exception is given statutory clarification by s. 3(2) of the Civil Evidence Act 1972: 'It is hereby declared that where a person is called as a witness in any civil proceedings, a statement of opinion by him on any relevant matter on which he is not qualified to give expert evidence, if made as a way of conveying relevant facts personally perceived by him, is admissible as evidence of what he perceived'.

These common law exceptions do not cover findings such as the ones mentioned above, and the formulation in s. 3(2) of the Civil Evidence Act 1972 does not cover them because the officer who conducted the inquiry did not personally perceive them: although an eye-witness might be permitted to give oral testimony at the trial of

4. Shipping Casualties and Appeals and Re-hearings Rules 1923, S.R. & O. 1923 No. 752.
5. See ss. 464 and 465 of the Merchant Shipping Act 1894. The phrase was taken by Gorrell Barnes J in *The Fulham* [1898] P 206 as being limited to within territorial waters. Section 55 of the 1970 Act substitutes for the phrase the words 'in the United Kingdom or the territorial waters thereof'. Nowadays, 'on or near' could well be interpreted on the basis that if damage is caused, the casualty was 'near'.
6. There was an investigation by a Committee of Scientists on the Scientific and Technological Aspects of the disaster: see *The Torrey Canyon* (HMSO, 1967); see also Cmnd. 3246.
7. *Sherrard v Jacob* [1965] NI 151 at 157–158, per Lord Macdermott; cited by Sir Rupert Cross, *Evidence* (4th ed.) 381.

the civil action as to what was the speed of ship X, or her course, a finding of the court of inquiry at which such evidence had already been given, to the same effect, would be inadmissible.

This exclusion is not affected by s. 1 of the Civil Evidence Act 1972, for, although it permits hearsay evidence of opinion to be given by extending the provisions of ss. 2 and 4 of the Civil Evidence Act 1968, it is necessary to start the chain of record with a matter of which direct oral evidence would be admissible – and as has been seen, direct oral evidence by the officer who held the inquiry would be inadmissible.

It therefore appears that the findings of the marine inquiry, which are potentially so valuable to prospective parties to a civil action for oil pollution damage, would be inadmissible in those proceedings.

Certain perhaps less valuable elements of the report will not be opinion evidence, but will be hearsay – for instance, the recorded evidence of eye-witnesses as to what actually took place. This too will be excluded at common law unless it can be fitted into one of the recognised exceptions to the hearsay rule. The question arises, therefore, whether statements of this nature contained in the report are within the 'public documents' exception to the hearsay rule.

There is a longstanding exception, retained for civil proceedings by the Civil Evidence Act 1968[8], that public documents, including inquisitions, surveys, assessments, reports and returns, are admissible but not conclusive as to their contents when made under public authority. For a document to qualify under this exception, it must be one produced as a result of 'a judicial or quasi-judicial duty to inquire by a public officer'[9]. Further, it will only be a public document if it is made for the purpose of the public making use of it, and to enable the public to refer to it[10].

Despite the formal nature of the inquiry and the statutory basis thereof, it is difficult to find this object in the proceedings. Section 466(6) of the 1894 Act requires that, in the usual case, the report shall be made 'to the Department of Trade' (although copies must be given to parties to the proceedings on application[11]) and it is only when there is a question as to the cancelling or suspending of a certificate that the court must state in open court the decision to which they have come[12]. The lack of conclusive evidence as to the purpose of these inquiries could prove fatal to a party seeking to adduce a report produced by

8. Section 9(2)(c). By s. 9(6) the words used in s. 9 do not alter the common law rules, but merely identify them.
9. *Phipson on Evidence* (12th ed., 1976) para. 1099, citing Lord Blackburn in *Sturla v Freccia* (1880) 5 App Cas 623. Remarks of Lord Blackburn applied in *Thrasyvoulos Ioannou v Papa Christoforos Demetriou* [1952] AC 84, [1952] 1 All ER 179, PC.
10. E.g. in *Sturla v Freccia* (1880) 5 App Cas 623, and *Ioannou v Demetriou* [1952] AC 84, [1952] 1 All ER 179, PC.
11. Shipping Casualties and Appeals and Re-hearing Rules, S.R. & O. 1923 No. 752, r. 18.
12. Section 470(2) of the Merchant Shipping Act 1894. Even then there is no provision to the effect that the report must be published, or kept in a record office open to the public.

one. Of course, in other countries the basis may be more clearly established as being public in the required sense.

In view of the doubtful admissibility of these parts of the report at common law, it becomes specially relevant to consider the statutory position. There are provisions in the Merchant Shipping Act itself, and in the Civil Evidence Acts 1968 and 1972.

Section 695(1) of the Merchant Shipping Act 1894 provides that 'Where a document is by this Act declared to be admissible in evidence, such document shall, on its production from the proper custody, be admissible in evidence in any court or before any person having by law or consent of parties authority to receive evidence, and, subject to all just exceptions, shall be evidence [and in Scotland sufficient evidence][13] of the matters stated therein in pursuance of this Act or by any officer in pursuance of his duties as such officer'. It is noticeable that, while s. 484(2) makes the report of a naval court[14] admissible, s. 466 makes no similar provision for non-military inquiries. Such omission is in line with earlier decisions on the Merchant Shipping Act 1854, which Act had contained wider rules on admissibility which were restricted by the courts[15]. It may therefore be firmly concluded that s. 695(1) of the 1894 Act does not affect the common law rules discussed above insofar as reports of civil marine inquiries are concerned.

The Civil Evidence Act 1968 is of much greater use, for it appears to allow in evidence those parts of the report which are hearsay only – e.g. recorded evidence given to the inquiry, such as where A/B Smith states that 'ship X sounded three blasts at 0842 hrs'. It seems likely that such evidence would be admissible either under s. 2(1) or s. 4(1)[16], although it may need to be proved in a manner authorised by the court, for the proviso to s. 2(3) requires this where 'the statement in question was made by a person while giving oral evidence in some other legal proceedings' – and a Merchant Shipping Act Inquiry may well be a 'legal proceeding' within the definition of s. 18(2)[17]. This admissibility is extended to the record of original opinion evidence to the inquiry, by s. 1 of the Civil Evidence Act 1972, if the opinion

---

13. Added by the Merchant Shipping Act 1970, s. 100(1), Sch. 3, para. 3.
14. As to the constitution etc. of naval courts, see the Merchant Shipping Act 1894, ss. 480–485. These provisions are prospectively repealed by the Merchant Shipping Act 1970, s. 100(1) and Sch. 5, on the recommendation of the Pearson Report, Cmnd. 3211, para. 183, and are not re-enacted.
15. See *Nothard v Pepper* (1864) 17 CBNS 39; *The Little Lizzie* (1870) LR 3A & E 56; *McAllum v Reid* (1870) cited in LR 3 A & E 57n; *The Henry Coxon* (1878) 3 PD 156.
16. In *Taylor v Taylor* [1970] 2 All ER 609, [1970] 1 WLR 1148, the Court of Appeal allowed the transcript of evidence given in a criminal prosecution to be given in evidence at a subsequent civil trial, on the grounds that both sections allowed it.
17. Section 18(2): 'In this Act – ... "legal proceedings" includes an arbitration or reference, whether under an enactment or not'. Cf. section 18(1): 'In this Act "civil proceedings" includes ... (b) an arbitration or reference, whether under an enactment or not, but does not include civil proceedings in relation to which the strict rules of evidence do not apply'.

reasonable: if the defence of novus actus interveniens can be rejected so often on the grounds that the event relied on as breaking the chain of causation was reasonably foreseeable[10], then this argument can be rejected on the grounds that the taking of reasonable preventive measures was foreseeable. Of course, the action taken by the plaintiff must be weighed in the balance with the threat posed, in order to decide what is reasonable in these cases[11]; and so it is not difficult to imagine circumstances in which preventive measures might well be irrecoverable. For instance, suppose the oil is spilled 100 miles out to sea, and starts to blow towards the shore, at which point the armada sets off; the wind changes direction and blows it out to sea where it is broken up by natural forces; here, the cost of any detergent spraying so far offshore would probably be too remote[12].

On the basis of the 'rescue' cases cited above in section 9.8.1.2, it would seem likely that it does not matter that the person who has incurred the expense of taking reasonable preventive measures is not the person whose land might have been oiled had the measures not been taken.

It must nonetheless be admitted that the conclusion that reasonable preventive measures are recoverable rests on reasoning by analogy: there is a paucity of precedent. Perhaps for this reason the UK law was confirmed by statute in 1971. Section 15(1) of the Merchant Shipping (Oil Pollution) Act 1971 provides that

'where –
   (a) after an escape or discharge of persistent oil from a ship, measures are reasonably taken for the purpose of preventing or reducing damage in the area of the United Kingdom which may be caused by contamination resulting from the discharge or escape; and
   (b) any person incurs, or might but for the measures have incurred, a liability, otherwise than under section 1 of this Act[13], for any such damage;
then, notwithstanding that subsection (1)(b) of that section does not apply, he shall be liable for the cost of the measures, whether or not the person taking them does so for the protection of his interests or in the performance of a duty'.

---

10. *D'Urso v Sanson* [1939] 4 All ER 26; *Steel v Glasgow Iron and Steel Co* 1944 SC 237; *Hyett v Great Western Rly Co* [1947] 2 All ER 264.
11. *Sayers v Harlow UDC* [1958] 2 All ER 342, [1958] 1 WLR 623, CA.
12. A not unsimilar case occurred following the collision between the *Olympic Alliance* and *H.M.S. Achilles*, on 12 November 1975. The Dutch spent £16,000 spraying the slick with detergent while it was proceeding parallel to the coast and then out to sea. See IMCO Doc. MEPC/Circ. 31. The UK and French reports on the same incident are contained in MEPC/Circ. 32 and 33 respectively.
13. Section 1 of the Act provides for strict liability where a tanker carrying oil in bulk as cargo has spilled oil.

The requirement both in this section and at common law that the cost of measures taken can only be recovered if the measures were reasonable is a necessary protection for the shipowner: the *Torrey Canyon* disaster indicated a propensity to over-react. In practice, the onus of taking very early preventive measures is on the shipowner himself, for on the whole the earlier action is taken, the more effective it is and the more money will be saved.

b) *Cost of cleaning oiled birds and other wildlife*
The voluntary activities of commendable organisations like the Royal Society for the Protection of Birds in cleaning oiled seabirds and in trying to prevent environmental damage generally is too remote, because no interest in property is being rescued[14].

c) *The fisherman's lost profits*
In *Attorney-General for British Columbia v Attorney-General for Canada*[15], Viscount Haldane LC, giving the advice of the Privy Council, reviewed the authorities on fishing rights of all kinds[16] and concluded that '... the subjects of the Crown are entitled as of right not only to navigate but to fish in the high seas and tidal waters alike'[17] and that this right can be taken away only by competent legislation[18]. The fact that for over a century there have been UK regulations on how sea fishing may be conducted, and where[19], it does not detract from the existence of the right. It would therefore appear that an oil pollution incident which prevents a member of the public from exercising this right constitutes a public nuisance, so long as the criteria discussed above in section 9.4.1 are fullfilled[20].

However, for a fisherman to have an action for damages in public nuisance he must show special damage – see above, section 9.4.2. Where a public right of fishery has been interfered with, all members of the public alike suffer interference, and it is difficult to see how a

14. See above, section 9.8.1.1.
15. [1914] AC 153.
16. Lord Hale, *De Jure Maris: Neill v Duke of Devonshire* (1882) 8 App Cas 135; *Malcomson v O'Dea* (1863) 10 HL Cas 593.
17. [1914] AC 153 at 169.
18. [1914] AC at 170. See also *McRae v British Norwegian Whaling Co Ltd* [1927–31] Nfld LR 274, declaring the right.
19. The legislation is voluminous and complicated, but the main instruments are the Sea Fish (Conservation) Act 1967 and the Sea Fisheries Act 1968, and subordinate legislation made thereunder.
20. *McRae v British Norwegian Whaling Co Ltd* [1927–31] Nfld LR 274 (waters polluted by whaling factory preventing exercise of public right of fishing held to be a public nuisance); *Fillion v New Brunswick International Paper Co* [1934] 3 DLR 22 (almost identical facts as in *McRae* – held a public nuisance); *Hickey v Electric Reduction Co of Canada Ltd* (1970) 21 DLR (3d) 368 (discharge of poisonous materials into Placentia Bay affecting public right of fishing held on a preliminary point of law to be a public nuisance).

professional fisherman could show that element of discrimination or peculiarity needed, unless perhaps he was actually fishing at the time of the spill, and had to stop as a result[1]. In the leading case of *Rose v Miles*[2], where a carrier brought an action on the case to recover the expense of having to unload his barges and transport their cargo by land due to the defendant's obstruction of a public navigable waterway, Lord Ellenborough CJ said:

'In *Hubert v Groves* (1794) 1 Esp 147 the damage might be said to be common to all, but this is something different, for the plaintiff was in the occupation, if I may so say, of the navigation; he had commenced his course upon it, and was in the act of using it when he is obstructed. It did not rest merely in contemplation. Surely this goes one step farther; this is something substantially more injurious to this person, than to the public at large, who might only have it in contemplation to use it. And he has been impeded in his progress by the defendants wrongfully mooring their barge across, and has been compelled to unload and to carry his goods over land, by which he has incurred expense, and that expense caused by the act of the defendants. If a man's time or his money are of any value, it seems to me that this plaintiff has shown a particular damage'[3].

It is, perhaps, just as well that this is so, for if it were otherwise, every fisherman within reach of the spill area could claim that he was going to have to fished there but for the spill, and thus 'cash in' on the disaster. The disadvantage of the operation of the rule here is, of course, that the genuine fisherman who really has had his habitual ground seriously affected goes without a remedy.

Would it make any difference if, on the morning following the casualty, a fisherman proceeds deliberately to the fishing ground polluted by oil, and there catches a tainted catch? While this might constitute special damage on the above principles, the conclusion that the plaintiff has been 100% contributorily negligent seems inescapable. Alternatively, the point may be phrased in causative terms by saying that the cause of the plaintiff's loss is not the defendant's act, but his own.

d) *The hotelier's lost profits*
If before 1970 there was some room for debate on the question of the status of pure economic loss in the law of torts, it seems that the two recent cases in the Court of Appeal, *SCM (United Kingdom) Ltd v W.*

1. In all three cases of *McRae*, *Fillion* and *Hickey*, above, the claims of fishermen were rejected as being too remote, for special damage could not be shown.
2. (1815) 4 M & S 101.
   (1815) 4 M & S 101 at 103.

J. Whittall & Son Ltd[4], and *Spartan Steel and Alloys Ltd v Martin &
Co (Contractors) Ltd*[5], in which all the authorities were reviewed[6],
have established quite clearly that normally a plaintiff can recover for
loss of profit consequent on physical or material damage, but not for
economic loss in circumstances where such damage, or its equivalent,
is absent[7]. Thus, in the latter case, where the defendant had
negligently caused the plaintiff's factory to suffer a power loss, the
plaintiffs suffered depreciation of £368 on a lost 'melt' in process at
the time the power was cut, £400 lost profit on that melt, and a
further £1,767 lost profit on four further melts they would otherwise
have been able to perform during the time the power was cut off; they
recovered only the first two items.

In *Hickey v Electric Reduction Co of Canada Ltd*, Furlong CJ held[8],
obiter, that the principle applied as well in nuisance cases as in
negligence.

It therefore seems that the common law will rarely provide a
remedy for the hotelier, innkeeper, tour operator or even the
holidaymaker himself who has suffered economic loss. The rare cases
where this head of damage might be recoverable are those where the
hotelier or innkeeper owns a waterfront premises which is contaminated by oil, and which he has to close while it is being cleaned-
up. It is quite clear from the two recent Court of Appeal cases and
from earlier ones too[9] that the basis of the rule is pure policy: that
there must be a limit to the extent of damage for which a person may
be held liable. As Lord Denning MR remarked[10], '... Where is the
line to be drawn? Lawyers are continually asking that question. But
the judges are never defeated by it. We may not be able to draw the
line with precision, but we can always say on which side of it any
particular case falls'.

4. [1971] 1 QB 337, [1970] 3 All ER 245.
5. [1973] QB 27, [1972] 3 All ER 557, Edmund Davies LJ dissenting.
6. Notably *Cattle v Stockton Waterworks Co* (1875) LR 10 QB 453 (loss of profit on a contract
   too remote); *Electrochrome Ltd v Welsh Plastics Ltd* [1968] 2 All ER 205 (duty of care not
   owed to plaintiff, whose financial loss was, in the circumstances, too remote); *Weller & Co v
   Foot and Mouth Disease Research Institute* [1966] 1 QB 569, [1965] 3 All ER 560 (duty of care
   not owed to auctioneers who suffered loss as a result of escape of virus).
7. Per Lord Denning MR, [1971] 1 QB 337 at 345–346: 'I must not be taken, however, as
   saying that economic loss is always too remote. There are some exceptional cases when it is
   the immediate consequence of the negligence and is recoverable accordingly ... see *Hedley
   Byrne & Co Ltd v Heller & Partners Ltd* [1964] AC 465, [1963] 2 All ER 575 [for instance].
   Another [case] is when the defendant by his negligence damages a lorry which is carrying the
   plaintiff's goods. The goods themselves are not damaged, but the lorry is so badly damaged
   that the goods have to be *unloaded* and carried forward in some other vehicle. The goods
   owner suffers economic loss only, namely, the cost of unloading and carriage, but he can
   recover it from the defendant because it is immediate and not too remote. It is analogous to
   physical damage: because the goods themselves had to be unloaded'.
8. (1970) 21 DLR (3d) 368 at 372.
9. Especially *Cattle v Stockton Waterworks Co* (1875) LR 10 QB 453, per Blackburn J.
10. [1971] 1 QB 337 at 346.

9.8.2 LIMITATION OF LIABILITY

The origins of the shipowner's right to limit his liability, and the early policies on which the right was based, are not wholly clear[11]. This is not, however, a matter of concern here, and so no attempt will be made to unravel the mystery. It is sufficient for present purposes to give a brief account of the policies behind the current international conventions.

There have been three attempts by the international community of states to unify their laws relating to limitation of liability towards third parties. The first was in Brussels in 1924, and gave rise to the International Convention for the Unification of Certain Rules Relating to the Limitation of the Liability of Owners of Sea-going Vessels 1924[12]. The second was in 1957 (again in Brussels), and this conference gave rise to the International Convention Relating to the Limitation of the Liability of Owners of Sea-going Ships 1957[13]; lastly, a Conference held in London from 1 to 19 November 1976 under the auspices of IMCO adopted the Convention on Limitation of Liability for Maritime Claims 1976[14]. Each of the two latter instruments is designed to replace the previous uniform provisions as between parties to the Convention[15]. Unfortunately, at present not every party to the 1924 Convention is a party to the 1957 Convention, and so there are two co-existent regimes to consider[16]; when the 1976 Convention enters into force[17], there will doubtless be three. It is greatly to be hoped that the 1976 Convention will achieve a popularity which its two predecessors have failed to achieve, by attracting all maritime and coastal nations as parties.

The problem facing the delegates to the 1924 Conference was primarily one of lack of uniformity, and so the instrument adopted was one which sought a compromise between the interests of the shipper, the passenger, the shipowner and his insurer, within the context that in many countries the shipowner could limit his liability to the value of his ship, its freight and accessories[18]. In 1957, however, the problem was rather different, the main task being to revise the limits upwards by reference to the ship's tonnage – the value of the ship had been a figure difficult to ascertain.

11. *Marsden's The Law of Collisions at Sea* (11th ed., London, 1961 (ed. K. C. McGuffie)) paras. 168–174, where the contract of *commande* (joint venture of shipowners and merchants), protection, *noxae deditio* (deodand), division of loss and arrest are all mentioned.
12. See below, section 9.8.2.1.
13. See below, section 9.8.2.2.
14. See below, section 9.8.2.3.
15. Article 17(4) of the 1976 Convention; Article 16 of the 1957 Convention.
16. This has lead to a wide variation in limitation laws. A short summary of the rules in selected states is contained in Plinio Manca, *International Maritime Law* (Antwerp, 1970, Vol. 1) 124–127. Many states are party to neither Convention, and in such cases purely national principles are followed which may or may not grant the right to limit.
17. Not expected before 1980.
18. C. J. Colombos, *The International Law of the Sea* (6th ed., London, 1967) 352–355.

By 1976, so many problems had developed within the existing system that a complete overhaul was called for. The two previous conferences had proceeded on the basis that a shipowner's interest in the maritime adventure should be limited to the value of his ship, however that be ascertained. A new policy based the discussion in 1976, namely that limitation should be at a figure as high as that against which the shipowner can insure at reasonable cost. This principle gave rise to a dramatic rise in the real value of the limits, whereas the upward revision of 1957 had really only accounted for the inflation which had taken place since 1924.

Oil pollution was mentioned only at the 1976 Conference, and it is quite likely that it was hardly thought of as a special possibility at the previous two, yet today it is still quite possible that a claim for oil pollution damage in a particular jurisdiction will be limitable, if at all, under the 1924 or 1957 Conventions. Of course, in those jurisdictions whose governments are parties to CLC 1969, claims for liability thereunder are generally limitable only thereunder[19]: but even in these jurisdictions there are likely to be claims for oil pollution damage when the incident is not covered by CLC, and these claims will possibly be limitable under the 1924 or 1957 Conventions if the government is a party to them. In the United Kingdom, limitation of claims arising outside CLC is governed by the 1957 Convention as enacted into national law[20].

In the case of each Convention, therefore, three questions must be asnwered: (1) Does the shipowner have the right to limit his liability for oil pollution damage? (2) If so, in what circumstances will this be denied? (3) What are the limits of liability? The question of limitation of indemnities is more conveniently dealt with in connection with CLC[1].

9.8.2.1 The 1924 Brussels Convention[2]

a) *The right to limit*
By Article 1, 'The liability of the owner[3] of a seagoing vessel is limited...in respect of: (1) Compensation due to third parties by reason of damage caused, whether on land or on water, by the acts or

19. See below, sections 10.2.2.1 and 10.2.2.2.
20. Merchant Shipping Act 1894, s. 503, as amended, in particular by the Merchant Shipping (Liability of Shipowners and Others) Act 1958.
 1. See below, section 10.2.2.1.
 2. LNTS, Vol. 120 (1931), 125; N. Singh, *International Conventions of Merchant Shipping* (2nd ed., London, 1973) 1342. By 1 January 1968 the following states had ratified or acceded to it: Belgium*, Brazil, Denmark*, Dominican Republic, Finland*, France*, Hungary, Monaco*, Norway*, Poland*, Portugal*, Spain*, Sweden*, Turkey, Malagasy Republic*.
    * denotes also a party to the 1957 Convention.
    The 1924 Convention entered into force 21 June 1931.
 3. Article 10 extends the right to limit to certain others, including a bareboat charterer.

faults of the master, crew, pilot, or any other person in the service of the vessel;...'. This clearly encompasses oil pollution damage from ships.

b) *Denial of the right to limit*
By Article 2, 'The limitation of liability laid down in the foregoing article does not apply: (1) To obligations arising out of acts or faults of the owner of the vessel;...'. It would seem clear, therefore, that where the oil pollution has arisen due to the unseaworthiness of the ship there will be no right to limit under this Convention. It will be for the lex fori to decide what further circumstances are within the phrase.

c) *The limits of liability*
By Article 1, the shipowner's liability is limited 'to an amount equal to the value of the vessel[4], the freight[5], and accessories[6] of the vessel.... Provided that, as regards the cases mentioned in No. 1... the liability referred to in the preceding provisions shall not exceed an aggregate sum equal to 8 pounds sterling per ton of the vessel's tonnage[7].' However, by Article 7, the limit of liability for death and personal injury claims is £8 per ton. By Article 15, the pound referred to means the gold value thereof, which is to be translated into the currencies of states where the pound is not a monetary unit at a rate chosen by the state. Evaluation of this limitation figure in 1977 is difficult. On the one hand it is arguable that the value of a pound should be the current market value of the gold content of a sovereign; on the other hand, that such an approach is only relevant in countries where the pound sterling is not lawful money[8]. Hence, £8 could currently be taken as £8 or as something in excess of £32.

If for purposes of argument the latter figure is taken (bearing in mind that the question would never arise in the United Kingdom), since the value of most ships would today exceed even £32 per ton, the limitation amounts would work out as follows. For a ship with a limitation tonnage of 1,000 tons, the sum would be about £32,000; for a ship of the size of the *Torrey Canyon* (say 48,500 limitation tons), the sum would be £1,552,000; for a VLCC (say 100,000 limitation tons) it would be £3,200,000.

4. Article 3 deals with the method of valuation.
5. By Article 4 'the freight... is deemed, as respects vessels of every description, to be a lump sum fixed at all events at 10 per cent of the value of the vessel at the commencement of the voyage. That indemnity is due even though no freight be then earned by the vessel'.
6. See Article 5 for the definition of accessories. Importantly, 'payments on policies of insurance... are not deemed to be accessories'. So if the ship is lost, the shipowner can claim on his hull policy but does not have to make this sum available to those others who have suffered loss.
7. Tonnage is defined by Article 11.
8. *Scrutton on Charterparties* (18th ed., 1974) 449 contains a discussion of the same problem which arises in connection with the Hague Rules. See further on the problems of gold values, section 10.2.2.3.

While the cost of oil pollution claims is difficult to discover in individual cases since figures are rarely published[9], it is probably true to say that these limits would nowadays allow limitation in a large number of cases, expecially where the vessel responsible was small.

9.8.2.2 The 1957 Brussels Convention[10]

This Convention is at present the one most widely in force, and is the one which regulates UK law[11].

a) *The right to limit*

By Article 1(1), 'The owner[12] of a seagoing ship may limit his liability in accordance with Article 3 of this Convention in respect of claims arising from any of the following occurrences ... (b) loss of life of, or personal injury to, any other[13] person, whether on land or on water, loss of or damage to any other[13] property or infringement of any rights caused by the act, neglect or default of any person on board the ship for whose act, neglect or default the owner is responsible or any person not on board the ship for whose act, neglect or default the owner is responsible: provided however that in regard to the act, neglect or default of this last class of person, the owner shall only be entitled to limit his liability when the act, neglect or default is one which occurs in the navigation or the management of the ship or in the loading, carriage or discharge of its cargo or in the embarkation, carriage or disembarkation of its passengers.'

This clearly covers oil pollution damage from ships, although the wording has given rise to problems in connection with professional salvors not operating from a ship: these are discussed below in Chapter 13.

9. The information before the 1969 Conference is contained in LEG/CONF/6, Annex III. The cost of claims has clearly greatly escalated since 1969.

10. UKTS No. 52 of 1968 (Cmnd. 3678); 57 AJIL 268 (1963). By 1st July 1978 the following states had ratified or acceded to it: Algeria, Barbados, Belgium, Denmark, Fiji, Finland, France, FGR, Ghana, Guyana, Iceland, India, Iran, Israel, Japan, Lebanon, Malagasy Republic, Mauritius, Monaco, Netherlands, Norway, Poland, Portugal, Singapore, Spain, Sweden, Switzerland, Syria, Tonga, UAR, UK, Zaire. The Convention has been extended to: Isle of Man, Bahamas, Bermuda, British Antarctica, Belize, Solomon Islands, Falkland Islands, Gibraltar, Gilbert and Ellis Islands, Hong Kong, Seychelles, Virgin Islands, Guernsey and Jersey, Cayman Islands, Dominica, Granada, Montserrat, St Lucia, St Vincent, Turks and Caicos Islands, New Hebrides. Entered into force 31 May 1968.

11. Merchant Shipping Act 1894, s. 503, as amended, in particular by the Merchant Shipping (Liability of Shipowners and Others) Act 1958. See also the Merchant Shipping (Oil Pollution) Act 1971, s. 8A, inserted by the Merchant Shipping Act 1974, s. 9.

12. As with the 1924 Convention, the scope is extended. By Article 6(2) 'the charterer, manager and operator of the ship, and ... the master, members of the crew and other servants of the owner, charterer, manager or operator acting in the course of their employment' may limit their liability, and the master and members of the crew may do so even if guilty of actual fault or privity.

13. Subparagraph (a) had referred to persons and property on board the ship.

b) *Denial of the right to limit*

Article 1(1) grants the right to limit as above, 'unless the occurrence giving rise to the claim resulted from the actual fault or privity of the owner', the burden of proof of which is, by Article 1(6), for determination by the lex fori (in UK law, it is for the shipowner to disprove actual fault or privity[14]). Unfortunately, this phrase has lead to widely differing interpretations in different jurisdictions, and has lead in some states to the situation where in practice the shipowner is almost always denied the right to limit. In UK law as in other systems, the cases on the subject are voluminous[15]; a recent and important decision of the Court of Appeal in *The Eurysthenes*[16] held that the word privity means with knowledge and consent; so that, if the ship is sent to sea in an unseaworthy state, with the knowledge and concurrence of the shipowner personally, the right to limit will be denied. It is likely that this decision will be followed in future because it is based on a well-reasoned analysis of previous caselaw; but there still remains ample scope for a judge to deny the right to limit in applying this concept to the particular facts before him.

c) *The limits of liability*

By Article 3,

'(1) The amounts to which the owner of a ship may limit his liability under Article 1 shall be:

(a) where the occurrence has only given rise to property claims an aggregate amount of 1,000 francs for each ton of the ship's tonnage[17];

(b) where the occurrence has only given rise to personal claims an aggregate amount of 3,100 francs for each ton of the ship's tonnage;

(c) where the occurrence has given rise both to personal claims and property claims an aggregate amount of 3,100 francs for each ton of the ship's tonnage, of which a first portion amounting to 2,100 francs for each ton of the ship's tonnage shall be exclusively appropriated to the payment of personal claims and of which a second portion amounting to 1,000 francs for each ton of the ship's tonnage shall be appropriated to the payment of property claims: provided however that in cases where the first portion is insufficient

14. *Lennard's Carrying Co Ltd v Asiatic Petroleum Co Ltd* [1915] AC 705; *Paterson Steamships Ltd v Robin Hood Mills Ltd* (1937) 58 LlL Rep 33; *The Norman* [1960] 1 Lloyd's Rep 1.
15. See cases cited in *Temperley's The Merchant Shipping Acts* (7th ed. by M. Thomas and D. Steel, London, 1976) para. 431.
16. [1977] QB 49, [1976] 3 All ER 243. The decision was on the word privity used in the Marine Insurance Act 1906.
17. See Article 3(7) for the definition of tonnage. By Article 3(5), the tonnage of a ship of less than 300 tons shall be deemed to be 300 tons.

to pay the personal claims in full, the unpaid balance of such claims shall rank rateably with the property claims for payment against the second portion of the fund.

(2) In each portion of the limitation fund the distribution among the claimants shall be made in proportion to the amounts of their established claims.'

The franc referred to is the Poincaré franc[18]; the amounts of 1,000 and 3,100 francs translated in February 1978 into £43.62 and £133.66 respectively[19]. The effect of the system enacted by Article 3 is that in no circumstances can claimants for oil pollution damage to property get more between them than £43.12 per ton, and, where as a result of the same incident there are personal claims in excess of 2,100 francs (£90.54) per ton, they will get less.

Taking the same examples as with the 1924 Convention, the amount of money likely to be available in 1978 to oil pollution claimants had improved from £32,000 to £43,120 for a 1,000 limitation ton coastal tanker; from £1,552,000 to £2,091,320 for a vessel the size of the *Torrey Canyon*; and from £3,200,000 to £4,312,000 for a VLCC of 100,000 limitation tons.

It was found in the survey of oil pollution incidents available to the 1969 Conference on Oil Pollution Damage[20] that between 1960 and 1968 there were only two out of 850 cases investigated where the 1957 limits were exceeded (or would have been exceeded if applicable). However, subsequent inflation has again reduced the efficacy of these limits somewhat, so that, particularly for smaller ships, there would in 1977 be far more cases of oil pollution where the 1957 limits might give the plaintiffs a poor percentage of their costs.

9.8.2.3 The 1976 Limitation Convention[1]

a) *The right to limit*

The claims which are limitable are set out in Article 2(1): 'Subject to Articles 3 and 4 the following claims, whatever the basis of liability may be, shall be subject to limitation of liability: (a) claims in respect of loss of life or personal injury or loss of or damage to property (including damage to harbour works, basins and waterways and aids to navigation), occurring on board or in direct connexion with the

18. Article 3(6). On the problems of gold values, see below, section 10.2.2.3.
19. Merchant Shipping (Various Enactments) (Sterling Equivalents) Order 1978, S.I. 1978 No. 54.
20. LEG/CONF/6, Annex III.
 1. IMCO Sales No. 77.04E; IMCO Doc. LEG/CONF. 5/10 of 19 November 1976. By 31 December 1976 no states had ratified or acceded to it. It is not expected to enter into force before 1980.

operations of the ship or with salvage operations, and consequential loss resulting therefrom;... (f) claims of a person other than the person liable in respect of measures taken in order to avert or minimise loss for which the person liable may limit his liability in accordance with this Convention, and further loss caused by such measures[2]'. The persons entitled to limit their liability are enumerated in Article 1, and include the owner, charterer, manager and operator of a seagoing ship, and a salvor[3], and also any person for whose act, neglect or default they are responsible. It is therefore clear that, subject to any exception, claims for oil pollution damage would be limitable under the Convention.

Articles 3(b) and 17(4) and (5) make considerable exceptions in the oil pollution field. Article 17(5)(b) completely excludes floating platforms constructed for the purpose of exploring or exploiting the natural resources of the sea-bed or the subsoil thereof. This resolves the doubts existing in the two previous Conventions[4] against the offshore installation. Drillships are of course outside Article 17(5)(b), but are dealt with separately by Article 17(4): 'The Courts of a State Party shall not apply this Convention to ships constructed for, or adapted to, and engaged in, drilling: (a) when that State has established under its national legislation a higher limit of liability than that otherwise provided for in Article 6; or (b) when that State has become party to an international convention regulating the system of liability in respect of such ships'.

It is Article 3(b) which provides the major exception for oil pollution damage: 'The rules of this Convention shall not apply to:... (b) claims for oil pollution damage within the meaning of the International Convention on Civil Liability for Oil Pollution Damage, dated 29 November 1969 or of any amendment or Protocol thereto which is in force;...'.

The inclusion of such a provision, and its precise wording, were matters of considerable concern at the Conference, simply because for some states the whole question of oil pollution is such a political matter that they took firm positions from the start[5].

2. By Article 2(2), claims under paragraph 1(f) 'shall not be subject to limitation to the extent that they relate to remuneration under a contract with the person liable'.

3. Article 1(3) defines salvor as 'any person rendering services in direct connexion with salvage operations'. Thus a salvor not operating from a ship may limit. Article 6(4) provides a special limit in such circumstances. The Conference thus deliberately reversed the situation arising in *The Tojo Maru* (see below, Chapter 13).

4. The use of the word 'vessel' in the 1924 Convention is ambiguous with respect to offshore installations. The word 'ships' in the 1957 Convention gives rise to similar difficulty.

5. See LEG/CONF. 5/C. 1/SR. 6, pp. 4 to 11 (Committee of the Whole). A small Working Group was set up, but could not agree on a text: LEG/CONF. 5/C. 1/SR. 14, pp. 13 to 15. It did, however, elaborate a text which was approved by the Committee of the Whole by 23 to 7 with 4 abstentions: LEG/CONF. 5/C. 1/SR. 23, p. 5. After a change in wording by the Drafting Committee (LEG/CONF. 5/C. 3/1/Add. 1), and despite objections in Plenary by the DDR, the text was finally adopted by 22 to 7 with 8 abstentions: LEG/CONF. 5/SR. 4, p. 7.

The effect of the wording would appear to be that a claim of the type described in CLC as being one for oil pollution damage[6] is not limitable under the Convention, whether or not CLC is in force in the jurisdiction in which limitation under the Convention is sought: this leaves states free to regulate limitation for claims of this type as they please, without being forced (by the back door, as it were) to become a party to CLC. The phrase 'would appear to be' has been used advisedly above because the matter is, on the wording of Article 3(b), not free from doubt.

Proceeding on this wide interpretation of the wording above, it may be concluded that many of the cases of oil pollution damage at present limitable under the 1957 Convention in states not party to CLC would not be limitable under the 1976 Convention. One example is simply where oil cargo escapes accidentally from an oil tanker and damages the shores of State A. However, if bunkers escape accidentally from a dry cargo ship and damage the shores of State A, the claim would currently be limitable because

a) it is not a claim for oil pollution damage 'within the meaning of' CLC; and

b) it is therefore not excluded from Article 2 of the 1976 Convention.

The detailed effect of Article 3(b) can only be worked out in conjunction with an analysis of the scope of CLC[7].

b) *Denial of the right to limit*
By Article 4 'A person liable shall not be entitled to limit his liability if it is proved that the loss resulted from his personal act or omission, committed with the intent to cause such loss, or recklessly and with knowledge that such loss would probably result'. This formula was adopted from Article 7 of the International Convention for the Unification of Certain Rules Relating to the Carriage of Passengers by Sea, 1961[8] and from Article 7 of the International Convention for the Unification of Certain Rules Relating to Carriage of Passenger Luggage by Sea, 1967[9]. It is generally regarded as making the right to limit unbreakable for most practical purposes[10], so eradicating the evils of differing interpretation to which the 1957 Convention's formula ('actual fault or privity') had fallen.

6. See section 10.2.1.
7. See below, sections 10.1 and 10.2.2.1.
8. N. Singh, *International Conventions of Merchant Shipping* (2nd ed., London, 1973) 1357.
9. N. Singh, *International Conventions of Merchant Shipping* (2nd ed., London 1973) 1362.
10. See CMI comments, IMCO Circular Letter No. 286 of 31 March 1976, Annex III, pp. 100 to 102, for the reasons behind using this wording.

c) *The limits of liability*

It was the main task of the Conference to substantially raise the limits from those of the 1957 Convention. The compromise formula finally adopted in Article 6 is too complicated to merit inclusion in full in this text, so a summary of its effect will be given instead. As with the 1957 Convention, two funds are adopted, one for personal claims and one for other claims (referred to below as property claims). Where the former fund is insufficient to meet all personal claims, Article 6(2) provides that the other fund shall be available to meet the unpaid balance, and such unpaid balance shall rank rateably with any property claims. Since oil pollution rarely gives rise to personal claims, we can concentrate on the property fund; but it must be remembered that, if the ship is lost and there are heavy human casualties as well as oil pollution, the amount of the property fund available for oil pollution victims may be drastically reduced.

The amount of the property fund is calculated on a sophisticated sliding scale. For a ship with a tonnage[11] not exceeding 500 tons, the amount is 167,000 SDRs[12], or about $200,000 (£117,647)[13]. For a ship with a tonnage in excess of 500 tons, the following amounts must be added to the above figure:

> for each ton from 501 to 30,000 tons, 167 SDRs ($200 or £118);
> for each ton from 30,001 to 70,000 tons, 125 SDRs ($150 or £88);
> for each ton in excess of 70,000 tons, 83 SDRs ($100 or £59).

It is now possible to work out the maximum liability for oil pollution damage to property under the Convention for the three ships taken as previous examples. The results are shown comparatively in Table 9.1.

These figures show a very dramatic rise in limits over those of the 1957 Convention. From the oil pollution point of view it must be remembered that the majority of incidents will not be limitable under the Convention at all, and that the question of limitation will therefore rest purely on the lex fori, which may or may not grant limitation. We shall see that, where a shipowner can limit oil pollution claims under the 1976 Convention, his limitation fund exceeds that of the 1969 Civil Liability Convention[14]! It would certainly appear that this time, the

11. The tonnage has been changed from the old limitation ton of the 1924 and 1957 Conventions to the gross tonnage calculated in accordance with the tonnage measurement rules contained in Annex I of the International Convention on Tonnage Measurement of Ships 1969: see Article 6(5). This has the effect of increasing the tonnage of a given vessel by an amount which varies with the type of ship, but which can be by up to 200%.
12. The Special Drawing Right as defined by the International Monetary Fund: see Article 8, where provision is made for the alternative use of the Poincaré Franc in certain circumstances.
13. Conversion rates used are 1 SDR = $1.20; £1.00 = $1.70.
14. See section 10.2.2.3 and Table 10.1.

TABLE 9.1 Comparison of maximum limit of liability for oil pollution damage to property

Limitation Tonnage*	1924 Convention**	1957 Convention	1976 Convention (when allowed)
1,000	£ 32,000	£ 43,120	£ 176,470
48,500	£1,582,000	£2,091,320	£5,220,588
100,000	£3,200,000	£4,312,000	£8,882,353

* It must be remembered that the limitation ton for the 1976 Convention is not the same as that used in the 1924 and 1957 Conventions. In calculating the figures in the last column, this fact has been ignored; in practice, the limitation amounts under the 1976 Convention given in the Table will be higher due to the change in tonnage used to calculate amounts.

** Only approximate figures. See section 9.8.2.1.

limits have been set so that the shipowner is saved only from catastrophy, and that in few pure oil pollution cases will he be entitled to limit. There would now appear to be no need for further raising the limits.

9.8.2.4 Preventive measures taken by shipowners

Where a ship has suffered a casualty and is leaking oil, the most important thing is to ensure that measures are taken as soon as possible to prevent or mitigate damage – even if, in the circumstances, all that needs to be done is to keep a close watch on the oil slick as it drifts out to sea. It was noted above[15] that preventive measures taken by a potential victim will only be recoverable at common law and by UK statute if they are reasonable; and that until there is a perceivable threat of damage, this requirement is unlikely to be fulfilled. This puts the emphasis for taking early preventive measures even more upon the shipowner than does the practical reality in a spill situation.

It would operate as a considerable financial inducement to the shipowner to act quickly if his own reasonable preventive measures could rank with other claims against the limitation fund subsequently set up. Naturally, this would operate at the expense of claimants, but this is probably only technically true: it is better for the shipowner to have a financial inducement to try to stop any harm occurring at all, than it is for such efforts not to be made, as a result of which claims are made and are satisfied either substantially or in full.

15. Section 9.8.1.3, *Cost of preventive measures.*

With this principle in mind for all claims, the CMI (which prepared the earliest draft Convention of 1976) included a provision which was not paralleled in the 1924 or 1957 Conventions, and which was drawn from CLC 1969, making the shipowner's reasonable preventive measures rankable in the limitation fund. The form in which it reached the Conference was as follows (Draft Article 12(5)): 'Where an incident occurs which causes or threatens to cause damage giving rise to liability subject to limitation under this Convention and the person liable for that damage voluntarily takes measures to prevent or minimise such damage, any expenses incurred, including loss resulting from sacrifices made, by him in taking those measures shall rank equally with any claims [in such part of the] . . . fund [as is not reserved for claims for loss of life or personal injury][16,17]'.

The Committee of the Whole twice discussed proposals to reject the whole paragraph, and twice the paragraph was narrowly retained on the simple majority required in Committee[18]. However, in Plenary the paragraph failed to attract the necessary two-thirds majority[19] and so the Convention is now without it. There has therefore been no change from the existing position, which from an oil pollution point of view is unfortunate.

As to whether the shipowner can recover such expenses under the 1971 Fund Convention, TOVALOP, CRISTAL or its P & I Club policy, see below, sections 11.2.2, 12.1 and 12.2.

9.9 Jurisdictional and practical problems

Where a foreign element is involved in a dispute, the court in which a remedy is sought must first decide whether it has jurisdiction to try the case; if it decides this affirmatively, the question will then arise as to what law should be chosen to apply to the determination of the dispute. The former question in England[20] in an oil pollution case would in practice centre around whether or not in an appropriate case

16. Square brackets indicated that these words would need special debate at the Conference.
17. IMCO Circular Letter No. 286, Annex I, p. 10.
18. See LEG/CONF. 5/C. 1/SR. 15, pp. 9–15 and LEG/CONF. 5/C. 1/SR. 24, p. 4.
19. See LEG/CONF. 5/SR. 4, p. 10.
20. Following the usage in Dicey and Morris, *The Conflict of Laws* (8th ed., London, 1973), in sections 9.9 and 9.10 unless the context otherwise requires 'England' means the territory of England, including the Principality of Wales and the town of Berwick-on-Tweed, and the territorial waters adjacent thereto, and any ship of the Royal Navy wherever situate. The territorial waters of England (and indeed of the United Kingdom) may be taken as three miles from the baselines from which it is to be measured. See Territorial Waters Jurisdiction Act 1878; Territorial Waters Order in Council 1964 of 25 September 1964 (*London Gazette*, 29/9/64, p. 8222).

a writ (or notice thereof) could be served out of the jurisdiction, and so
this question is dealt with in this section with respect to ships[1,2]
together with other matters of a practical nature. The second question,
being one of pure law, is dealt with separately in section 9.10.

If the defendant is within the jurisdiction[3], then he may be served
with a writ issued in the High Court irrespective of his nationality or
domicile[4], and irrespective of the time he is within the jurisdiction[5];
and this is so whether the action is in personam or in rem[6] (although
of course in the latter case the defendant would normally be a ship).
Having been served in due form, the courts have jurisdiction over
him[7].

Unfortunately for the potential plaintiff in an oil pollution case, the
chances of the ship which caused the damage or a sister ship[8] or its
owner or master being within the jurisdiction at some time after the
writ has been issued are not very great. Of course, it will quite often
be so, but far more often, the owner, master and ship will all be out of
the jurisdiction, and it is these cases which give rise to difficulties. In
such a case it is always open to the plaintiff to watch and wait to see if
any person or thing on which he can serve a writ appears within the
jurisdiction, but such option dies on the expiry of the relevant time
limit[9]. A further option is to see if such a person or thing turns up in
another jurisdiction where a writ can be issued and served[10], although
as has been pointed out by another writer, the possibilities of such
action by private individuals are in practice remote[11].

1. For jurisdiction over oil pollution emanating from the UK sector of the Continental Shelf,
   see s. 3, Continental Shelf Act 1964 and Continental Shelf (Jurisdiction) Order 1968, S.I.
   1968 No. 892, as amended by S.I. 1971 No. 721, S.I. 1974 No. 1490, S.I. 1975 No. 1708 and
   S.I. 1976 No. 1517.
2. For jurisdiction over foreign ships claiming sovereign immunity, see below, section 10.1.1.2.
3. A corporation is present here if it does business here, and there are detailed rules on when an
   agency will constitute presence, on oversea companies within the meaning of the Companies
   Act 1948, and on partnerships: see G. C. Cheshire, *Private International Law* (9th ed.,
   London, 1974) 79–84; Dicey and Morris, *The Conflict of Laws* (8th ed., London, 1973)
   Chapters 10 and 11.
4. For jurisdiction over foreign ships claiming sovereign immunity, see below, section 10.1.1.2.
5. *Maharanee of Baroda v Wildenstein* [1972] 2 QB 283, [1972] 2 All ER 689. But if a defendant
   is lured within the jurisdiction fraudulently or wrongly, service may be set aside: *Watkins v
   North American Land and Timber Co Ltd* (1904) 20 TLR 534.
6. *Castrique v Imrie* (1870) LR 4 HL 414.
7. 'The root principle of the English law about jurisdiction is that the judges stand in the place
   of the sovereign in whose name they administer justice, and that therefore whoever is served
   with the King's writ, and can be compelled consequently to submit to the decree made, is a
   person over whom the Courts have jurisdiction...' per Viscount Haldane in *John Russell &
   Co Ltd v Cayzer, Irvine & Co Ltd* [1916] 2 AC 298 at 302.
8. As to actions against sister ships, see below, section 9.9.2.
9. Normally six years from the accrual of the cause of action in tort cases, but if the claim is for
   personal injuries, normally three years: see the Limitation Act 1939, s. 2, as amended,
   especially by the Limitation Act 1975.
10. As was done by the UK Government in the *Torrey Canyon* case, the *Lake Poloinde*, a sister
    ship, was arrested in Singapore. As to the power to arrest sister ships, see section 9.9.2.
11. G. W. Keeton, *The Lessons of the Torrey Canyon* [1968] CLP 94 at 111.

within the jurisdiction. Most of what the learned judges[13] said in that case is, therefore, obiter, but none of it contradicts the conclusion of Winn J, in the *Cordova Land* case, and one statement of Goddard LJ is particularly damaging: 'In an action on the case, the cause of the action is the wrongful act or default of the defendant. The right to bring the action depends on the happening of damage to the plaintiff'[14]. In the case before him, 'the alleged tort which was committed was a wrongful act or default. It was the sale of what was said to be a dangerous article without warning as to its nature. That act was committed in America, not in this country'.

The courts are extremely unlikely to seek means of distinguishing such authorities even in an oil pollution case where sympathy for the plaintiff will be considerable, for, as Scott LJ said in the earlier case, 'service out of the jurisdiction at the instance of our courts is necessarily prima facie an interference with the exclusive jurisdiction of the sovereignty of the foreign country where service is to be effected...As a matter of international comity it seems to me important to make sure that no such service shall be allowed unless it is clearly within both the letter and the spirit of Order 11'[15].

It is difficult to see how these cases can be distinguished from the oil pollution situation being considered, except in the unlikely case where the court takes the view that the wrongful act was not the escape of the oil outside the jurisdiction but the failure within the jurisdiction to keep it from causing damage[16]. The reluctant conclusion must therefore be that, even where damage is suffered within the jurisdiction, and a fortiori where it is suffered outside the jurisdiction, the chances of the court being able under paragraph (h) to grant leave (in its discretion) to serve notice of the writ outside the jurisdiction are very slight indeed.

Paragraph (n): '...if the action begun by the writ is brought to enforce a claim in respect of a liability incurred under the Merchant Shipping (Oil Pollution) Act 1971'.

This paragraph was of course added as a result of the ratification of CLC by H.M. Government, and it will be considered again briefly in

13. A strong bench of Scott, Goddard and du Parcq LJJ.
14. [1944] KB 432 at 439, citing his own previous judgment in *Draper v Trist and Trisbestos Brake Linings Ltd* (1939) 56 RPC 429 at 442.
15. [1944] 1 KB 432 at 437. Du Parcq LJ concurred in the need for caution and strictness, at p. 441, citing *Societe Générale de Paris v Dreyfus Bros* (1885) 29 ChLD 239, as did Winn J in the *Cordova Land* case. See also Diplock LJ in *Mackender v Feldia AG* [1967] 2 QB 590 at 599, concurring on the need for caution and the basis in comity.
16. See above, section 9.7.1. In *Distillers Co (Biochemicals) Ltd v Thompson* [1971] AC 458, [1971] 1 All ER 694, the Privy Council, construing a similar provision in New South Wales law, took the view that an English Company who had failed to warn a potential purchaser of a drug manufactured in England that it would be dangerous for a pregnant person to take, had given the plaintiff a cause of action at the place of purchase. The court, applying *Jackson v Spittall* (1870) LR 5 CP 542, held that the test was whether the act on the part of the defendant which gave the plaintiff cause of complaint had occurred within the jurisdiction.

connection with the examination of that Convention in Chapter 10[17]. In this Chapter the question is whether, in situations governed by common law[18], the paragraph gives grounds for the exercise of the court's leave.

It will be remembered that in enacting the Merchant Shipping (Oil Pollution) Act 1971, the legislature exceeded its obligations under CLC by granting the right to recover preventive clean-up costs in certain non-convention cases: see section 15(1) of the Act[19]. There is no doubt that section 15(1) creates a liability – '. . . he shall be liable for the cost of the measures . . .' – and so there is no doubt that paragraph (n) would give the court grounds to exercise its discretion, whereas paragraph (h) probably denies it. Paragraph (n) is, however, limited in scope to the cost of preventive measures: it does not apply to physical damage, nor to economic loss consequent thereon[20].

9.9.1.2 Order 75, rule 4(1)

It is this rule which will govern the question of whether the court may grant leave to serve notice of the writ out of the jurisdiction in cases which are held to be 'arising out of' situations listed in Order 75, Rule 2(1)(a)[1], where the action is one in personam.

Order 75, rule 4(1), provides as follows:

> 'Subject to the following provisions of this rule, service out of the jurisdiction of a writ, or notice of a writ, containing any such claim as is mentioned in rule 2(1) is permissible with the leave of the Court if, but only if –
> (a) the defendant has his habitual residence or a place of business within England and Wales, or
> (b) the cause of action arose within inland waters of England and Wales or within the limits of a port of England and Wales, or
> (c) an action arising out of the same incident or series of incidents is proceeding in the High Court or has been heard and determined in the High Court, or
> (d) the defendant has submitted or agreed to submit to the jurisdiction of the High Court. . . .'

The case under specific consideration is where the defendant is abroad and life is difficult for the plaintiff, and so paragraphs (a) and

17. See below, section 10.3.1.
18. Enumerated above, section 9.1.
19. Above, section 9.8.1.3, *Cost of preventive measures*.
20. It is settled law that a plaintiff cannot litigate an issue not within RSC Ord. 11, r. 1(1), when he has successfully brought another issue within it: see *The Siskina* [1978] 1 Lloyd's Rep 1, HL.
 1. Above, section 9.9.1.

(d) may be noted without comment. Paragraph (c) is unlikely to be of use to an oil pollution claimant. The best way of explaining why is to take an illustration. Suppose a Liberian tanker, Ship A, collides with a British vessel, Ship B, causing oil to spill from Ship A and cause pollution damage to P within England. If Ship B wishes to sue Ship A in the High Court, precisely the same alternatives will be open to him as will subsequently be open to P; so, if Ship B's action can proceed in the High Court, it will be able to do so for a reason which would equally well allow P's action. So paragraph (c) is not relevant. If, on the other hand, Ship A were to wish to sue Ship B in the High Court, paragraph (c) might enable P to serve Ship A out of the jurisdiction where otherwise he could not; but, in considering whether or not to sue Ship B in the High Court, Ship A will undoubtedly have regard to the consequences of this course vis-a-vis P!

The paragraph potentially of use to an oil pollution claimant is paragraph (b). Order 75, rule 4(1), states that 'In this pagagraph "inland waters" and "port" have the same meanings as in section 4(1) of the Administration of Justice Act 1956', the important point in the definitions for oil pollution purposes being that 'inland waters' excludes 'territorial waters'. Hence in this very important respect Order 75, rule 4(1), is narrower than Order 11, rule 1(1)(h), for the latter does at least definitely allow service out of the jurisdiction where the whole tort is committed within territorial waters.

9.9.2 ACTIONS IN REM

In accordance with Articles 2 and 4[2] of the International Convention Relating to the Arrest of Seagoing Ships, 1952[3], a writ in rem, which is the only way in which an action in rem may be begun[4], may never be served out of the jurisdiction, nor, by implication, may notice thereof[5].

However, a powerful new weapon was placed in the hands of some maritime claimants in the form of Article 3 of the 1952 Arrest

---

2. Article 2: 'A ship flying the flag of one of the Contracting States may be arrested *within the jurisdiction* of any of the Contracting States...'. Article 4: 'A ship may only be arrested under the authority of a Court or of the appropriate judicial authority of the Contracting State in which the arrest is made'.
3. 439 UNTS 193; UKTS No. 47 of 1960 (Cmnd. 1128). As at 1 January 1971, the same states had become parties to the Convention as had become parties to the 1952 Collision Convention (above, section 9.9.1) with the exception of Argentine and the addition of Haiti. The same extensions had been made. Entered into force, 24 February 1956.
4. RSC Ord. 75, r. 3(1).
5. RSC Ord. 75, r. 4(1), does not apply to an action in rem: see RSC Ord. 75, r. 4(3). RSC Ord. 75, rr. 8 and 11, dealing with service, make no mention of the possibility of service out of the jurisdiction and are worded in such a way as to make nonsense if service out of the jurisdiction were possible.

Convention, whereby in certain cases a sister ship might be arrested:
'(1) Subject to the provisions of para. (4) of this Article[6] and of Article
10[7], a claimant may arrest either the particular ship in respect of which
the maritime claim arose, or any other ship which is owned by the
person who was, at the time when the maritime claim arose, the owner
of the particular ship, even though the ship arrested be ready to
sail;...'. The maritime claims in respect of which the power is granted
are listed in Articles 1(1)(a) to (n), and include claims arising out of
'damage caused by any ship either in collision or otherwise' (Article
1(1)(a)).

Does this include oil pollution damage? Certainly the phrase is
capable of a wide enough interpretation to cover oil pollution damage
if more weight is given to the words 'or otherwise' than to the words
'by any ship'; but equally, if the weighting is reversed, the conclusion
would be that oil pollution damage is caused, not by a ship, but by oil,
and so is excluded. If the phrase is taken in the context of the purpose
of the whole Convention, it should be interpreted to cover oil pollution
damage, for the object of the Convention is clearly to allow the arrest
of a ship where the claim has a legitimate connection with it.

The UK ratifying legislation is the Administration of Justice Act
1956. Section 3(4) provides as follows: 'In the case of any such claim
as is mentioned is paragraphs (d) to (r) of subsection (1) of section one
of this Act, being a claim arising in connection with a ship, where the
person who would be liable on the claim in an action in personam[8]
was, when the cause of action arose, the owner or charterer of, or in
possession or in control of, the ship, the Admiralty jurisdiction of the
High Court may (whether the claim gives rise to a maritime lien on
the ship or not) be invoked by an action in rem against – (a) that ship,
if at the time when the action is brought it is beneficially owned as
respects all the shares therein by that person; or (b) any other ship
which, at the time when the action is brought, is beneficially owned as
aforesaid.' Paragraph (d) of section 1(1), following earlier legislation on
Admiralty jurisdiction[9], lists 'any claim for damage done by a ship',
but section 3(4) itself provides that this may be a claim 'arising in
connection with a ship'.

The phrase 'damage done by a ship' has long been the subject of
litigation, and, as in other cases where the real issue is one of
causation, it is difficult to abstract a single pre-eminent principle from

6. Which protects the owner's ships from arrest where a person other than the registered owner
(e.g. a bareboat charterer) is liable for the maritime claim.
7. Which grants states certain rights of reservation.
8. By section 3(8), in determining whether a person would be liable in an action in personam, it
shall be assumed that he has his habitual residence or a place of business within England and
Wales.
9. Supreme Court of Judicature (Consolidation) Act 1925, s. 22(1)(a)(iv), replacing Admiralty
Court Act 1861, s. 7.

them. In two early cases, *The Vera Cruz (No. 2)*[10] and *Currie v M'Knight*[11], a fairly direct connection seemed required. In the former case, the administratrix of the master of the *Agnes* sued under Lord Campbell's Act the owners of the *Vera Cruz* which had collided with and sunk the *Agnes*. The Court of Appeal held that section 7 of the Admiralty Court Act 1861 did not give the court jurisdiction because, in the words of Brett MR, 'the real cause of action is in fact pecuniary loss caused to these persons, it is not a cause of action for anything done by a ship, which is only one ingredient in the right of action'[12]. In the latter case an equally harsh decision was made. There, the *Dunlossit* was moored between the *Easdale* and another ship. When a gale blew up, occasioning a serious threat by contact with the other two, the crew of the *Dunlossit* cut the mooring rope of the *Easdale* and the *Dunlossit* steamed out. The *Easdale* was unable to get up steam and so was driven ashore and damaged. The House of Lords held that there was no connection between the damage suffered by the *Easdale* and the *Dunlossit* itself. Lord Halsbury LC said: '... the phrase that it must be the fault of the ship itself is not a mere figurative expression, but it imports, in my opinion, that the ship against which a maritime lien for damages is claimed is the instrument of mischief, and that in order to establish the liability of the ship itself to the maritime lien claimed some act of navigation of the ship itself should either mediately or immediately be the cause of the damage[13].'

However, other cases, two of which are more recent, indicate that a looser view may be taken of the causative link. In *The Industrie*[14] Sir Robert Phillimore had held that damage was done by a ship if it was navigated so negligently as to cause another ship to go aground in the process of taking reasonable avoiding action. In *The Chr. Knudsen*[15] Bateson J held that expenses incurred by a dock company in removing a barge sunk by collision with the defendant vessel, was 'damage done by a ship'; and in *The Minerva*[16] the same judge held that damage done by part of a ship was within the phrase.

In the most recent case, *The Jade, The Eschersheim*[17] the House of Lords unanimously approved *The Vera Cruz* and *Currie v M'Knight*, in a case in which neither *The Industrie*, nor *The Chr. Knudsen* nor *The Minerva* were cited, and yet in which the result was a far wider interpretation of the phrase than even the uncited cases would have

10. (1884) 9 PD 96.
11. [1897] AC 97.
12. (1884) 9 PD 96 at 100.
13. [1897] AC 97 at 101.
14. (1871) LR 3 A & E 303.
15. [1932] P 153.
16. [1933] P 224.
17. [1976] 1 All ER 920, [1976] 1 WLR 430, HL, affirming [1976] 1 All ER 441, [1976] 1 WLR 339, CA, affirming [1974] 3 All ER 307, [1975] 1 WLR 83 (Brandon J).

allowed. The interest of the case is heightened by the fact that pollution claims were involved. The facts were that the *Erkowit* collided in the Bay of Biscay with a German vessel and was badly holed. Three hours later a salvage tug, the *Rotesand* arrived and entered into a salvage agreement with the *Erkowit*, which she towed towards La Coruna, and beached for repairs on an open beach. The salvors attempted to patch her with canvas and wood, but this proved ineffective, and the *Erkowit* was broken up by the waves and her cargo swept away. Some of the cargo consisted of drums of insecticide which allegedly caused pollution of local fisheries.

The owners of the *Erkowit* and her cargo owners brought actions in rem against sister ships of the *Rotesand* claiming, inter alia, negligence on the part of the salvors in beaching the *Erkowit* in a place exposed to wind and waves and in patching her with canvas and wood instead of steel.

At first instance Brandon J adopted *Currie v M'Knight* as giving the true interpretation to be made, and in applying it to the facts found that the *Rotesand* was not the physical instrument of any of the damage complained of[18]. The Court of Appeal and the House of Lords, however, both approving *Currie v M'Knight*, applied it to the facts with the opposite conclusion[19]. Two judges in the Court of Appeal were explicit in finding that the pollution damage was capable of being proved to have been damage done by the *Rotesand*[20]. Lord Diplock in the House of Lords, with whom all the judges concurred, may be taken to have included the pollution claims[1]. The reasoning of Lord Diplock is worth repeating here because it greatly favours claimants in oil pollution cases, even if some might find it difficult to agree with his application of the principle he adopts to the facts before him. He said:

> 'Strictly speaking this makes it unnecessary to decide whether the shipowners' and cargo owners' claims also came within para (d), viz "damage done by a ship" or, as it is phrased in art. 1 of the convention, "damage caused by any ship either in collision or otherwise"; but as this was a matter on which The Court of Appeal differed from Brandon J, I will express my views on it briefly. The figurative phrase "damage done by a ship" is a term of art in maritime law whose meaning is well settled by authority (*The Vera Cruz*; *Currie v M'Knight*). To fall within the phrase not only must the damage be the direct result or natural consequence of something done by those engaged in the navigation of the ship, but the ship itself must be the actual

18. [1974] 3 All ER 307 at 314, 315.
19. [1976] 1 All ER 441 CA, [1976] 1 All ER 920.
20. Per Sir Gordon Willmer, [1976] 1 All ER at 460; per Scarman LJ, concurring at p. 454.
  1. [1976] 1 All ER at 927.

instrument by which the damage was done. The commonest case is that of collision, which is specifically mentioned in the convention; but physical contact between the ship and whatever object sustains the damage is not essential – a ship may negligently cause a wash by which some other vessel or some property on shore is damaged.

In the instant case the act of casting off the *Erkowit* in such a way as to beach her on an exposed shore was something done by those engaged in the navigation of the *Rotesand*, as a result of which the *Erkowit* and her cargo were left exposed to the risk of being damaged by wind and wave if the weather worsened before she could be removed to a more sheltered position.

I do not understand it to be claimed that the actual beaching caused any physical damage to ship or cargo, but for the purposes of this appeal it must be assumed that the chain of causation is unbroken between the beaching of the *Erkowit* and her subsequent breaking up by wind and wave. Had the damage been caused by the beaching, there could in my view have been no question but that the *Rotesand* could properly be regarded as the actual instrument by which that damage was done. Although for my part I find this a borderline case, I do not think that the intervening failure of the salvors to take steps to avert the risk of damage, which forms the subject of the alternative grounds of negligence, prevents the *Rotesand* from remaining the actual instrument by which the damage subsequent to the beaching was done. I accordingly agree with the Court of Appeal that the shipowners' and cargo owners' claims also fall under para. (d) of s. 1(1) of the 1956 Act[2].'

There is now, therefore, clear authority for the proposition that where a ship is at fault and oil leaks from her causing a plaintiff damage, that is 'damage done by a ship' within paragraph (d) of s. 1(1) of the Administration of Justice Act 1956; and the case is further authority for the proposition that where Ship A causes Ship B to leak oil, the pollution damage is 'done by' Ship A.

The Court of Appeal and the House of Lords unanimously held that the damage suffered by the *Erkowit* was 'done by' the *Rotesand*, but it is clear from the decision on the facts of *Currie v M'Knight* that the court had in that case a far more restrictive interpretation of the principle in mind. However, the wider approach is supported by *The Industrie*, *The Chr. Knudsen* and *The Minerva*, and so it seems likely that it will be followed in future.

One may note that in practice, the chances of the plaintiff being able to find a sister ship to arrest have been considerably reduced since

2. [1976] 1 All ER 920 at 926 and 927.

1952 by the formation of single-ship companies – a device employed partly to defeat the power of arrest of sister ships.

9.9.3 CONCLUSION

The oil pollution claimant is placed in a peculiarly difficult situation when it comes to actually mounting an action against a foreign defendant. He cannot benefit from the limited right to service out of the jurisdiction granted by Order 11, rule 1(2), and so is forced (along with most other types of claimant) to seek the leave of the court under Order 11, rule 1(1). The scope of paragraph (h) is limited to cases where the tort has been committed wholly within the jurisdiction, which will by no means always be the case, and so his ability to rely on that paragraph is affected by the precise positioning of the offending vessel inside or outside the three-mile limit – while the damage he suffers is the same irrespective of this circumstance.

As a by-product of the adoption of section 15 of the Merchant Shipping (Oil Pollution) Act 1971, paragraph (n) of Order 11, rule 1(1), gives the court power in non-CLC cases to grant leave to serve out of the jurisdiction where the damage suffered is the cost of preventive measures, but not where the oil has succeeded in causing physical damage or economic loss consequent thereon, as respects such damage. It may be noted that section 15 is a provision adopted in excess of the government's obligations under CLC, so that other contracting parties will not necessarily have seen fit to pass similar measures[3].

If the court were to find that in certain cases involving more than one ship[4], the Admiralty jurisdiction of the High Court should apply, the circumstances in which leave to serve out of the jurisdiction will be granted are, in oil pollution cases, even narrower than under Order 11, rule 1(1), and the benefit of Order 11, rule 1(1)(n), will in particular be denied.

Although a writ in rem may never be served out of the jurisdiction, oil pollution claims are probably within that class of claims for which there is a right to arrest sister ships.

Two further points are worthy of note. First, the offending ship may well be insured against oil pollution risks, but there is no right of direct recourse against the insurer, even though he is within the jurisdiction, apart from the provisions of CLC[5]. Second, it is now clear

3. The Bahamas has adopted the UK legislation wholesale, including section 15: see the Bahamas Merchant Shipping Act 1976.
4. As to joint and several liability, see section 10.4.
5. See below, section 10.5. Some states have enacted their own direct recourse legislation, e.g. the USA and Canada.

that the resources needed to prosecute an oil pollution claim against a defendant not within the jurisdiction are beyond the private claimant. Not only that, but private and public claimants alike may find that, even after overcoming all the obstacles, the defendant forces execution abroad of the judgment finally obtained.

9.10 Choice of law

Once the English court[6] has jurisdiction over the defendant by virtue of his having been duly served with process, the question arises whether any law apart from English law is to be applied to the case. More specifically, three situations may be supposed, and the problem of choice of law considered in respect of each:

1) A ship within English territorial waters spills oil which causes damage within English territorial waters;
2) A ship on the high seas and outside the territorial waters of any state[7] spills oil which causes damage within English territorial waters;
3) A ship in foreign territorial waters spills oil which causes damage in English territorial waters.

9.10.1 A SHIP WITHIN ENGLISH TERRITORIAL WATERS SPILLS OIL WHICH CAUSES DAMAGE WITHIN ENGLISH TERRITORIAL WATERS

Here, the lex fori and the lex loci delicti coincide, and the only fact which might raise a doubt as to the applicability of English law to the full case is if the ship is registered abroad. There is no authority for the proposition that the law of the flag should apply to an oil pollution claim in these circumstances, and there is the authority of a defamation case to the contrary[8]. There is further no reason to disagree with Professor Cheshire that, even after *Chaplin v Boys*[9], 'it

6. No attempt is made here to analyse the choice of law which a foreign court apprised of the case might make. G. O. Z. Sundstrom, in *Foreign Ships and Foreign Waters* (Almquist and Wiksell, Stockholm, 1971) makes a comparative analysis of British, American, German and Scandinavian conflict law (in collision cases only).
7. In older cases the high seas are regarded as being all waters upon which great ships go – see Sundstrom, *Foreign Ships and Foreign Waters* (Almquist and Wiksell, Stockholm, 1971) 42–44, but now a distinction is made: see, e.g. the use of the phrase 'on the high seas outside territorial waters' by Brandon J in *The Esso Malaysia* [1975] QB 198 at 204.
8. *Szalatnay-Stacho v Fink* [1947] KB 1, [1946] 2 All ER 231.
9. [1971] AC 356, [1969] 2 All ER 1085.

would seem unlikely that an English court could avoid the application
of English law to a tort committed in England'[10].

9.10.2 A SHIP ON THE HIGH SEAS AND OUTSIDE THE TERRITORIAL WATERS OF ANY STATE SPILLS OIL WHICH CAUSES DAMAGE WITHIN ENGLISH TERRITORIAL WATERS

It is well established that, assuming proper service has established
jurisdiction over the defendant, the High Court has jurisdiction over
acts which took place on the high seas, notwithstanding the fact that
neither plaintiff nor defendant nor any ship involved is English[11]. It is
therefore no defence to plead that the act or omission on which the
plaintiff relies occurred on the high seas. This does not, however,
affect the question of which law is to regulate liability.

The cases support a distinction between acts or omissions whose
effect is confined to the ship, and those which have an effect external
to the ship. With respect to the former, the lex loci delicti is the law of
the port of registry[12]. Thus, it has been held in Canada that where the
plaintiff brings an action for personal injuries caused on board due to
the negligence of an officer[13] or the master[14], the rule in *Phillips v
Eyre*[15] applies, and the plaintiff must show that the negligence is
actionable by the lex fori and is not justifiable by the lex loci
delicti – although if the defendant does not plead any difference
between the two laws, the plaintiff may rely on a presumption that
they are the same.

In collision cases, it is clear that the rule is quite different. Here the
law governing is the common law of England as applied in maritime
cases[16], or, to express it differently, the general maritime law as
administered in England. As Brett LJ said in *The Gaetano and
Maria*[17]: 'Now the first question raised on the argument before us was
what is the law which is administered in an English Court of

10. *Private International Law* (9th ed. (ed. P. M. North), London, 1974) 288.
11. *The Tubantia* [1924] P 78; *Chartered Mercantile Bank of India, London and China v
Netherlands India Steam Navigation Co Ltd* (1883) 10 QB 521; *The Esso Malaysia* [1975]
QB 198, [1974] 2 All ER 705.
12. *Canadian National Steamships Co v Watson* [1939] 1 DLR 273; *Gronlund v Hansen* (1969) 4
DLR (3d) 435. And see Merchant Shipping Act 1894, s.265, seemingly enacting the same
rule, but repealed without replacement from 1 January 1973 by the Merchant Shipping Act
1970, s. 100, Sch. 5, and the Merchant Shipping Act 1970 (Commencement No. 1) Order
1972, S.I. 1972 No. 1977.
13. *Canadian National Steamships Co v Watson* [1939] 1 DLR 273 (SC of Canada).
14. *Gronlund v Hansen* (1969) 4 DLR (3d) 435 (British Columbia CA).
15. (1870) LR 6 QB 1.
16. *Lloyd v Guibert* (1865) LR 1 QB 115; *Chartered Mercantile Bank of India v Netherlands India
Steam Navigation Co* (1883) 10 QBD 521. And see cases cited in *Marsden's The Law of
Collisions at Sea* (11th ed. (ed. K. C. McGuffie) London, 1961) para. 262.
17. (1882) 7 PD 137.

Admiralty, whether it is English law, or whether it is that which is called the common maritime law, which is not the law of England alone, but the law of all maritime countries. About that question I have not the smallest doubt. Every Court of Admiralty is a court of the country in which it sits and to which it belongs. The law which is administered in the Admiralty Court of England is the English maritime law. It is not the ordinary municipal law of the country, but it is the law which the English Court of Admiralty either by Act of Parliament or by reiterated decisions and traditions and principles has adopted as the English maritime law, and about that I cannot conceive that there is any doubt'[18]. Thus, the question of whether an Act of Parliament is to have effect for high seas collisions between vessels of any flag is one of construction of the particular statute[19], but, as one writer says, it is clear that the English maritime law 'includes those principles of English law which determine the consequences of wrongful acts in such matters as vicarious liability and damages'[20].

The question remains whether this is the rule in all cases where damage external to the ship is suffered, or whether it is confined to collision cases only. The scant authority on the point would suggest the former alternative. In *The Submarine Telegraph Co v Dickson*[1], the plaintiffs were possessed of a cable stretching across the sea bed of the English Channel between Dover and Calais. The defendants' vessel (of Swedish registry) was alleged to have been negligently navigated so that its anchor fouled and injured the cable outside the three-mile limit. It was conceded that the court had jurisdiction over the matter, and it was held that the question was purely one of negligence. Willes J, concurring with Erle CJ and Williams J, said: 'Mr. Archibald [counsel for the plaintiffs] admits that there is nothing in the allegation as to the three miles: The rights and duties of persons navigating vessels apply equally whether in port or on the high seas. It is the duty of the persons navigating so to exercise their rights as to do no damage to the property of others. I see no substantial difference between a telegraphic-cable and another ship . . .'[2].

This case was followed and approved in another case[3] on similar facts, where the question was purely of jurisdiction under section 7 of the Admiralty Court Act 1861, and the principle is in accord with

18. (1882) 7 PD 137 at 143.
19. See e.g. *The Esso Malaysia* [1975] QB 198, [1974] 2 All ER 705, on the construction of the Fatal Accidents Acts.
20. *Dicey and Morris on The Conflict of Laws* (9th ed. (ed. J. H. C. Morris) London, 1973) 974, citing *Davidsson v Hill* [1901] 2 KB 606 and *The Arum* [1921] P 12. See also *The Leon* (1881) 6 PD 148; and *The Esso Malaysia* [1975] 1 QB 198, [1974] 2 All ER 705.
1. (1864) 15 CBNS 759.
2. (1864) 15 CBNS 759 at 779.
3. *The Clara Killam* (1870) LR 3 A & E 161. And see *The Tubantia* [1924] P 78 where there was no question of applying any law other than the maritime law. The plaintiffs were granted an injunction restraining British defendants from interfering with their possession of a wreck below water fifty miles from the English coast.

common sense: if in such cases an attempt was made to apply a lex loci delicti, the task would be next to impossible where two or three ships become involved[4], all of different flags. The only practical alternative to applying the collision case rule would be the application of the rule in *Phillips v Eyre*[5], but, as one learned author has commented, 'it seems a little strained to treat the law of the flag in maritime wrongs as being equivalent to the lex loci delicti comissi in the case of torts on land. The reason why English law requires proof that a wrong committed in a foreign country is actionable by the lex loci is that the offending act has been committed within the exclusive jurisdiction of a foreign sovereign, but, as Brett LJ has shown, there is no such thing as exclusive jurisdiction over the high seas[6,7].

It may therefore be concluded with a certain degree of confidence, all too rare in the conflict of laws, that where a ship on the high seas and outside the territorial waters of any state spills oil which causes damage within English territorial waters, the law to be applied by an English court is the maritime law of England as described above.

9.10.3 A SHIP IN FOREIGN TERRITORIAL WATERS SPILLS OIL WHICH CAUSES DAMAGE IN ENGLISH TERRITORIAL WATERS

Subject to rights prescribed by international law, the territorial sea of a state is regarded as being within its sovereignty[8]. It is clear that where the tort is committed wholly within the territorial sea of a foreign state, the normal English conflict rule applies, and the plaintiff must satisfy both limbs of the rule in *Phillips v Eyre*[9]. This may be stated notwithstanding the remarks of Lord Denning MR in *Sayers v International Drilling Co NV*[10] where he applied a doctrine of the proper law of the tort to a case of personal injury sustained by an employee aboard an offshore drilling rig in Nigerian territorial waters. It is a delicate point of jurisprudence as to whether his remarks were obiter, but they were not concurred in by Salmon and Stamp LJJ, and

---

4. The example often cited is *Aberdeen Arctic Co v Sutter* (1862) 4 Macq 355, where two Scottish vessels disputed the property in a whale speared in the Northern fishing grounds.
5. (1870) LR 6 QB 1.
6. *Chartered Mercantile Bank of India, London and China v Netherlands India Steam Navigation Co. Ltd* (1883) 10 QBD 521 at 536–537.
7. *Cheshire's Private International Law* (9th ed. (ed. P. M. North), London, 1974) 295.
8. See e.g. Article 1 of the Geneva Convention on Territorial Sea and Contiguous Zone 1958.
9. *The Mary Moxham* (1876) 1 PD 107 (English ship damaged a Spanish pier: Spanish law applied); *The Arum* [1921] P 12 (defence of compulsory pilotage by common law applicable in Gibraltar allowed in respect of a collision in Gibraltese waters); *The Waziristan* [1953] 2 All ER 1213, [1953] 1 WLR 1446 (defence of compulsory pilotage under Iraqi law allowed in respect of a collision in Iraqi waters).
10. [1971] 3 All ER 163 at 166.

This chapter will analyse the Convention in detail, and will make reference to the corresponding UK law where appropriate. The United Kingdom has extended the provisions of her ratifying Act[5] to her overseas territories[6], and so, unless otherwise stated, statutory provisions mentioned in this chapter as relating to the United Kingdom may be taken also to apply in those overseas territories.

10.1 Sphere of application

10.1.1 THE RULE OF LIABILITY: ARTICLE III(1)

10.1.1.1 The words used to express the rule of liability

Article III(1) provides that 'Except as provided in paragraphs 2 and 3 of this Article[7], the owner of a ship at the time of an incident, or where the incident consists of a series of occurrences at the time of the first such occurrence, shall be liable for any pollution damage caused by oil which has escaped or been discharged from the ship as a result of the incident'.

It can be seen at once that the rule is tortious in nature, and is one of strict liability within its sphere of operation. That sphere is delineated not only by the exceptions contained in paragraphs 2 and 3[7] but also by the words used in the body of Article III(1).

Ship[8] is defined in Article I(1) as 'any sea-going vessel and any seaborne craft of any type whatsoever, actually carrying oil in bulk as cargo'. This includes combination carriers laden with bulk oil cargo, but excludes them when they are carrying oil only in the form of slops. Thus, where an OBO has changed from an oil cargo to a dry cargo and has retained oil residues on board in a slop tank, any subsequent escape of oil from the slop tank or bunker tanks would not be covered

---

5. The Merchant Shipping (Oil Pollution) Act 1971, as amended by the Merchant Shipping Act 1974, s. 9.
6. Jersey (S.I. 1975 No. 2184), Guernsey (S.I. 1975 No. 2185), Isle of Man (S.I. 1975 No. 2186), Akrotiri and Dhekelia (S.I. 1975 No. 2171), Belize (S.I. 1975 No. 2164), British Indian Ocean Territory (S.I. 1975 No. 2171), Cayman Islands (S.I. 1975 No. 2166), Falkland Islands (S.I. 1975 No. 2167), Gibraltar (S.I. 1976 No. 53), Gilbert Islands (S.I. 1975 No. 2168), Montserrat (S.I. 1975 No. 2170), Pitcairn (S.I. 1975 No. 2171), St Helena (S.I. 1975 No. 2171), Seychelles (S.I. 1975 No. 2172 – now that the Seychelles are independent, by virtue of the Seychelles Act 1976, s. 5, the law contained in S.I. 1975 No. 2172 takes effect until repeal by the new legislature), Solomon Islands (S.I. 1975 No. 2173), Turks and Caicos Islands (S.I. 1976 No. 223), Tuvalu (S.I. 1975 No. 2174), Virgin Islands (S.I. 1975 No. 2175).
7. These exceptions are discussed in section 10.1.4.
8. For exempt ships, see below, section 10.1.1.2.

by the Convention. However, the escape of any oil from a combination
carrier partly laden with bulk oil cargo and partly with dry cargo is
caught by Article III(1).

River and lake vessels carrying bulk oil cargoes, offshore installations (e.g. semi-submersible or submerged oil storage installations, drilling barges and semi-submersible, fixed or floating
platforms) and pipelines are all excluded. CLC is thus almost
exclusively a tanker Convention: the only dry cargo vessels covered by
it being those few carrying oil in their deep tanks, for instance for
places too out-of-the-way to merit a special tanker visit. However, it is
only laden tankers which are covered: a tanker on the ballast voyage,
even though she carries bunkers and slops, is not covered by Article
III(1)[9], whereas a tanker carrying oil in bulk as cargo is covered
even where the oil which actually escapes and causes damage is bunker
oil.

The scope of Article III(1) is further limited by the definition of *oil*
in Article I(5): '...any persistent oil such as crude oil, fuel oil, heavy
diesel oil, lubricating oil and whale oil, whether carried on board a
ship as cargo or in the bunkers of such a ship'. Two important
questions are raised by this definition: what is the meaning of
persistent, and are slop and bilge oils included?

The word *persistent* is nowhere defined in the Convention, and so
may be interpreted in accordance with Articles 31 to 33 of the Vienna
Convention on the Law of Treaties 1969[10]. The Preamble to CLC
twice refers to 'pollution', a phrase usually taken to import an element
of harm[11]. Few, if any straight-chain paraffin or other animal or
vegetable oils leave a residue which can be regarded as harmful. The
specific inclusion of whale oil at the instigation of the Japanese[12] seems

9. Hence the damage caused by the oil escaping from the bunker tanks of the *Olympic Bravery*,
   which went aground off Ushant in March 1976, would not have been covered by CLC
   because she carried no oil as cargo at the time: see *The Daily Telegraph*, 19.3.76, p. 6, for an
   account of the incident.

10. 8 ILM 679. The Convention had not entered into force as at 31 December 1975, thirty-five
    ascessions or ratifications being needed. At that date, the following 24 states had deposited
    instruments of ratification or accesion: Argentina, Australia, Barbados, Canada, Central
    African Republic, Greece, Italy, Jamaica, Kuwait, Lesotho, Mauritius, Mexico, Morocco,
    New Zealand, Niger, Nigeria, Paraguay, Phillipines, Spain, Sweden, Syrian Arab Republic,
    Tunisia, United Kingdom, Yugoslavia.

11. The UN Conference on the Human Environment 1972 adopted the following definition of
    marine pollution (UN Doc. A/CONF. 48/8, para. 197): '...the introduction by man, directly
    or indirectly, of substances or energy into the marine environment (including estuaries)
    resulting in such deleterious effects as harm to living resources, hazards to human health,
    hindrance to marine activities including fishing, impairment of quality for use of sea water
    and reduction of amenities'.

12. Whale oil was not included in the Draft Articles, LEG/CONF/4, *OR* 437 at 444. The
    Japanese proposed its introduction, LEG/CONF/C. 2/SR. 14, *OR* 701 at 713, becuase whale
    oil had the same persistence and viscosity as heavy oil and was carried in bulk; the proposal
    was adopted by 13 votes to 8 with 15 abstentions. In Plenary this amendment was carried
    unanimously without debate: LEG/CONF/SR. 5, *OR* 91 at 93.

to have been based on a misapprehension of the environmental effects of whale oil: it is clear from the *travaux preparatoires* that the other delegations were not informed about whale oil. All the preparatory work and consultation was done in collaboration only with the hydrocarbon mineral oil industry, and no ratifying legislation published to date[13] has sought to include any animal or vegetable oil apart from whale oil. Further, the definition of oil adopted in the Public Law Convention[14] drawn up at the same conference completely omits animal and vegetable oils, and even excludes whale oil. Thus it would seem that 'persistent' should be limited to hydrocarbon mineral oils and whale oil. The hydrocarbon mineral oils to be covered, apart from those listed, may be scientifically taken to be those which, after evaporation has ceased, leave a harmful residue[15]. An alternative suggestion by one writer[16], that oil be taken to be persistent if it has actually caused damage, suffers from one defect, namely that it is necessarily applicable only ex post facto; it does not solve the question of whether a plaintiff can recover if his clean-up has been so successful that no damage (as opposed to loss) has been suffered.

It is not clear from Article I(5) whether slop and bilge oils are included. This depends on whether the words 'whether carried on board a ship as cargo or in the bunkers of such a ship' are taken restrictively or illustratively. The phrase began life as 'whether carried as cargo or in bunkers', in Draft Article I(4)[17], and was amended only by the Drafting Committee. The *travaux preparatoires* do not, therefore, afford any assistance. The corresponding definition in the Public Law Convention[18] omits the clause altogether, indicating the inclusion in that Convention of slop oil and bilge oil, although the latter could scarcely constitute a 'grave and imminent danger' to a coastline and so attract the provisions of that Convention. There is no sound reason for excluding slop oil or bilge oil from CLC, and there are good reasons for including them: it would be unnecessarily arbitrary to include the bunkers of laden tankers but to exclude slops and bilges carried in laden tankers[19]. On balance, it would seem that

---

13. That of Bahamas, Greece, FGR, Liberia, New Zealand, Norway, Panama, Spain, Sweden, UK and USSR.
14. See above, section 5.4.
15. Private communication from Dr D. R. Blaikley, Environmental Adviser, Amoco (Europe) Inc.
16. A. L. Doud, 'Compensation for Oil Pollution Damage: Further Comment on the Civil Liability and Compensation Fund Conventions' (1973) 4 *J Mar L & Comm*, 525 at 533.
17. LEG/CONF/4, *OR* 437 at 444.
18. See above, section 5.4.
19. Slop oil will only rarely be carried in laden tankers. The sort of situation where it might be so carried is where a tanker has discharged part of her cargo at Port A and is proceeding to Port B to discharge the balance. After washing the tanks from which cargo was discharged at Port A, she will have slop oil collected in her slop tank.

the clause should be taken illustratively, so that oil is not limited to oil carried as cargo and as bunkers[20,1].

For the Convention to apply, the oil must have *'escaped or been discharged'* from the ship, so that both accidental and intentional discharges are covered; but the discharge must have been *'from the ship'*. Consequently, where the oil has escaped due to a burst in a pipe connecting a tanker either to a terminal, or to a single buoy mooring, or even to another ship, the Convention would appear not to apply. However, it is open to a legislature or a court to interpret the phrase as including a part of a ship, and to hold that the pipe is a part of the ship[2].

The Convention will further only apply where the oil has escaped *'as a result of the incident'*. Incident is defined widely in Article I (8) to be '... any occurrence, or series of occurrences having the same origin, which causes pollution damage'.

10.1.1.2 Persons liable and exempt from liability

a) *Owners and others*
By Article III(1), it is the *owner* of the ship who is liable. Owner is defined in Article I(3) as '... the person or persons[3] registered as the owner of the ship or, in the absence of registration, the person or persons owning the ship. However, in the case of a ship owned by a State and operated by a company which in that State is registered as the ship's operator, "owner" shall mean such company'. It is therefore clear that the Convention places no liability whatsoever either upon any person salving the ship from which oil has escaped, or upon the owner's servants such as the master and crew. However, the owner is liable irrespective of his residence or domicile, or of the state in which his ship is registered.

In an attempt to channel the liability to the owner, Article III(4) provides that 'No claim for compensation for pollution damage shall be made against the owner otherwise than in accordance with this Convention. No claim for pollution damage under this Convention or otherwise may be made against the servants or agents of the owner'.

---

20. The United Kingdom and the Bahamas have both included slop and bilge oil carried in laden tankers – see the UK Merchant Shipping (Oil Pollution) Act 1971, s. 1, and the Bahamian Merchant Shipping (Oil Pollution) Act 1976, s. 20.
1. See further, section 10.6.1.
2. In *The Minerva* [1933] P 224, Bateson J held that 'damage done by a ship' in s. 22(1)(a)(iv) of the Supreme Court of Judicature (Consolidation) Act 1925 included damage done by part of a ship, in this case part of the elevator on a grain elevator barge.
3. Article I(2): ' "Persons" means any individual or partnership or any public or private body, whether corporate or not, including a State or any of its constituent subdivisions'.

recent cases[10]. The best conclusion to be drawn at present is that in an action in rem for oil pollution damage, the plea would be refused if the ship were a pure trading vessel; in an action in personam, the matter is more open to doubt, but the balance of probabilities is that the same result would follow.

In the United Kingdom the matter has been resolved beyond doubt by the State Immunity Act 1978[11], section 10(2) of which applies to Admiralty proceedings on any claim which could be made the subject of such proceedings, and which states that 'a State is not immune as respects—(a) an action in rem against a ship belonging to that State; or (b) an action in personam for enforcing a claim in connection with such a ship, if, at the time when the cause of action arose, the ship was in use or intended for use for commercial purposes'[12].

10.1.2 THE TERRITORIAL LIMITS OF THE RULE OF LIABILITY: ARTICLE II

Article II limits the geographical scope of the Convention: 'This Convention shall apply exclusively to pollution damage caused on the territory including the territorial sea of a Contracting State and to preventive measures taken to prevent or minimise such damage'.

The sole criterion is, therefore, territorial: the nationality, domicile or residence of the defendant is irrelevant. Under this provision, if a ship goes aground on the high seas and oil pollutes the shores of State A (a contracting party) and State B (a non-contracting party), the Convention will apply only to the former damage, but this will include damage suffered in State A by State B or her nationals. Additionally, reasonable preventive measures[13] taken on the high seas or on the territorial sea of States A or B and designed to prevent or minimise pollution damage in State A are covered, irrespective of who took them. It is therefore clear that a benefit is conferred on non-contracting states or their nationals if they suffer pollution damage covered by Article II[14].

There is one area excluded by Article II which is becoming increasingly important. Offshore installations, such as rigs and single

---

10. *The Philippine Admiral* [1977] AC 373, [1976] 1 All ER 78; *Thai-Europe Tapioca Service Ltd v Government of Pakistan* [1975] 3 All ER 961, [1975] 1 WLR 1485; *Trendtex Trading Corpn v Central Bank of Nigeria* [1977] QB 529 [1977] 1 All ER 881; *The I Congreso del Partido* [1978] 1 All ER 1169, [1977] 3 WLR 778.
11. The Act enters into force on a day to be appointed.
12. See further for the case of the USSR, the USSR–UK Treaty on Merchant Navigation of 3 March 1968, UKTS No. 67 of 1972 (Cmnd. 5008), 7 ILM 1037; and the Protocol thereto (not yet in force): Soviet Union No. 1 of 1974 (Cmnd. 5611).
13. For the definition of 'preventive measures' see below, section 10.2.1.
14. See E. D. Brown, *The Legal Regime of Hydrospace* (London, 1971) 169: 'It would seem to follow that the intention of the parties is clearly to create a *benefit*, if not a right, for non-contracting States'.

buoy moorings, and possibly mollusc beds, are frequently outside the territorial sea of the state under whose control they lie. Reasonable preventive measures taken to prevent contamination to them, wherever such measures are taken, would seem to be excluded by Article II when they are outside the territorial sea, for such places do not qualify as the 'territory' of the state in question. However, offshore installations and single buoy moorings can rarely suffer serious damage from an oil spill, and mollusc beds are rarely below the high seas.

10.1.3 SUMMARY OF AREAS NOT COVERED BY THE RULE OF LIABILITY

The more important areas not attracting the attention of the rule of liability are as follows:

1) Oil escaping from river and lake vessels, offshore installations, and installations and pipelines.
2) Oil escaping from dry cargo ships and tankers not carrying oil in bulk as cargo.
3) Damage caused by non-persistent oils.
4) Damage suffered by installations outside the territory or territorial sea of a contracting state and all damage suffered on the territory or territorial sea of a non-contracting state.
5) Claims against salvors and bareboat charterers.

10.1.4 SPECIFIC EXEMPTIONS FROM LIABILITY: ARTICLES III(2) AND (3)

Paragraph 2 of Article III contains certain exceptions which are meant to represent uninsurable risks. Since the Convention makes insurance against liability under it compulsory, as a practical matter those risks thought to be uninsurable had to be excluded. The exceptions now contained in sub-paragraphs (b) and (c) were known at the Conference as 'the British exceptions'[15], and the UK delegation made it clear that insurance was available on the London market if, but only if, those exceptions to liability were adopted[16].

The owner will not, therefore, be liable if he proves that the damage '(a) resulted from an act of war, hostilities, civil war, insurrection, or a natural phenomenon of an exceptional, inevitable and irresistable character'.

The natural phenomenon referred to[17] began life as 'a grave natural

15. LEG/CONF/C. 2/WP. 6, *OR* 564.
16. LEG/CONF/C. 2/WP. 35, *OR* 596.
17. LEG/CONF/4, *OR* 437 at 460.

disaster of an exceptional character'[18] and took its present form by compromise[19]. As Lord Hawke pointed out in the UK House of Lords, the key word is, therefore, 'irresistible'[20], and the exception is more limited than the more familiar concept of Act of God[1]. It seems clear that the phrase does not cover hurricanes, for these are negotiable by some ships, but would encompass tidal waves. One writer has submitted that for the defence to be established, the defendant must show that in no circumstances could anyone have avoided the accident[2], and this is in accordance with Lord Hawke's interpretation. It is clear that the exemption is far narrower than the defence of 'inevitable accident' allowed in maritime law, which is that the accident could not have been avoided by the exercise of ordinary care and maritime skill[3].

A French study of tanker accidents occurring between 1960 and 1970 (inclusive) found that 17·7% of them were caused by exceptional circumstances beyond the control of the ship's company[4]. The study analysed this group of accidents and found four main causes: strong current (2·8%), difficulty in steering in bad weather (25·0%), fatigue of ship in bad weather (66·6%), and anchor chain breaking in bad weather (5·6%). This does not, unfortunately, tell us how many would have been covered by the exception contained in the Convention, because 'bad weather' is not further explained; but from it one may surmise that the exception will not prove to be purely hypothetical.

The owner will also escape liability if he proves that the discharge '(b) was wholly caused by an act or omission done with intent to cause damage by a third party'[5]. This clearly covers the sadly increasing occurrence of terrorist action. Both pipelines and rigs have been the subject of attacks or threats[6], and it is perhaps only a matter of time before a tanker is seized. The inclusion of the word 'wholly' keeps outside the scope of the exclusion the situation where a government deliberately damages the stricken ship, thereby causing a discharge or further discharge; for in such a case the discharge will be at least partly caused by the ship being stricken.

The last exception in paragraph (2) is where the owner can prove that the discharge '(c) was wholly caused by the negligence or other wrongful act of any Government or other authority responsible for the

---

18. The 1971 Fund Convention compensates plaintiffs and shipowners in this case: see section 11.2.2.
19. LEG/CONF/C. 2/SR. 18, *OR* 738 to 741.
20. 315 H of L Deb., col. 23.
 1. See also the remarks of Lord Drumalbyn, 315 H of L Deb., Col. 24.
 2. M. Forster, 'Civil Liability of Shipowners for Oil Pollution' [1973] *JBL* 23 at 26.
 3. See generally K. C. McGuffie, *Marsden's The Law of Collisions at Sea*, (11th ed.) paras. 9–15.
 4. IMCO Doc. MP XIII/2(a)/9 of 13 June 1972, entitled 'Accidental Pollution of the Sea by Oil', Vol. III, p. 29.
 5. But the 1971 Fund Convention will compensate victims in this case: see section 11.2.2.
 6. *The Times*, 13.9.75 (pipeline attack); *The Times*, 28.8.75 (offshore installation: threat).

maintenance of lights or other navigational aids in the exercise of that function'[7].

It would seem that this clause applies only to negligence or other wrongful acts performed in connection with the *maintenance* of the navigational aids, so that if the government in question has failed to place a light on a particular hazard, such failure is outside the scope of the exception; whereas if it has placed a light there but has failed to maintain it so that it goes out, it will be within the exception, and a shipowner whose ship thereby goes aground can claim exemption. Other parts of the clause which could lead to litigation, and on which it is difficult to come to any usefully conclusive view, are the meanings of the phrases 'other wrongful act' and 'other authority'.

By paragraph (3), 'if the owner proves that the pollution damage resulted wholly or partially either from an act or omission done with intent to cause damage by the persons who suffered the damage or from the negligence of that person, the owner may be exonerated wholly or partially from his liability to such person'.

The intentional conduct of the victim must clearly be excluded because no person should be able to be indemnified against or to profit from his own wickedness. The negligence part of this exception was not dictated by insurance considerations but seems to have been introduced[8] on grounds of fairness, despite anxieties on the part of some that it would weaken the concept of strict liability[9]. The phrase uses the words 'may be', rather than 'shall be', which probably indicates that the competent court has a discretion.

10.2 Damages recoverable

10.2.1 REMOTENESS OF DAMAGE

Article III(1) imposes liability on the shipowner only for '*pollution damage*'. This phrase is defined by Article I(6) as meaning 'loss or damage caused outside the ship carrying oil by contamination resulting from the escape or discharge of oil from the ship, wherever such escape or discharge may occur, and includes the costs of preventive measures and further loss or damage caused by preventive measures'. There are, therefore, three separate elements to the definition[10]: (1) loss or damage by contamination, (2) costs of preventive measures and (3) further loss or damage caused by preventive measures. One may

7. See above, note 5.
8. LEG/CON/C.2/WP.41, para. 3 *OR* 601.
9. LEG/CONF/C. 2/SR. 18, *OR* 738 et seq.
10. These are separately enumerated in the Merchant Shipping (Oil Pollution) Act 1971, s. 1(1).

note that the definition in Article I(6) is exclusive: it begins with the words ' "Pollution damage" *means*' and not ' "Pollution damage" *includes*'.

10.2.1.1 Loss or damage by contamination

It is clear that damage caused by the oil subsequently igniting[11] or exploding is not caused by contamination, and so is irrecoverable under the Convention[12]. This kind of damage will therefore be recoverable only under the lex fori unrelated to CLC, although where a vessel has exploded or caught fire and as a result oil has escaped and caused damage by contamination, such damage will be recoverable under CLC. The limitation to loss or damage by contamination would also appear to exclude the claim of a shipowner whose ship has had to take action to avoid floating oil, whether or not ignited, which has been discharged from another ship[13]. However, there is no rule of foreseeability involved: the test of remoteness, within the sphere of the definition, is purely one of causation.

It may be inferred that personal injury caused by unignited oil is recoverable[14], for this is essentially a kind of damage caused by contamination, but how far other types of loss are to be recoverable is not clear. The use of the phrase 'loss or damage' clearly indicates that more than just physical damage caused by contamination is recoverable. The words 'by contamination' must qualify 'loss' as they qualify 'damage', but what is to be understood by 'loss' is unclear. Certainly, there are strong grounds for holding (with the common law[15]) that economic loss consequent on physical damage sustained by the plaintiff and caused by contamination is recoverable, but whether the fisherman's lost profits, or the hotelier's lost profits in other cases are recoverable is in doubt. A similar doubt pertains to the costs of cleaning oiled birds and other wildlife. The interpretation of the word 'loss' is one for the lex fori, and it is probable that variations will arise from jurisdiction to jurisdiction. In the United Kingdom, it is likely that loss by contamination[16] will be limited to cases where the loss is caused directly by the contamination, and to cases where loss would

11. Oil floating on the water has subsequently ignited and caused damage in three reported cases: *The Wagon Mound* [1961] AC 388 and (*No. 2*) [1967] AC 617; *The Kazimah* [1967] 2 Lloyds Rep 163; and *Eastern Asia Navigation Co Ltd v Fremantle Harbour Trust Comrs.* (1951) 83 CLR 353.
12. Such damage was specifically included in the Draft Articles, LEG/CONF/4, *OR* 437 et seq., but the Committee of the Whole II excluded it by 21 votes to 9 with 6 abstentions (LEG/CONF/C. 2/SR. 15, *OR* 714) on a UK proposal, LEG/CONF/C. 2/WP. 9, *OR* 566.
13. It was this situation which gave rise to the claims in *The Kazimah* [1967] 2 Lloyds Rep 163.
14. See the remarks of Mr Kerry, (UK), LEG/CONF/C. 2/SR. 15, *OR* 715.
15. See above, section 9.8.1.3, *The hotelier's lost profits.*
16. See the Merchant Shipping (Oil Pollution) Act 1971, ss. 1(1), 20(1).

otherwise be allowable, so that in the three doubtful cases mentioned, recovery would be denied (as it is at common law[17]).

10.2.1.2 Costs of preventive measures

Preventive measures are defined by Article I(7) as 'any reasonable measures taken by any person after an incident has occurred to prevent or minimise pollution damage'. The requirement of reasonableness is an important safeguard for the shipowner. As has been seen[18], by Article II the cost of such measures taken on the high seas is recoverable, but only if they are taken to prevent or minimise damage inside the territory or territorial sea of a contracting state; so if detergent is sprayed on the high seas on a slick which is being blown out to sea, and there are no grounds for thinking that the slick will turn towards the shore, the costs will be irrecoverable. An owner may well argue that he should not have to pay for clean-up costs when the sea would have broken down the slick on its own. Hence, in the situation posed above in section 9.8.1.3[19], the cost of the detergent spraying would be irrecoverable under CLC, just as it was seen to be at common law. Again, the use of too much detergent or otherwise inordinate measures would be unreasonable and so irrecoverable.

Article I(7) defines preventive measures as being only those taken 'after an incident has occurred'; 'an incident' is defined in Article I(8) to be 'any occurrence, or series of occurrences having the same origin, which causes pollution damage', so that we are forced back to the definition of pollution damage to establish the full meaning of 'preventive measures'. Article I(6) states that pollution damage 'means loss or damage... *resulting from the escape or discharge of oil from the ship*'. It is therefore implied that any measures taken before oil actually spills from the ship are irrecoverable under CLC. So, if a ship has stranded but no oil has spilled, the cost of sending out boats with detergent spraying capability, and of laying booms and of other such measures, will be irrecoverable.

10.2.1.3 Further loss or damage caused by preventive measures

In 1969 the detergents used to disperse oil slicks were often highly toxic to marine life, and in some cases were capable of causing more environmental damage than the oil itself. Although modern dispersants are of much reduced toxicity, it is still technically possible that

17. See above, section 9.8.1.3.
18. Section 10.1.2.
19. Under the heading *Cost of preventive measures*.

their use could cause physical damage, and loss consequent thereon could be suffered. To be recoverable, this loss or damage does not itself need to be caused by contamination but merely by the preventive measures. It is therefore possible that a wider interpretation is here to be placed on the word 'loss' than in the first limb of the definition of pollution damage.

10.2.2 LIMITATION OF LIABILITY

10.2.2.1 The right to limit

By Article V(1), 'The owner of a ship shall be entitled to limit his liability under this Convention in respect of any one incident...'. The two significant points here are that it is only the owner who may limit[20], and it is only his liability under the Convention which he may limit under Article V. It is, of course, only upon the owner that the Convention imposes any liability (see above, section 10.1.1.2), but the absence of the right to limit on the part of others creates certain anomalies.

Consider a situation where a salvor negligently causes oil to escape from a ship which has stranded without the actual fault or privity of the shipowner. A plaintiff (for instance, a government) who has incurred heavy clean-up costs may sue both the shipowner (under CLC) and the salvor (in negligence)[1]. The shipowner will be able to limit his liability to the plaintiff under CLC, and the salvor may or may not be able to limit his liability under another Convention or provision of the lex fori[2]. In this way, the plaintiff will make fuller recovery of his costs than if the same discharge had been made without the involvement of the salvor.

The question then arises as to whether the shipowner could bear the burden of both limitation amounts by the operation of an indemnity clause such as PIOPIC[3]. That will depend on whether the shipowner can include the salvor's claim under PIOPIC in the CLC limitation fund – if he cannot, and must have recourse to a separate limitation fund under another Convention or provision of the lex fori, then he will bear a burden of more than the CLC limitation amount.

CLC grants the shipowner the right to limit only 'his liability under this Convention'. That liability is, by Article III(1), 'for any pollution

---

20. Just as the Convention imposes liability on owners not resident or domiciled in a contracting state, so it accords them the right to limit.
1. Under UK, Bahamian, Norwegian and Danish law, the action against the salvor would be barred: see above, section 10.1.1.2.
2. See above, section 9.8.2.
3. As to PIOPIC see Chapter 13. As to the rights of contribution in the absence of contract between several tortfeasors, see below, section 10.4.

damage caused by oil which has escaped or been discharged from the ship as a result of the incident'. Is, then, the liability of the shipowner to the salvor a liability 'for pollution damage'? This depends on the definition of 'pollution damage', which is by Article I(6) 'loss or damage caused outside the ship by contamination'. 'Pollution damage' is, therefore, actual loss or damage, and is not itself a *liability* for actual loss or damage[4]. The claim of a salvor under an indemnity clause is a contractual claim for indemnity against *liability* for pollution damage – it is not a claim for pollution damage. The shipowner would not have been liable to the salvor in the absence of contract, and there is nothing in CLC to suggest that his liability to the salvor in contract is a liability 'under this Convention'. It appears, then, that there are strong grounds for holding that the shipowner cannot limit his liability to the salvor under an indemnity clause under CLC. He may, however, be entitled to establish a separate limitation fund under another Convention or provision of the lex fori.

Consider now a situation where the shipowner has demise chartered the vessel, so that the master and crew are servants of the charterer. The ship goes aground due to the master's negligence, causing heavy oil clean-up costs to the plaintiff. The shipowner is liable to the plaintiff under CLC, but may limit that liability under CLC. The charterer is also liable to the plaintiff in negligence[5], and may perhaps limit his liability under a different Convention or provision of the lex fori. The plaintiff here again makes fuller recovery of his costs than if the vessel had not been demise chartered.

Can the charterer include any claim of the shipowner[6] for indemnity under a clause in the demise charter[7] in the same limitation fund as that which he sets up against the plaintiff? This will depend on the particular provisions under which he seeks limitation. Take as an example the case where he can rely on the 1957 Brussels Limitation Convention[8]. By Article I(1), as applied by Article 6 of that Convention, he may limit his liability 'in respect of claims arising from' occurrences such property damage. The shipowner's contractual claim certainly arises from the occurrence of property damage, as does the plaintiff government's tort claim. Thus, where the total clean-up

---

4. The distinction between damage and liability therefore was made by the Court of Appeal in *Drinkwater v Kimber* [1952] 2 QB 281, [1952] 1 All ER 701, in denying a plaintiff contribution under the Law Reform (Contributory Negligence) Act 1945, s. 1(1), and by Willmer J in *The Kirknes* [1975] P 51, [1975] 1 All ER 97, (Merchant Shipping Act 1894, s. 503).
5. Under UK and Bahamian law, the action against the charterer would in most cases be stayed and under Norwegian and Danish law it would be barred – see above, section 10.1.1.2.
6. Article III(5) expressly provides that nothing in CLC shall prejudice any rights the shipowner may have against third parties.
7. As to rights of contribution in the absence of contract between several tortfeasors, see below, section 10.4.2.2.
8. See above, section 9.8.2.2.

costs are equal to, say, 3,000 francs per ton, the plaintiff government may recover 2,000 francs per ton from the shipowner under CLC, and the charterer may establish a limitation fund of 1,000 francs per ton under the 1957 Convention[9]. The plaintiff government's balance of costs unrecovered from the shipowner under CLC (1,000 francs per ton) ranks rateably with the shipowner's indemnity claim against the charterer of 2,000 francs per ton. Hence, if there are no other claims, the charterer will pay to the plaintiff government 333 francs per ton, and to the shipowner 667 francs per ton. The total cost is thus borne as follows:

	Francs per ton
Plaintiff government (3,000 less recovery of 2,000 and 333)	667
Charterer (limitation fund amount)	1,000
Shipowner (2,000 CLC less recovery of 667)	1,333
	3,000

The plaintiff government has recovered 2,333 francs per ton as against the 2,000 francs per ton it would have recovered had the vessel not been demise chartered.

10.2.2.2 Denial of the right to limit

By Article V(2) 'if the incident occurred as a result of the actual fault or privity of the owner[10], he shall not be entitled to avail himself of the limitation provided in paragraph 1 of this Article'. This phraseology is identical to that contained in the 1957 Convention[11], and so the right to limit under CLC will be denied in the same situations as under that Convention. Article V(2) must also be regarded as just as breakable as Article 1(1) of the 1957 Convention, and is therefore likely to give rise to as wide variations in interpretation as occurred in the case of the 1957 Convention.

The UK and the Bahamas have denied the right to limit under CLC to those ships registered in a country which is party to the 1957

---

9. The position under the UK Merchant Shipping Act 1894, s. 503, would appear to be narrower than under legislation reproducing the exact wording of the 1957 Convention. The Convention accords the right to limit in respect of 'claims arising from' certain specified occurrences, but s. 503 only accords the right to limit liability to *damages*; hence it would not appear to cover indemnity claims in contract: see *The Kirknes* [1957] P 51, [1957] 1 All ER 97 (Willmer J).

10. As to the position regarding limitation in cases of co-ownership, see K. C. McGuffie, *Marsden's The Law of Collisions at Sea* (19th ed., London, 1961) para. 196.

11. See above, section 9.8.2.2. under the heading *Denial of the right to limit*.

Convention but which is not party to CLC[12]. This preserves treaty obligations under the 1957 Convention towards such countries, and has the effect of considerably reducing the amount for which a shipowner is liable: in situations where only oil pollution damage has been suffered, the reduction is 50% (from 2,000 to 1,000 francs per ton). In countries where no specific equivalent provision has been made, Article XII of CLC would appear to accord ships registered in countries not party to CLC but party to the 1957 Convention a similar privilege of being able to rely on the latter Convention, for Article XII states that 'This Convention shall supersede any International Conventions in force or open for signature, ratification or accession at the date on which the Convention is opened for signature, but only to the extent that such Conventions would be in conflict with it; however, nothing in this Article shall affect the obligations of Contracting States to non-Contracting States arising under such International Conventions'.

10.2.2.3 The limits of liability

By Article V(1), the limits to which a shipowner may limit his liability under the Convention in respect of any one incident are 'an aggregate amount of 2,000 francs for each ton of the ship's tonnage. However, this aggregate amount shall not in any event exceed 210 million francs'. The franc referred to is the Poincaré franc and was adopted at the conference in the hope that it would ensure uniformity in the real value of a fund, in whichever country it was established. In earlier conventions there had been a problem in deciding whether or not this amount should be converted into the currency of payment at the official rate or at a free market rate[13], and so on the verbal suggestion in Plenary of Mr W. Muller of Switzerland, the official rate was chosen[14]. Article V(9) now provides that 'the amount mentioned in [Article V(1)] shall be converted into the national currency of the state in which the fund is being constituted on the basis of the official value of that currency . . .'.

Unfortunately the world currency crisis which lead to the major currencies floating on the markets destroyed the efficacy of this formula, and so at a Conference held in London from 17 to 19 November 1976, there was adopted a Protocol to the Convention[15]

---

12. UK Merchant Shipping (Oil Pollution) Act 1971, s. 8A, as inserted by the Merchant Shipping Act 1974, s. 9; Bahamian Merchant Shipping (Oil Pollution) Act 1976, s. 28.
13. See T. M. C. Asser, *'Golden Limitations of Liability in International Transport Conventions and the Currency Crisis'* (1973/4) 5 *J Mar L & Comm*, 646; P. P. Heller, *'The Value of the Gold Franc – a Different Point of View'* (1974/5) 6 *J Mar L & Comm*, 73.
14. LEG/CONF/SR. 5, *OR* 91 at 105.
15. Protocol to the International Convention on Civil Liability for Oil Pollution Damage 1969, IMCO Sales No. 77.05.E, UK Misc. No. 26 of 1977 (Cmnd. 7028).

which alters the unit of account from Poincaré francs to the Special Drawing Right as defined by the International Monetary Fund. However, if a state which is not a member of the IMF cannot under its own law convert the SDR into local currency, the Poincaré franc may be used and the conversion 'shall be made in such a manner as to express in the national currency of the Contracting State as far as possible the same real value' for the limitation amounts as is expressed in the Protocol in SDRs[16]. The amounts of 2,000 francs and 210 million francs in Article V(1) of CLC are expressed in SDRs by the Protocol as 133 and 14 million respectively. When the Protocol enters into force[17], the problems of floating currencies in relation to limitation amounts should be solved.

The limits of liability for oil pollution damage under CLC and its Protocol for the three ships taken as previous examples[18] may now be compared with the limits under the other Conventions discussed above. The results are given in Table 10.1.

TABLE 10.1 Comparison of maximum limit of liability for oil pollution damage to property

Limitation Tonnage*	1924 Convention	1957 Convention	1976 Convention	1969 CLC (francs)**
1,000	£ 32,000	£ 43,120	£ 176,470	£ 85,690
48,500	£1,552,000	£2,091,320	£5,220,588	£4,155,965
100,000	£3,200,000	£4,312,000	£8,882,353	£8,569,000

*The limitation ton in the 1976 Convention is not the same as that used in the 1924, 1957 and 1969 Conventions. This fact has been ignored in calculating the figures.

**Figures in this column taken at the rate declared in S.I. 1978 No. 54.

A feature of the limitation provisions of CLC is the maximum limit of 210 million francs. This represented the maximum insurable liability in 1969 (about $14 million). The market capacity has since expanded so that P & I Clubs can now offer up to $50 million any one oil pollution incident. This capacity could well contract if the limits in CLC were raised. However, it would appear from Table 10.1 that the increase of 100% over the 1957 Convention's per ton limit is still adequate to cover most oil spills: the problem, if there is one, is at the

16. Article II of the Protocol, amending Article V of CLC.
17. This is not expected before 1980. The entry into force conditions (Article V) are the same as those for CLC (see below, section 10.7).
18. See above, Table 9.1 in section 9.8.2.3.

lower end of the tonnage scale, and this is solved by the 1971 Fund Convention[19].

10.2.2.4 Preventive measures taken by shipowners

In marked contrast to the position under other Conventions[20], Article V(8) of CLC provides that 'claims in respect of expenses reasonably incurred or sacrifices reasonably made by the owner voluntarily to prevent or minimise pollution damage shall rank equally with other claims against the fund'. The restriction to the prevention or minimisation of 'pollution damage' restricts the application of Article V(8) to preventive costs incurred by the shipowner after the oil has escaped onto the sea, for 'pollution damage' is defined in Article I(6) as 'loss or damage . . . resulting from the escape or discharge of oil from the ship . . .'. Any costs incurred by the shipowner in attempting salvage before the oil spills onto the sea and causes pollution damage (or claims therefor) may not rank in the limitation fund.

It is possible that there will be some problem with the interpretation of the word 'voluntarily'. If, for instance, under the law of the flag or coastal state the owner is under a duty to take preventive measures in the event of an oil spill, it could be said that such measures were not taken voluntarily[1].

10.2.2.5 Establishment of the limitation fund

By Article V(3), to avail himself of the right to limit, the owner must establish a fund for the total sum representing his limit of liability under the Convention with the court or other competent authority of any one of the contracting states in which action is brought under Article IX[2]. The fund must be distributed among the claimants in proportion to the amounts of their established claims (Article V(4)), and there is provision for subrogation in certain cases (Articles V(5) to (7)).

The effect of establishing a fund is that it becomes the sole source of satisfaction of claims under the Convention, and any arrested property must be released[3]. Claims for damage other than pollution damage

---

19. See below, Chapter 11.
20. See above, section 9.8.2.4.
  1. The duty on the owner to act in the event of a spill is at present rare, but it could well become more common in future. For an example see s. 16 of the Canadian Arctic Waters Pollution Prevention Act 1970 (Canada is not a party to CLC). Duties to report the existence of a spill to coastal authorities exist in the legislation of almost every country with special oil pollution legislation, but these duties do not normally extend to actually taking clean-up or other action.
  2. Article IX is discussed below, section 10.3.1.
  3. Articles VI and IX(3).

suffered in contracting states, and all claims for damage suffered in non-contracting states, are unaffected by the establishment of a CLC fund. Consequently, where an incident pollutes the shores of one contracting state and one non-contracting state, the owner's liability can exceed the CLC amount because he does not have the privilege of establishing only one fund. If, however, both states are contracting states, Articles V and VI will apply to all claims and the owner may establish one fund only in either country. This illustrates the great advantage to shipowners in as many states as possible becoming party to the Convention, even though it means that liability will be strict rather than based on fault.

10.3 Jurisdictional provisions

10.3.1 FORUM OF THE PLAINTIFF'S ACTION

By Article IX(1), 'where an incident has caused pollution damage in the territory, including the territorial sea of one or more Contracting States, or preventive measures have been taken to prevent or minimise pollution damage in such territory including the territorial sea, actions for compensation may only be brought in the Courts of any such Contracting State or States...'. By Article IX(2), each contracting state 'shall ensure that its Courts possess the necessary jurisdiction to entertain such actions for compensation'.

The policy of Article IX(1) attempts to solve the problems associated with bringing an action in the jurisdiction where the defendant happens to be, and Article IX(2) ensures that in respect of claims under the Convention the jurisdictional problems encountered in Chapter 9 do not apply[4]. The corollary to giving jurisdiction to the place where the damage was suffered is to deny it to other fora – hence the use of the word 'only' in Article IX(1).

It appears that, taken literally, Article IX(1) goes too far, by denying the right to bring an action for compensation outside the place where damage has been suffered in all cases where 'pollution damage' has been suffered; Article IX(1) would therefore prohibit, on its face, the bringing of an action for pollution damage against a demise charterer or salvor in a contracting state other than the one in which damage has been suffered. This cannot have been the intention of the conference, since the scheme of CLC is to place liability upon the shipowner and to deal with the way in which that liability is to be established. Thus it appears reasonable to interpret the phrase 'actions

4. Thus RSC Ord. 11, rule 1(1)(n), allows for service of a writ or notice thereof out of the jurisdiction in CLC cases.

for compensation' as meaning 'actions for compensation under this Convention'.

Even this interpretation leaves a loophole, for if the shipowner is resident in a non-contracting state there is unlikely to be any provision in the law of that state to prevent the plaintiff suing him there. The conference was aware of the problem, and of the fact that it was powerless to do anything about it[5].

10.3.2 TIME LIMIT FOR THE PLAINTIFF'S ACTION

Article VIII states that 'Rights of compensation under this Convention shall be extinguished unless an action is brought thereunder within three years from the date when the damage occurred. However, in no case shall an action be brought after six years from the date of the incident which caused the damage. Where this incident consists of a series of occurrences, the six years' period shall run from the date of the first such occurrence'.

10.3.3 RECOGNITION AND ENFORCEMENT OF JUDGMENTS

Article X provides that

'(1) Any judgment given by a Court with jurisdiction in accordance with Article IX which is enforceable in the State of origin where it is no longer subject to ordinary forms of review, shall be recognized in any Contracting State, except:
(a) where the judgment was obtained by fraud; or
(b) where the defendant was not given reasonable notice and a fair opportunity to present his case.
(2) A judgment recognized under paragraph 1 of this Article shall be enforceable in each Contracting State as soon as the formalities required in that State have been complied with. The formalities shall not permit the merits of the case to be reopened.'

This important provision is a major incentive to governments to become party to the Convention, for it solves the problem of enforcement of judgments in other contracting states. It does not, of course, have effect where the defendant is present in a non-contracting state.

---

5. LEG/CONF/C. 2/SR. 19, *OR* 745 at 755. The point is dramatically illustrated by the case of the *Amaco Cadiz* where French plaintiffs including the government instituted actions in the United States. France was a party to CLC at the time of the incident (16 March 1978).

10.4 Joint and several liability

It will be remembered from section 10.1.1.2 that by Article IV 'when oil has escaped or has been discharged from two or more ships, and pollution damage results therefrom, the owners of all the ships concerned, unless exonerated under Article III, shall be jointly and severally liable for all such damage which is not reasonably separable'. Before turning to examine the situations in which this Article does and does not apply, we may recall that it appears from Table 3.1 that collisions account for just under one third of all tanker accidents causing oil spillage, and for a somewhat smaller proportion of oil actually spilled. Unfortunately, there are no figures relating to the number of incidents where both ships have spilled oil.

10.4.1 WHERE ARTICLE IV APPLIES

The situation clearly envisaged by Article IV is where two tankers, A and B, collide, and their cargoes spill into one slick, which causes P damage. The fact that P may be unable to show that x% of his damage is due to A and the remainder to B is irrelevant because he is entitled to judgment for all his damage against both A and B; subject to A or B limiting their individual liabilities, P could recover in full from either of them. This, it may be noted, is identical to the English common law and Admiralty rule in collision cases where vessel C is damaged by a collision between vessels A and B for which they are both to blame[6].

But this does not mean that in common law or other countries Article IV will be superfluous, for there would without it be no guarantee that the rule would apply in the unusual situation dealt with by the Convention. For instance, in the United Kingdom several defendants have been held severally liable for all P's damage which is reasonably separable in some cases[7], but not in others[8]. Article IV ensures that the rule will apply.

6. *The Devonshire* [1912] AC 634; and see G. L. Williams, *Joint Torts and Contributory Negligence* (London, 1951) 23–32. Article IV is enacted into United Kingdom law by section 1(3) of the Merchant Shipping (Oil Pollution) Act 1971.
7. E.g. *Grant v Sun Shipping Co Ltd* [1948] AC 549, [1948] 2 All ER 238, HL; see especially per Lord Parcq at 563: '... when separate and independent acts of negligence on the part of two or more persons have directly contributed to cause injury and damage to another, the person injured may recover damages from any one of the wrongdoers, or from all of them'; and see also *Fleming v Gemmill* 1908 SC 340 (several defendants contributing to sewage pollution of a stream jointly and severally liable in nuisance).
8. Notwithstanding the indivisibility of damage, liability was apportioned as between several defendants in *Croston v Vaughan* [1938] 1 KB 540, [1937] 4 All ER 249, CA (road accident) and in *Pride of Derby and Derbyshire Angling Association Ltd v British Celanese Ltd* [1952] 1 All ER 1326 (river pollution).

Even where Article IV does apply there are matters arising in connection with such an incident which are not dealt with by the Convention and which are therefore left for the lex fori. Such matters, which include contribution, the effect of limitation and the principles on which separation of damage will be made, are now considered with reference to English law.

10.4.1.1 Contribution

In English law the Maritime Conventions Act 1911 affords no ground for contribution because it applies where the loss has been suffered 'on board a vessel' (section 3(1))[9], but the Law Reform (Married Women and Tortfeasors) Act 1935 does apply[10], section 6 of which is as follows:

'(1) Where damage is suffered by any person as a result of a tort (whether a crime or not) –

(a) ...

(b) ...

(c) any tortfeasor liable in respect of that damage may recover contribution from any other tortfeasor who is, or would if sued have been, liable in respect of the same damage, whether as a joint tortfeasor or otherwise, so, however, that no person shall be entitled to recover contribution under this section from any person entitled to be indemnified by

---

9. In accordance with Article 1 of the International Convention for the Unification of Certain Rules of Law with Respect to Collisions between Vessels 1910, UKTS No. 4 of 1913 (Cmnd. 6677), whose ratifying Act it is.

10. The question of whether an English Act has effect with respect to acts occurring outside the jurisdiction is one which has created a voluminous and somewhat conflicting caselaw. There are many cases where the courts have denied the extension of an Act of Parliament to acts occurring on the high seas or abroad (e.g. *Yorke v British and Continental SS Co.* (1945) 78 Ll L Rep 181, CA (Docks Regulations 1934); *C. E. B. Draper Ltd & Son v Edward Turner & Son Ltd* [1965] 1 QB 424, [1964] 3 All ER 148, CA (Fertilisers and Feeding Stuffs Act 1926)), just as there are many which have granted such extension (e.g. *Davidsson v Hill* [1901] 2 KB 606 (Fatal Accidents Acts); *The Esso Malaysia* [1975] QB 198, [1974] 2 All ER 705 (Fatal Accidents Acts)). Dicey and Morris, *Conflict of Laws* (9th ed., London, 1973) suggest at page 952 that 'Statutes which create new rules of conduct must in this respect be distinguished from those which remove exceptions to common law liabilities, such as the defence of common employment or of compulsory pilotage, or which attach new liabilities to the violation of existing rules of conduct, such as the Fatal Accidents Acts'. This was expressly approved by Brandon J in *The Esso Malaysia* [1975] QB 198 at 206, and this distinction does bring a measure of principle to the confusing state of the authorities. Since the Act of 1935 removes exceptional defences to a common law action, and also attaches new liabilities to existing rules of conduct, it would seem likely to be held to have extra-territorial effect. Further, the provisions of s. 6(1)(a) and (b) may be regarded as purely procedural, and so not presenting a conflict of laws at all. If the 1935 Act were not to apply extra-territorially, the absurd position would result that the law in *Brinsmead v Harrison* (1872) LR 7 CP 547 and *Merryweather v Nixan* (1799) 8 Term Rep 186, would still apply.

him in respect of the liability in respect of which contribution is sought.

(2) In any proceedings for contribution under this section the amount of the contribution recoverable from any person shall be such as may be found by the court to be just and equitable having regard to the extent of that person's responsibility for the damage; and the court shall have power to exempt any person from liability to make contribution, or to direct that the contribution to be recovered from any person shall amount to a complete indemnity[11].'

It is clear from section 6(2) that the amount of contribution is discretionary, but that it should be based on the defendant's responsibility for the damage. At various times and in various circumstances the courts have made apportionment according to the fault of the vessels[12], the number of vessels involved[13], and the supposed degree of causation of each defendant[14]. What test should be adopted in an oil pollution situation here? The causation test seems totally impossible to apply if only because, while it may be possible to ascertain what quantities have escaped from each vessel, it will normally be impossible to show what has been their fate at sea before causing the damage. Ideally, this test should therefore be rejected[15]. The culpability test, which probably is the current legal interpretation of the word 'responsibility' in the section, is easier to apply where the tortfeasors have been negligent[16], even if it is somewhat arbitrary. But where both parties have been guilty of a strict duty (although they may also have been negligent) the idea of culpability seems inapt. The rule that each ship should bear equal blame is no more helpful, for it would in many cases lead to manifest injustice.

In cases which have involved two defendants, one of whom has been in breach of a strict duty, the other of whom has been in breach of a common law duty (either of care, or that care be taken), the courts

11. For detailed consideration of this section see G. L. Williams, *Joint Torts and Contributory Negligence* (London, 1951) 148–174.
12. E.g. *The Koursk* [1924] P 140. This is the normal rule of tort. See cases cited by Williams, *Joint Torts and Contributory Negligence* (London, 1951) 159. Apportionment by fault is also the rule under the Maritime Conventions Act 1911, s. 3, as interpreted by *The Cairnbahn* [1914] P 25, CA; a recent example of such apportionment is *Miraflores v George Livanos* [1967] AC 826, [1967] 1 All ER 672, HL (3 ships, 40/20/40).
13. The Admiralty rule of Division of Loss is the prime example: *The Milan* (1861) Lush 388; *The City of Manchester* (1879) 5 PD 3 and 221; *The Drumlanrig* [1911] AC 16. See generally as to the rule, K. C. McGuffie, *Marsden's The Law of Collisions at Sea* (11th ed., London, 1961) Chapters 4 and 5.
14. E.g. *Collins v Hertfordshire County Council* [1947] 1 KB 598, [1947] 1 All ER 633 (Hilbery J following his own decision in *Smith v Bray* (1939) 56 TLR 200).
15. On the general question, both Stephen Chapman (1948) 64 LQR 26 and G. L. Williams, *Joint Torts and Contributory Negligence* (London, 1951) 157–158, concur.
16. E.g. *Weaver v Commercial Process Co Ltd* (1947) 63 TLR 466 (Hallett J) following *Daniel v Rickett, Cockerell & Co Ltd and Raymond* [1938] 2 KB 322, [1938] 2 All ER 631.

have tended to award the former a complete indemnity[17], although they have not always done this[18]; and in the only case I have found where both defendants have been in breach of a strict duty[19], Tucker J apportioned liability 75/25 on the basis that the first defendant had at all times had complete control of the stairway which caused the damage.

It is quite possible that if, in an oil pollution situation, there is evidence before the court that one or both of the parties were negligent, apportionment would be made on that basis, despite the fact that the actions are founded on breaches of strict duties. Such a course would have legal precedent, and there seems no moral reason why it should not be adopted – the 1969 Conference was keen only that the plaintiff should not have to prove negligence. If such evidence is not before the court, or if the judge finds that as a matter of fact neither party was negligent, the court is likely to apply the causation test, however inaccurate that will be, simply because there is little else it can do! The problems it would face in that task are amply demonstrated in this example: Suppose A was a 100,000 dwt ton tanker full of crude, and after the incident only 95,000 tons remain in her; B was a 200,000 dwt tons tanker full of crude, and after the incident only 195,000 tons remain in her. It will be impossible to say what tonnage from either A or B will have been degraded before causing damage, or was dispersed before causing damage, or sank, or drifted out to sea, or became dissolved in the water column. A division on the basis of the amounts spilled (1/3, 2/3) cannot reliably be made.

10.4.1.2 Limitation of liability

By Article IV, P has an independent cause of action against A and B because they are made severally liable. It is quite clear that without limitation provisions, P could sue A for all he is worth, and if this does not satisfy P's claim, then he could go on to recover the balance against B. Would the position be any different where A limits his liability under the Convention? The entitlement to limitation under Article V is designed not to limit P's ability to recover, but to limit the owner's maximum liability so as to enable him to obtain insurance.

---

17. See e.g. *Whitby v Burt, Boulton and Haywood Ltd* [1947] 1 KB 918, [1947] 2 All ER 324 (Factories Act 1937, s. 26(1), employers' liability); *Hosking v De Havilland Aircraft Co Ltd* [1949] 1 All ER 540 (Factories Act 1937, ss. 25(1), 26(1), employers' liability); *Witchard v Whitehead Iron and Steel Co*, unreported, [1965] CLY 2724.

18. E.g. *Whincup v Joseph Woodhead & Sons (Engineers) Ltd* [1951] 1 All ER 387 at 389, per McNair J, 'As regards contribution inter se, I can see no reason for making any distinction between the two defendants. I hold that the contribution inter se should be limited to fifty per cent of the liability of each'.

19. *Rippon v Port of London Authority and J Russel & Co* [1940] 1 KB 858, [1940] 1 All ER 637.

There seems no moral reason, then, why P should not recover his full loss if the aggregate of A's and B's limitation funds amounts to, or exceeds his full loss. The wording of the Convention would not contradict this – if there is more than one plaintiff (a likely circumstance) all would share rateably in each fund (but it is clearly not the intention to enable a plaintiff to recover twice over).

The position in English law before the passing of the Law Reform (Married Women and Tortfeasors) Act 1935 was clearly as just stated[20]. The question is whether or not it has now been affected by section 6(1)(b) of that Act, which provides as follows:

> 'Where damage is suffered by any person as a result of a tort (whether a crime or not) –
> (a) ...
> (b) if more than one action is brought in respect of that damage by or on behalf of the person by whom it was suffered ... against tortfeasors liable in respect of the damage (whether as joint tortfeasors or otherwise) the sums recoverable under the judgements given in those actions by way of damages shall not in the aggregate exceed the amount of damages awarded by the judgement first given; ...'.

This subsection was enacted to ensure that a plaintiff did not exercise his right to sue a second concurrent tortfeasor as a method of appealing against the quantum of damages awarded him in an action against a first defendant. On the face of it, it does not apply when P institutes proceedings against A and B in the same action, so that without more it might be concluded that, at any rate in that case, the old rule had not been altered. But in two recent cases of high authority[1], it has been held that paragraph (a) of section 6(1)[2], which also on the face of its wording does not apply where P institutes a single action against A and B, does so apply; and this casts doubt on a literal interpretation of paragraph (b). If we suppose for the purposes of argument that paragraph (b) will apply even when P institutes a single action against both A and B, then it appears that paragraph (b) does abolish the old rule, and P will be unable to recover his full loss where A and B limit their liabilities.

This undesirable conclusion can be avoided, however, by holding that the words 'that damage' in paragraph (b) mean 'the same damage'. Such an interpretation cannot be supported by authority, but

---

20. *Morris v Robinson* (1824) 3 B & C 196 (trover); *Ellis v Stenning & Son* [1932] 2 Ch 81 (conversion); *The Koursk* [1924] P 140, especially at 153–154 (negligence–collision at sea).
1. *Wah Tat Bank Ltd v Chan Cheng Kum* [1975] AC 507, [1975] 2 All ER 257, applied in *Bryanston Finance Ltd v de Vries* [1975] QB 703, [1975] 2 All ER 609, CA.
2. This paragraph is reproduced below in section 10.4.1.3.

then neither can it be so refuted – and it accords not only with justice, reason and common sense, but also with the reality of the situation: in the second action (or, if there is but one, then as regards B) P is claiming for damage (i.e. the damage in excess of A's limitation fund) which he has suffered, and for which he has had no redress against A because A has limited his liability. The damage he claims against B is not, therefore, the same damage as that which he claims against A.

10.4.1.3 Part owners and limitation of liability

Part owners really form a separate example of their own, but are dealt with here because it is convenient. What happens, then, when one vessel owned partly by O1 and partly by O2 causes P oil pollution damage?

Beyond recognising in Article 1(3) that ships can be in part ownership ('"Owner" means the person or persons registered as the owner of the ship'), the Convention is silent, leaving the position to the lex fori.

In English law, the part owners are joint tortfeasors, and so P does not have several causes of action against each of them, but one action against them all. Before 1935 this meant that P could not recover judgment against O2 if he had done so against O1, even if it remained unsatisfied[3], and even if only one action had been instituted[4]. Therefore, P would have been unable to sue O2 for the balance of his damage before 1935 – judgment against O1 extinguished his cause of action. Now, section 6(1)(a) of the Law Reform (Married Women and Tortfeasors) Act 1935 provides that 'where damage is suffered by any person as a result of a tort (whether a crime or not) – (a) judgment recovered against any tortfeasor liable in respect of that damage shall not be a bar to an action against any other person who would, if sued, have been liable as a joint tortfeasor in respect of the same damage'. The Privy Council[5] and Court of Appeal[6] (obiter) have both recently held that the section applies even when P has sued both joint tortfeasors in the same action, despite the fact that on its face the section clearly contemplates only the situation where P has instituted two actions. Taking the law as these cases interpret the section, the old rule is now abolished.

Cases on limitation under other Acts show that where O1 is unable

3. *King v Hoare* (1844) 13 M & W 494; *Brinsmead v Harrison* (1872) LR 7 CP 547.
4. *Gouldrei, Foucard & Son v Sinclair and Russian Chamber of Commerce in London* [1918] 1 KB 180 at 191.
5. *Wah Tat Bank Ltd v Chan Cheng Kum* [1975] AC 507, [1975] 2 All ER 257.
6. *Bryanston Finance Ltd. v de Vries* [1975] QB 703, [1975] 2 All ER 609.

to limit his liability because of his actual fault or privity, O2 is not deprived of his entitlement to limitation[7].

10.4.1.4 Separation of damage

Article IV applies only to damage which is not reasonably separable, just as at common law several concurrent tortfeasors will only be concurrently liable for damage which is indivisible[8]. The principles on which damage is to be separated, left to the lex fori by the silence of the Convention, must therefore be considered.

In order to decide when damage will be found to be indivisible it is not possible to rely on cases where *liability* has been apportioned, because quite separate evidence is needed in such cases to that needed here. To apportion fault you will normally look to the quality of the parties' acts before the collision[9]; to separate damage, you look to the nature of events taking place after the collision.

One eminent writer has concluded that 'whether injury is susceptible to apportionment seems to depend on pragmatic rather than purely theoretical considerations'[10]. This opinion is not only based on a formidable review of caselaw, but it accords with what one would naturally expect. It is not, therefore, possible to give any guidance on when in a particular case damage will be separable[11].

10.4.2   WHERE ARTICLE IV DOES NOT APPLY

10.4.2.1 Example 1 : laden tanker and dry cargo vessel collide

Suppose C, a tanker, collides with D, a dry cargo vessel or empty tanker, and oil spills from C's cargo and from D's bunker tanks, causing P damage. Here, oil has not escaped from 'two or more ships' (in the words of Article IV) because 'ship' is defined in Article I(1) as

---

7. *The Spirit of the Ocean* (1865) 12 LT 239 (Merchant Shipping Act 1854); *The Obey* (1866) LR 1 A & E 102 (obiter on Merchant Shipping (Amendment) Act 1862); *Wilson v Dickson* (1818) 2 B & Ald 2 (53 Geo III, c. 159).
8. J. G. Fleming, *The Law of Torts* (4th ed., Australia, 1976) 174; H. Street, *The Law of Torts* (6th ed., London, 1976) 476; R. F. V. Heuston, *Salmond on the Law of Torts* (16th ed., London, 1973) 451–452; *Winfield and Jolowicz on Tort* (10th ed., (ed. W. H. V. Rogers) London, 1975) 545. And see generally *Baker v Willoughby* [1970] AC 467, [1969] 3 All ER 1528, HL.
9. See above section 10.4.1.1.
10. J. G. Fleming, *The Law of Torts* (4th ed., Australia, 1976).
11. It seems, however, that insofar as apportionment was made in *Pride of Derby and Derbyshire Angling Association v British Celanese Ltd* [1952] 1 All ER 1326 and *Croston v Vaughan* [1938] 1 KB 540, [1937] 4 All ER 249, they were wrongly decided – P was deprived of the benefit of a judgment for the full amount against each of several tortfeasors, in cases where damage was held to be inseparable.

a vessel actually carrying oil in bulk as cargo. There has been an escape from only one 'ship', namely C. Article IV does not, therefore, apply to this situation. C will still incur a liability under Article III; but D's liability, if any, will be governed by the lex fori. Another situation akin to this one is the perhaps more common one where no oil spills from D, but where D has negligently caused the collision and hence the spillage from C.

At common law, C and D would be several (and not joint) tortfeasors[12]. The English law relating to the question of contribution is, therefore, as discussed above in section 10.4.1.1, with the added likelihood that D's fault will make the culpability test more apt, and will increase C's chances of a complete indemnity.

Questions of limitation and separability are the same as those dealt with in sections 10.4.1.2 and 10.4.1.4.

10.4.2.2 Example 2: Owner and bareboat charterer

What is the position outside of contract as between an owner and a bareboat charterer if both are sued? The latter will, of course, incur no liability under the Convention, and Article IV cannot regulate the position because it applies only to 'the owners of all ships concerned...'. In English law, if the charterer has incurred a liability outside the Convention, the owner and he will be several concurrent tortfeasors, and the situation would have been the same as in *Example 1*, but for the enactment of section 7 of the Merchant Shipping (Oil Pollution) Act 1971, which provides as follows:

> 'Where, as a result of any discharge or escape of persistent oil from a ship, the owner of the ship incurs a liability under section 1 of this Act and any other person incurs a liability, otherwise than under that section, for any such damage or cost as is mentioned in subsection (1) of that section, then, if –
>
> (a) the owner has been found, in proceedings under section 5 of this Act, to be entitled to limit his liability to any amount and has paid into court a sum not less than that amount; and
>
> (b) the other person is entitled to limit his liability in connection with the ship by virtue of the Merchant Shipping (Liability of Shipowners and Others) Act 1958;
>
> no proceedings shall be taken against the other person in respect

---

12. *The Devonshire* [1912] AC 634. They will not normally be jointly liable (and so each liable for all of P's damage notwithstanding the fact that part may be exclusively attributable to one of them) because normally there will be no breach of a joint duty, no vicarious liability between them, nor any joint purpose or concerted action to a common end. See G. L. Williams, *Joint Torts and Contributory Negligence* (London, 1951) 6–16; and *The Koursk* [1924] P 140.

of his liability, and if any such proceedings were commenced before the owner paid the sum into court, no further steps shall be taken in the proceedings except in relation to costs.'

Section 3 of the Merchant Shipping (Liability of Shipowners and Others) Act 1958 enables a charterer to obtain the benefit of the limitation of liability provisions hitherto available only to shipowners (by section 503 of the Merchant Shipping Act 1894), in accordance with the International Convention relating to the Limitation of Liability of Owners of Sea-going Ships 1957[13]. Such benefit is only available in the absence of actual fault or privity. Therefore, in general the effect of section 7 will be that where neither owner nor bareboat charterer has been negligent or privy to causative negligence, the charterer will be totally free from all liability for oil pollution damage. If, on the other hand, either the owner has been guilty of actual fault or privity (extremely unlikely in practice) or the charterer has been guilty of it, the conditions in section 7 are unfulfilled and it would not apply[14]. The relationship between the two would, in that case, depend on whether the owner had negotiated an indemnity in the charter, for the proviso to s. 6(1)(c) of the Law Reform (Married Women and Tortfeasors) Act 1935 denies the right to contribution under that Act where the liability in respect of which contribution is sought is one in which the person seeking contribution is entitled to be indemnified. If there is no relevant indemnity, the court would, as seen in section 10.4.1.1, tend to lay the majority of the blame at the feet of the person who was in control of the ship or who had been negligent.

10.4.2.3 Example 3: Owner and salvor

Section 3 of the Merchant Shipping (Oil Pollution) Act 1971 grants the salvor complete exemption[15]. Had it not done so, the position would have been as in *Example 1*.

10.4.3 CONCLUSION

The conference must be taken to have intended to have left the matters discussed in section 10.4 to the lex fori; in so doing, at least as far as English law is concerned, and quite possibly so far as many other legal systems are concerned, the influence of fault has crept into

13. See section 9.8.2.2.
14. Section 7 would not appear to grant the bareboat charterer immunity from an action by the shipowner for a contractual or statute-based indemnity.
15. See above, section 10.1.1.2. The law in the Bahamas, Norway and Denmark is the same.

the structure of the strict liability regime created by the Convention. We have seen that the fact that the Convention makes the owner strictly liable does not necessarily mean that it is the owner who will bear all the ultimate burden. This is only right and proper, and can be taken to have been envisaged by the conference in adopting Article III(5), which expressly reserves to the owner his right of recourse.

The English law to which resort must be had in dealing with the gaps in CLC is not entirely free from areas of doubt, notably as respects whether the 1935 Act would apply to collisions on the high seas, and as respects the basis of contribution where one or both parties are guilty only of strict duties. Other systems of law can be expected to be equally uncertain in various areas, but whether the situation merits uniform law provisions is doubtful.

10.5 Compulsory insurance and direct recourse

10.5.1 THE DUTY TO INSURE

Compulsory insurance is not a new concept in international or municipal law[16], but in the legal committee which prepared the draft Convention, there was a division of opinion as to whether or not to adopt the idea[17]. The division continued for two weeks at the Conference, after which the principle was finally adopted[18]. As will be seen, the drafting of these provisions has suffered from the haste with which they were eventually debated.

The formula finally worked out is contained in Article VII(1): 'The owner of a ship registered in a Contracting State and carrying more than 2,000 tons of oil in bulk as cargo shall be required to maintain insurance or other financial security, such as the guarantee of a bank or certificate delivered by an international compensation fund, in the sums fixed by applying the limits of liability prescribed in Article V, paragraph 1 to cover his liability for pollution damage under this Convention.'

The advantages of compulsory insurance are obvious, but there is one which deserves special mention. In the words of one of the US delegates to the Conference, 'there [are] such things as one-vessel companies, and in such cases the victim's only recourse would be

---

16. For early examples on compulsory insurance see, e.g. UK Road Traffic Acts 1930 to 1936; The International Convention for the Unification of Certain Rules relating to Damage Caused by Aircraft to Third Parties on the Surface, Rome 1933 (UK Misc. No. 6 of 1935, Cmd. 5056); and in the employment field, see UK National Insurance (Industrial Injuries) Act 1946.
17. LEG/CONF/4, OR 437 at 465; LEG/CONF/C. 2/SR. 14, OR 701 at 702.
18. LEG/CONF/C. 2/SR. 14, OR 701 at 705 – 30 votes to 3 with 3 abstentions.

against the vessel, which would probably not be available, having been damaged or sunk'[19]. Compulsory insurance does solve this very real problem.

The duty to insure (as opposed to the imposition of liability for pollution damage) arises only when the ship is carrying more than 2,000 tons of oil in bulk as cargo. Thus, where a tanker is on a ballast voyage carrying 2,000 tons of bunkers or more, no duty arises[20]. The figure of 2,000 tons was controversial at the conference, but seems to have been chosen so as to exclude the bulk of the coastal trade, and those dry cargo vessels which occasionally carry up to about 2,000 tons of oil in their deep tanks[1].

10.5.2 ENFORCEMENT

Compulsory insurance has its difficulties, and these were all vociferously mentioned at the Conference. The most serious one is the problem of enforcement. The solution adopted was that every ship to which the Convention applies must be issued with 'a certificate attesting that insurance or other financial security is in force in accordance with the provisions of this Convention'[2], by the state of the ship's registry[3]. The form of the certificate is laid down[4], and it must be carried on board[5].

There was felt to be a problem for the authorities of a flag state to estimate the financial security of an insurer who is regularly resident abroad, acting under foreign law and insurance conditions[6]. The procedure adopted does not really solve this problem. The Convention provides that the state of registry shall determine the conditions of issue and validity of the certificate[7]; and that those issued by a contracting state shall be accepted by other contracting states as having the same force as their own – but 'a Contracting State may at any time request consultation with the state of a ship's registry should it believe that the insurer or guarantor named in the certificate is not financially capable of meeting the obligations imposed by this Convention'[8]. Where the insurer is a well-known entity (e.g. a

19. LEG/CONF/C. 2/SR. 14, *OR* 701 at 703, per Mr Neuman.
20. But tankers are normally insured on an annual basis, and so in practice tankers who are insured against CLC liability while laden will also be insured against liability for pollution damage while in ballast.
  1. LEG/CONF/C. 2/SR. 14, *OR* 701 at 708/9.
  2. Article VII(2).
  3. This phrase is defined in Article I(4).
  4. Article VII(2) and (3) and Annex.
  5. Article VII(4).
  6. See e.g. LEG/CONF/4/Add. 1, *OR* 503 at 505.
  7. Article VII(6).
  8. Article VII(7).

Protection and Indemnity Association which is a member of the International Group of P & I Clubs) there will be no trouble, but if this is not the case, then delay will inevitably result in the granting of a certificate while the issuing state makes inquiries. It is therefore in the assured's best interest to take out cover with an internationally known organisation or underwriter.

Paragraphs 10 and 11 of Article VII provide the teeth of the enforcement system. By paragraph 10, 'a Contracting State shall not permit a ship under its flag to which this Article applies to trade unless a certificate has been issued under... this Article'. The French pointed out at the preparatory stage that the use of the words 'to trade' was unfortunate because they do not accurately reflect the desired objective, which is to prohibit a ship not provided with the necessary certificate from sailing. It would, in their view, have been preferable to have used the traditional maritime phraseology 'put to sea' – which is more precise and wider in scope[9]. In practice, however, this is probably what states will do[10].

There was considerable anxiety at the Conference that restrictions placed on ships registered in contracting states would make them competitively at a disadvantage[11]. But the form of paragraph 11 does not give grounds for these fears, because ships registered in non-contracting states also need certificates to enter contracting states: each contracting state 'shall ensure, under its national legislation, that insurance or other security to the extent specified in paragraph 1 of this Article is in force in respect of any ship, wherever registered, entering or leaving a port in its territory, or arriving at or leaving an offshore terminal in its territorial sea, if the ship actually carries more than 2,000 tons of oil in bulk as cargo'. In practice, no state is likely to refuse a ship entry on the grounds that it has no certificate, not only because this may involve exposing the vessel to undue dangers but also because until the ship reaches pilotage waters (at the earliest) there is no opportunity to discover whether or not there is a certificate aboard. But the state can and ought to prevent its departure until a certificate is produced.

The effect of paragraph 11 is that if any tanker, even one registered in a non-contracting state, wishes to enter a port or offshore terminal in a contracting state, she must have a certificate. Under paragraph 2 the certificate must be issued by the flag state, but under paragraph 7 only certificates issued by or certified under the authority of another contracting state must be regarded as having the same force as those issued by the recognising state. It seems to follow that certificates

9. LEG/CONF/4, OR 437 at 468.
10. This solution has been adopted by the UK – see the Merchant Shipping (Oil Pollution) Act 1971, s. 10(2).
11. See e.g. LEG/CONF/4/Add. 1, OR 503 at 506; LEG/CONF/C. 2/SR. 14, OR 701 at 702.

issued by non-contracting states to their own ships need not be recognised, and indeed a non-contracting state would probably not issue such a certificate as a matter of practice. The paragraphs are not so worded as to exclude the recognition of such certificates – it is just that they do not provide for them. This, doubtless, is a result of the late acceptance of the principle at the Conference, which left insufficient time for considering these provisions properly.

10.5.3 UNINSURED SHIPS

It is obvious that it is impossible for a Convention to make insurance compulsory (as a matter of law) for ships registered in non-contracting states, and so the Conference can be said to have done all it could under existing international law. The result is that it is still technically possible for a victim to suffer oil pollution damage in a contracting state and find that the responsible ship was uninsured. This would be the case where such a ship is on a voyage from one non-contracting state to another, and suffers an accident on the way. We may note that at 31 December 1977 no Gulf state was a party to the Convention; that six Mediterranean states had not ratified (Italy[12], Albania, Turkey, Israel, UAR and Libya); and that the following nations with significant tanker tonnage had not ratified (although some may have insurance regulations of their own): Italy[12], Cyprus, Somalia, Singapore and the USA. In practice, however, almost every tanker sailing the high seas is now insured against CLC liability.

10.5.4 CHANGE OF OWNERSHIP

The Legal Committee of IMCO (which produced the draft convention) recognised that there would be a problem if a change of ownership took place during the currency of an insurance policy. If pollution damage is to be continuously covered, the new owner would have to take out cover immediately he came into ownership of the vessel. This would create administrative difficulties, not the least of which is the fact that he cannot fill in the application forms for insurance until he owns the ship! It also had to be borne in mind that the change of ownership might take place while the vessel was at sea, and so could not receive a new certificate until she called at a convenient port. Paragraph 5 of Article VII tries to solve this problem, by forcing on insurers the duty to cover the new, and perhaps unidentified owner, for up to three months. As soon as possible, therefore, the change of ownership should be notified to the authorities

12. Italy has indicated her intention to ratify.

of the state of the ship's registry, the old certificate delivered up, and a new certificate evidencing a new insurance personal to the new owner issued.

10.5.5 GOVERNMENT SHIPS

Special provision is made by paragraph 12 for government ships – they must carry a certificate stating that the ship is owned by the state and that her liability is covered to Article V(1) limits.

10.5.6 PROCEEDS OF COMPULSORY INSURANCE

In jurisdictions where a shipowner may limit his liability to the value of the ship and freight, it has happened that, because the ship is a total loss, claimants have been left with virtually nothing, while the shipowner collects a large sum under his hull insurance. To avoid any possibility of claimants under CLC failing to get the benefit of the insurance made compulsory, Article VII(9) provides that 'any sums provided by insurance or by other financial security maintained in accordance with paragraph 1 of this Article shall be available exclusively for the satisfaction of claims under this Convention'. It is to be noted that this does not cover hull insurance.

10.5.7 DIRECT PROCEEDINGS AGAINST INSURERS

Since Article VII(8) provides that proceedings may be made directly against the insurer or other persons providing financial security for the owner's liability for pollution damage, and that the insurer may limit his liability (even in the case of actual fault or privity of the owner), Article V(11) provides that the insurer, when directly sued by a person suffering damage, may also establish a fund to effect limitation of his liability. Where the accident has occurred with the owner's actual fault or privity, the entitlement of the insurer to limit his liability in a direct suit does not detract from the plaintiff's remedies against the owner – if he has suffered greater loss than the insurer's limitation amount, he can pursue the owner for the balance.

Article VII(8) affords the insurer all the defences which the owner could have invoked, save the bankruptcy or winding-up of the owner, but no other defences which the insurer might otherwise have invoked against the assured are available to him, save one: that the pollution damage resulted from the wilful misconduct of the owner himself. One important defence thus excluded is that the ship concerned was sent to sea in an unseaworthy state with the privity of the assured. This defence is implied by statute into all time policies subject to the United Kingdom Marine Insurance Act 1906[13], and is often inserted into policies not so covered as an express clause. The exclusion of this and other defences does not, of course, affect the insurer's position when the *assured* makes a claim.

Making direct recourse against the insurer a possibility for all claims – against the will of the insurer and by operation of law – is extremely unusual in insurance law: for instance, the United Kingdom Third Parties (Rights against Insurers) Act 1930 makes this possible only in the case of the bankruptcy or winding-up of the assured. But at the Conference, the French[14] and others[15] regarded it as vital: 'Shorn of the right of direct action in all cases, insurance would lose its prime benefit'[16]. The United Kingdom was originally against such wide recourse against insurers: 'the shipowner would have little interest in assisting the insurer in a defence action and it would, in some cases, lessen the incentive for shipowners to take due care'[17]. But later she relented[18].

The complete defence of the owner's wilful misconduct was demanded by the London insurance market as a precondition for granting cover[19]. Lord Devlin (United Kingdom) explained that 'insurers would insist on that minimum defence in order to allay their fear that a shipowner might decide deliberately to destroy, wreck or strand his ship in order to collect his insurance money'[19].

The question arises, however, whether there are any other situations encompassed by the phrase. It is clear that no act done by the master or crew purely on their own initiative, nor any act done by a bareboat charterer or his servants is contemplated. But it is possible to imagine a situation which might easily occur where the defence would apply. The master may wish to discharge oil deliberately for a number of reasons, for instance because for some reason he cannot operate LOT and he does not want to waste time at the loading port discharging to shore reception facilities: in such a case he may be under instructions to discharge oil, or he may request and receive express or implied permission to discharge.

In this situation, if a plaintiff suffers pollution damage, has it 'resulted from the wilful misconduct of the owner himself' within the

13. Section 39(5). A P & I policy, being from 20 February to the 20 February following, is a time policy within the definition contained in s. 25(1): see *The Eurysthenes* [1977] QB 49 [1976] 3 All ER 243, CA.
14. LEG/CONF/4, OR 437.
15. E.g. Sweden, Greece, Liberia and West Germany – LEG/CONF/C. 2/SR. 14, OR 701 at 705 et seq.
16. LEG/CONF/4, OR 437 at 467.
17. LEG/CONF/4, 437 at 477; see also LEG/CONF/C. 2/SR. 14, OR 701 at 705.
18. LEG/CONF/C. 2/WP. 35, OR 596 at 598.
19. LEG/CONF/C. 2/SR. 17, OR 726 at 727 and 728.

meaning of Article V(8)? The answer will in practice be decided in accordance with the rules of interpretation of the lex fori.

The court will have to decide whether or not the defence is established merely by the insurer showing wilfulness as to the discharge or escape, or whether he must show wilfulness as to the pollution damage. Article VII(8) states that the only thing that has to be shown to be wilful is the misconduct; if the pollution damage resulted from that, the defence is complete. What, then, is the misconduct? Is it the giving of permission or instructions, or is it the discharge itself? It must be the former, because the latter will never be made by the owner himself. It follows that it will be enough for the insurer to show that the owner was wilful as to the discharge or escape, and that pollution damage resulted therefrom.

This interpretation is supported by the wording used in the United Kingdom's Merchant Shipping (Oil Pollution) Act 1971, section 12(2) of which provides as follows:

> 'In any proceedings brought against the insurer by virtue of this section it shall be a defence... to prove that the discharge or escape was due to the wilful misconduct of the owner himself.'

Misconduct and discharge are seen as being separate, and the latter must be due to the former.

There is one argument which might prevent the conclusion that in the imagined situation the defence applies. This rests on a comparison of the two phrases, wilful misconduct and actual fault or privity, both of which appear in the Convention. There should be a distinction between them, and the former is clearly worse than the latter. Particularly in view of the Court of Appeal decision in *The Eurysthenes*[20], where it was held that privity means with knowledge and concurrence, the imagined circumstances would constitute actual fault or privity but not wilful misconduct. Wilful misconduct should, so the argument goes, be confined therefore to the deliberate scuttling of the ship with the connivance of the owner.

Technically, there should be less difficulty in interpreting the phrases in English law than in any other, for they are drawn therefrom; and as Lord Devlin pointed out at the conference, wilful misconduct is a difficult phrase to translate and has no direct equivalent in many European legal systems[1]. Even in English law, however, little help is afforded by precedent because the phrases have never before arisen in connection with oil pollution damage. Nearly all the cases on wilful misconduct involve hull policies[2].

20. [1977] QB 49, [1976] 3 All ER 243.
  1. LEG/CONF/C. 2/SR. 17, *OR* 726 at 728.
  2. See e.g. where wilful misconduct was proved: *Visscherij Maatschappij NO v Scottish Metropolitan Assurance Co* (1922) 10 Ll L Rep 579, CA (scuttling); *Coulouras v British*

Neither the Convention nor the Merchant Shipping (Oil Pollution) Act 1971 mention scuttling. To interpret wilful misconduct as including acts other than scuttling is not to deprive actual fault or privity of content or scope; for instance, this phrase would seem to clearly cover the following four situations drawn from caselaw[3]: (1) failure of owners to act upon the habitual practice of the master of travelling at excessive speed in fog (discoverable from engine room and deck logs)[4]; (2) failure of owners to bring to master's attention precautions for deballasting tanks and cargo storage[5]; (3) the appointment of improperly qualified or incompetent crew[6]; (4) failure to communicate the latest navigational information to the ship at sea[7]. If any of these resulted in an accidental discharge, the damage resulting could be said to have occurred with the actual fault of privity of the owner.

In the context of the insurance policy a deliberate discharge of a substance likely to lead to a claim under the policy is as much an act striking at the good faith existing between assured and insurer as is a deliberate scuttling, and it is the context of the insurance policy which is the most important consideration here.

Thus it may be concluded that, in the imagined case, there are strong ground for holding that the shipowner has been guilty of wilful misconduct, and hence that the plaintiff would be denied direct recourse to the insurer.

10.6 Changes under current consideration by IMCO

At the 29th and 30th Sessions of IMCO's Legal Committee[8], held in London in July and September 1976 respectively, possible improve-

---

footnote 2 contd.

General Insurance Co Ltd (1922) 12 Ll L Rep 220 (scuttling); *Compania Naviera Martiartu v Royal Exchange Assurance Corpn* (1924) 18 Ll L Rep 247 and 19 Ll L Rep 95, HL (scuttling); where not proved: *Papadimitriou v Henderson* (1939) 64 Ll L Rep 345 (decision to proceed with voyage when risk of capture known); *Doriga Y Sanudo v Royal Exchange Assurance Corpn Ltd* (1922) 13 Ll L Rep 126 at 166 (poor seamanship and panic). On the question of evidence, see *Lemos v British and Foreign Marine Insurance Co Ltd* (1931) 39 Ll L Rep 275 and *Astrovlanis Compania Naviera SA v Linard* [1972] 2 QB 611, [1972] 2 All ER 647.

3. For full caselaw on actual fault or privity see *Temperley's The Merchant Shipping Acts* (7th ed. (eds. M. Thomas and D. Steel) London, 1976) para. 431.
4. *The Lady Gwendolen* [1965] P 294, CA.
5. *Standard Oil Co of New York v Clan Line Steamers Ltd* [1924] AC 100, HL.
6. *The Empire Jamaica* [1957] AC 386, [1956] 3 All ER 144, HL – the appointment was held on the facts not to have caused the collision.
7. *The Norman* [1960] 1 Lloyd's Rep 1, HL.
8. Reports, LEG XXIX/5 and XXX/6 respectively.

ments to the Convention were discussed with a view to the eventual adoption of a Protocol. These discussions were developed further at the 32nd Session[9] in April and May 1977, and at the 33rd Session (12–16 September 1977)[10]. Almost all the proposals have been for extension of the scope of the Convention, which, as we have seen, is strictly limited at present to spillage of persistent oil from certain vessels and to specified types of damage suffered in carefully delineated areas.

In this section the various proposals for change will be examined in some detail, as the implications of extending CLC are the most important in the field of civil liability for oil pollution since the adoption and subsequent entry into force of the Convention itself.

10.6.1 EXTENSION TO BUNKERS OF DRY CARGO SHIPS AND OF TANKERS NOT CARRYING OIL IN BULK AS CARGO, AND CLARIFICATION OF THE POSITION OF SLOPS

In view of the fact that large modern ships can carry considerable quantities of persistent oil as bunkers, it appeared to many that the Convention ought to cover pollution damage caused by such oil, just as it covers oil escaping from a tanker carrying oil in bulk as cargo. There is certainly an anomaly in the fact that a plaintiff's right to recover under the favourable strict liability regime of the Convention should depend on whether or not the source of the oil was a tanker carrying oil in bulk as cargo. Why, it is reasoned, should the pollution damage caused by another *Torrey Canyon*-type incident be within CLC but the pollution damage caused by the bunkers of the tanker *Olympic Bravery*[11] not be covered merely because she was in ballast at the time she stranded, or the pollution damage from a dry cargo vessel's bunkers be excluded because the vessel carries dry and not persistent oil cargo?

The international shipping industry[12] has recognised the validity of the point as respects tankers in ballast, but there are definitely problems in extending CLC to the bunkers of dry cargo vessels. One is that if such an extension is made, it would be logical to extend also the compulsory insurance provisions thereto; this would extend the number of ships covered by the duty to insure and by the certification

9. Report, LEG XXXII/10.
10. Report, LEG XXXIII/5.
11. *The Times*, 27.1.76, p. 8; *The Daily Telegraph*, 19.3.76, p. 6; the reference to this casualty in LEG XXX/6, para. 11, is probably inaccurate, in that the pollution damage resulting was highly unlikely to have exceeded the 1957 Limitation Convention limitation fund.
12. Through ICS, LEG XXXII/9/1/Add. 1, Annex I, p. 6; and BIMCO, LEG XXXII/9/1/Add. 1, Annex I, p. 1.

procedures attendant on it from about 5,200 ships at present to about 23,000, with a corresponding heavy increase in costs. A second is that extensions should only be made when the nature of the problem is large enough to warrant them, and while oil pollution incidents from dry cargo vessels are by no means insignificant, there is no evidence that they form a sufficiently large problem[13]. A third is that some way would have to be found to integrate dry cargo vessels into the 1971 Fund Convention[14] scheme, and while this could be done as respects tankers (because the oil industry, which pays for the 1971 Fund Convention compensation, has a definite interest in the tanker shipping industry which transports its oil), it would be very difficult to achieve as respects dry cargo vessels. The oil industry can legitimately be burdened with a proportion of the damage caused by the tanker industry, but there is no reason why it should pay for part of the pollution costs of an industry which merely uses oil and does not transport it.

A way out of the first objection would be not to extend the compulsory insurance provisions of CLC to dry cargo ships, and this has been suggested by BIMCO[15]. The only way round the second objection is simply to suggest that the extension is politically desirable, as no doubt some nations feel[16]. A way out of the third might be for governments themselves to fund the operation of the 1971 Fund Convention as respects dry cargo ships (a suggestion unlikely to be adopted in practice!)[17].

On balance, it would appear to present difficulties of too great a nature to merit extension to the bunkers of dry cargo ships however desirable this may be felt to be, and that it is perhaps best to leave these incidents governed by national legal regimes.

This is not to say that effecting an extension of CLC to the bunkers of unladen tankers is a simple matter which ought to be effected. One difficulty it involves is that, unless special provision is made in the Fund Convention or in CLC regarding the limitation amounts, an unladen tanker would find itself liable to a greater level than a laden one[18]. This would happen because a laden tanker can avail itself of shipowner relief under Article 5 of the Fund Convention, but an unladen tanker, on the current wording, could not[19]. The only way to

---

13. See BIMCO's paper in LEG XXXII/9/I/Add. 1, Annex I, p. 2, para. 7.
14. See Chapter 11.
15. LEG XXXII/9/1/Add. 1, Annex I, p. 1 and 2, para. 6.
16. E.g. Netherlands, DDR, Norway, USSR and Poland.
17. In this connection it may be noted that paragraph 8 of the Working Group's Report at the 1969 Conference, LEG/CONF/C. 2/WP. 45, OR 604, is as follows: 'The Working Group unanimously concluded that, for practical and theoretical reasons, no burden should be imposed on States'.
18. ICS has brought this problem to the notice of the Legal Committee: LEG XXXIII/2/Add. 2.
19. See section 11.2.3.

rectify this, apart from altering the definition of 'ship' in the Fund Convention as well as in CLC, is to provide a special limitation Article in CLC for unladen tankers, allowing a limit of 1,500 francs per ton or 125 million francs, whichever the less.

It was seen in section 10.1.1.1 that there is room for doubt as to whether CLC covers slop oil which causes pollution damage. It was proposed at the 32nd Session that the definition of 'oil' be amended to remove this doubt[20]. However, when a Working Group at the 33rd Session considered the problem, it recommended that no change be made to the existing definition as respects slop oil, because 'the existing text has been widely interpreted as including mixtures in the ordinary, as opposed to scientific, sense of this word. If a reference to mixtures is included, this could have an unwanted limiting effect on the scope of the existing Convention'[1]. It is likely that as a result no clarification will be adopted.

10.6.2 PRE-SPILL PREVENTIVE MEASURES

It was seen in sections 10.2.1 and 10.2.2.4 that CLC does not cover preventive measures taken either by a government (or other plaintiff), or by a shipowner, in a situation where there is merely a threat of oil spillage and as yet no actual escape of oil.

It was suggested by OCIMF[2] that this situation should be remedied so that CLC, like the industry scheme TOVALOP[3], covered the pre-spill situation. There is no doubt that it is in the early stages of an incident that most can be done to minimise pollution, and that as the law stands the onus is very much on the shipowner to take preventive measures in the early period of an incident[4]. It may be argued that, just as it was wise to give the shipowner an incentive to take his own preventive action after a spill by enacting Article V(8)[5], it would be wise to extend that Article to the pre-spill situation.

The main danger here is that any extension of Article V(8) would obviously need to be accompanied by a corresponding extension in Article III to allow plaintiffs to recover their pre-spill costs (this could be done merely by changing the definition of 'preventive measures' in Article I(7)); and this could very easily lead to the shipowner paying for the cost of a coastal state's gross over-reaction to a grounding off

20. LEG XXXII/10, para. 29 and Annex III.
  1. LEG XXXIII/5, Annex.
  2. LEG XXXII/9/1/Add. 1, Annex I, p. 11.
  3. See Chapter 12.
  4. See section 9.8.1.3, under the heading *Cost of preventive measures*.
  5. See section 10.2.2.4.

its shores. How is one to tell what is reasonable in the way of preventive action when there is no actual oil spillage?

The Legal Committee did not have time to discuss this extension and so reached no conclusion on it[6], and it could well be rejected if and when it is further discussed.

10.6.3 EXTENSION TO NON-PERSISTENT OILS

It was seen in section 10.1.1.1 that Article I(5) limits the definition of oil to persistent oil. Perhaps the most important extension at present under consideration is the proposal that CLC should cover non-persistent oils (NPOs). Whether such an extension, if desirable, should be achieved by reference to a list (such as that contained in Annex I of the International Convention for the Prevention of Pollution from Ships 1973[7]), or a generic term[8], is not of concern here. The important question is whether such an extension ought to be made at all.

The major characteristic of NPOs is that, as their name accurately implies, they are non-persistent. When spilled on the surface of the sea, almost all the substance either evaporates, or dissolves in the water column (with a very heavy emphasis on the former). There is rarely, if ever, a residue left that is harmful, and, if there were, the substance would not be non-persistent! One would not expect NPOs to present an environmental problem in these circumstances, and indeed, as OCIMF report[9], a detailed examination by the oil industry in conjunction with the P and I Clubs failed to discover any cases of damage by non-persistent oil except for a few in-harbour incidents, all of which were covered by national legislation. Yet, at the 32nd Session there was considerable support, probably due to purely political background pressure, for an extension of CLC to these substances[10].

This extension would, if adopted, cause problems and would achieve almost no benefit. There would be almost no benefit because of the rarity of incidents involving NPOs which cause damage; there would be the problem of suitably amending the 1971 Fund Convention[11] and of administrating the compulsory insurance scheme,

6. LEG XXXII/10, para. 36.
7. See section 2.3.2.4.
8. Both means were suggested at the 32nd Session: see LEG XXXII/10, para. 33.
9. LEG XXXII/9/1/Add. 1, Annex I, p. 12.
10. France, USSR, USA, Canada, and with hesitation Poland and DDR all supported extension to NPOs. Five nations expressed doubt as to the need for such an extension and two were against it.
11. See Chapter 11.

which would need corresponding extension[12]. There would be a considerable risk that the only effect it would have would be to raise insurance premiums, and this might not even have a corresponding benefit of claims being paid (because there would be few, if any, claims). It is greatly to be hoped that this extension will not be adopted.

10.6.4 EXTENSION TO FIRE AND EXPLOSION

The 1969 Conference expressly rejected the coverage of this type of damage[13], and, although it reared its head again as a possible subject for extension, the Legal Committee again rejected it at its 32nd Session[14]. As BIMCO had pointed out[15], 'CLC is a Convention designed to protect the environment by providing compensation for damage by contamination, which encourages prompt and effective clean-up. Extension to fire and explosion would take the Convention into an entirely new field, namely the compensation of property damage and personal injury unrelated to environmental dangers. If oil should spill from a vessel which for some reason has exploded or caught fire, pollution damage caused by the oil will already be covered by CLC as it now stands. To extend the Convention in this way is therefore inappropriate'. The Committee's rejection is therefore welcomed.

10.6.5 EXTENSION TO THE EXCLUSIVE ECONOMIC ZONE

The Exclusive Economic Zone (EEZ) is a new concept in international law proposed at the third UN Conference on the Law of the Sea. In view of the fact that it is proposed that states should have jurisdiction within their EEZ with regard to the preservation of the marine environment (including pollution control), some delegations to the Legal Committee suggested that it would be desirable to extend the scope of the Convention delineated in Article II[16] to the EEZ[17]. However, at its 32nd Session the Committee decided that it would be

12. Since NPOs are often carried in small coastal tankers, the number of vessels not at present covered by compulsory insurance which would need certification would be high.
13. LEG/CONF/C. 2/SR. 15, *OR* 714.
14. LEG XXXII/10, para. 26.
15. LEG XXXII/9/1/Add. 1, Annex I, p. -
16. See section 10.12.
17. LEG XXX/6, paras. 19 and 20.

best to await the outcome of the Law of the Sea Conference before deciding this question[18].

10.6.6 POSITION OF BAREBOAT CHARTERERS AND OTHERS

The anomalous position of bareboat charterers and others, noted above[19], was drawn to the attention of the Legal Committee by BIMCO[20], and was felt by Poland, Italy and the UK to be an important question[1]. Little time was devoted to discussing this topic, which was a pity from the purely legal point of view, as the situation is untidy. From the practical point of view, the anomaly will become more serious when the 1976 Limitation Convention enters into force in CLC countries, for the liability of demise charterers for oil pollution damage will then be unlimited, unless the country makes special provision for limitation, either by exemption or otherwise.

10.6.7 EXISTING LIMITS TO BE RAISED

The Netherlands and the USA suggested at the 32nd Session that, if the Committee were to adopt a new Protocol, a revision of the limits should be included[2]. It was seen in section 10.2.2.3 and Table 10.1 that the limits in CLC compare very favourably with those of previous Conventions and even with those of the 1976 Limitation Convention. However, there have been incidents on a small scale which have exceeded the CLC limits, due to the small tonnage of the ship, and it was this aspect of the problem whose remedy was recommended by OCIMF[3]. There is no doubt that the problem of small ships was recognised at the 1976 Limitation Conference, and was reflected in the relatively high limits for them set in the Convention it adopted[4]. OCIMF recommended another dose of the same medicine for this small shipowner.

Raising the CLC limits for small ships, especially if other extensions to CLC go through, would probably increase the insurance premiums they have to pay, and might cause hardship to some companies, for

18. LEG XXXII/10, para. 27.
19. Sections 10.1.1.2, under the heading *Owners and others*, 10.2.2.1, 10.4.2.2 and 10.4.2.3.
20. LEG XXXII/9/1/Add. 1, Annex I, p. 3.
  1. LEG XXXII/10, para. 36.
  2. LEG XXXII/10, para. 28.
  3. LEG XXXII/9/1/Add. 1, Annex I, p. 11.
  4. See section 9.8.2.3.

this would come on top of the increases which the entry into force of the 1976 Limitation Convention will cause. This, and the fact that the number of incidents to date when even small ships have caused the CLC limits to be exceeded is very small, indicate that it would be best to leave these limits as they are. However, at the other end of the scale, the *Amoco Cadiz* incident will undoubtedly lead to further calls for a raising of limits, or their abandonment altogether.

10.7 Final clauses and status of the Convention

Articles XIII to XXI contain the final clauses, and deal with the mode of becoming party to the Convention, entry into force, denunciation, amendment and other matters, none of which call for comment here.

As at 31 December 1977, the following governments had become party to the Convention: Algeria, Bahamas, Belgium, Brazil, Chile, Denmark, Dominican Republic, Ecuador, Fiji, France, Federal Republic of Germany, Greece, Ivory Coast, Japan, Lebanon, Liberia, Monaco, Morocco, Netherlands, New Zealand, Norway, Panama, Poland, Portugal, Senegal, South Africa, Spain, Sweden, Syrian Arab Republic, Tunisia, USSR, United Kingdom, Yugoslavia. The Convention has been extended to: Belize, Bermuda, British Indian Ocean Territory, British Virgin Islands, Caiman Islands, Falkland Islands and Dependencies, Gibralter, Gilbert Islands, Guernsey, Isle of Man, Hong Kong, Jersey, Montserrat, Pitcairn, St Helena and Dependencies, Seychelles, Solomon Islands, Turks and Caicos Islands, Tuvalu, Akrotiri and Dhekelia Sovereign Base Areas in Cyprus.

10.8 Conclusion

Now that it appears possible that IMCO will adopt a Protocol to extend CLC to the bunkers of tankers in ballast, a major defect in the Convention would appear to be in the process of being cured. That an extension to non-persistent oils appears less likely is no bad thing: the best way to protect the marine environment from these hazards is to prohibit their operational discharge and to reduce the likelihood of their accidental spillage. The former has been done by the 1973 Convention[5]; the latter is part of a more general problem, but about

5. Section 2.3.2.4.

which action is nonetheless being taken[6]. There seems no need for a strict liability regime for non-persistent oils.

It is accepted that the standard rate per ton system of calculating the limitation amount gives rise to problems in relation to small ships, which are capable of causing quite serious oil pollution damage. On the other hand, the 1971 Fund Convention[7], does go a very long way to mitigating this problem. Again, although there can be said to be a casus omissus insofar as the Convention does not cover pre-spill measures, this is not as serious as it might otherwise be without the existence of sue-and-labour clauses in P & I insurance policies and without the existence of TOVALOP[8]. The dangers of writing pre-spill measures into CLC indicate that this could well be an area more apt for the operation of commercial practice than of law.

The Convention may be regarded as a very good one, despite the existence of a few blemishes. Its main features of strict liability and compulsory insurance are not mitigated by a profusion of exceptions[9], and the areas it fails to cover nearly all have good reasons for being omitted. The environmentalist can therefore welcome it, and hope for as wide an acceptance of it as is possible. The advantages to shipowners of such a wide acceptance are surprisingly great, largely because the alternatives are so grim. Thus, a wide acceptance of the uniform laws of CLC would reduce the chances of a shipowner having to establish more than one limitation fund in cases where one or more states have been polluted[10]. It provides certainty, and a disincentive to forum-shopping. Perhaps above all, acceptance of CLC by a state prevents it enacting draconian or unreasonable measures.

There are three main advantages of adherence to CLC from a government's point of view, in addition to the contribution this makes to the orderly development of private international law. One is an improvement in jurisdictional and procedural matters; another is access to the 1971 Fund Convention, which can only be ratified by states party to CLC; the third is that ships registered in states party to CLC may be issued with certificates which must be recognised by other contracting states.

6. See generally Chapter 3.
7. See Chapter 11.
8. See Chapters 12 and 13.
9. It is worth noting that the Conference rejected the defence (available under the 1954 Convention) of discharge in order to save life or damage to the ship – LEG/CONF/C. 2/SR. 18, *OR* 738 at 742.
10. If the USA had been a party to CLC, the French Government and others would have been unable to sue the owners of the *Amoco Cadiz* in New York and Chicago.

11 The International Convention on The Establishment of an International Fund for Compensation for Oil Pollution Damage 1971

11.1 Background to the adoption of the Convention

At the Conference of 1969 there had been a protracted debate on the main issues of strict or fault liability and of who was to bear that liability – the shipowner, the cargo owner or both[1]. At one stage it had begun to look as if the negotiations might completely break down in deadlock, but a series of votes on the important principles[2] evinced a majority view in favour of strict liability on the ship, combined with liability on the cargo interests in the form of a fund. In order to facilitate this compromise formula, a Working Group was set up[3] to examine the question of liability based on an international fund. It was apparent by the time the group produced its report[4] that there was no hope of formulating an instrument to set up such a fund, and so the Conference adopted a Resolution[5] that IMCO put the matter in hand immediately, and call a Diplomatic Conference not later than 1971 to consider and adopt a suitable Convention.

The origins of the 1971 Fund Convention[6] are thus to be found in the conflicts at the 1969 Conference: without the promise of a fund, the 1969 Conference would very probably have failed at adopt an instrument at all.

The Resolution of the 1969 Conference, 'recognising the view having emerged during the Conference that some form of supplementary scheme in the nature of an international fund is necessary to ensure that adequate compensation will be available for victims of large-scale oil pollution incidents', directed that the future work on the fund should be conducted in accordance with two guiding principles:

1. LEG/CONF/C. 2/SR. 2 to 8, *OR* 623 to 660; SR. 9, *OR* 664 to 667; SR. 10 to 13, *OR* 671 to 695.
2. LEG/CONF/C. 2/SR. 9, *OR* 662 to 666.
3. LEG/CONF/C. 2/SR. 9, *OR* 666 and SR. 11, *OR* 686 to 688.
4. LEG/CONF/C. 2/WP. 45, *OR* 604. Presented to Committee of the Whole, LEG/CONF/C. 2/SR. 20, *OR* 762 to 764, and to Plenary LEG/CONF/SR. 5, *OR* 100.
5. *OR* 185.
6. UK Misc. No. 26 of 1972 (Cmnd. 5061); (1972) 11 ILM 284. For the status of this Convention, see section 11.2.5.

(1) that victims should be fully and adequately compensated under a system based upon the principle of strict liability; (2) that the fund should in principle relieve the shipowner of the additional financial burden imposed by CLC. These two principles are reflected not only in the Preamble to the 1971 Fund Convention, but in Article 2 thereof (aims of the Fund) and in the two major compensatory provisions – Articles 4 and 5.

11.2 The main provisions of the Convention

11.2.1 INTRODUCTION[7]

Article 2 establishes an International Fund for compensation for pollution damage, to be named 'The International Oil Pollution Compensation Fund' ('the Fund'), which shall be recognised in each contracting state as a legal person capable under the laws of that state of assuming rights and obligations and of being a party in legal proceedings before the courts of that state.

The provisions of the Fund Convention are directly tailored to supplement those of CLC, so that, wherever possible, the same definitions are adopted, and the principle on which the provisions proceed is, generally speaking, that where CLC liability ends, Fund liability begins. The two fundamental compensatory provisions are Articles 4 and 5. Article 4 seeks to compensate plaintiffs (subject to a maximum limit) for pollution damage which they have suffered but for which they have been unable to recover full and adequate compensation under CLC for specified reasons, and also to a certain extent to reimburse shipowners for their voluntary clean-up expenses. Article 5 seeks to remove from the shipowner's shoulders the slice of his liability under CLC between 1,500 and 2,000 francs per ton, subject to maximum limits. Articles 6 to 9 contain supplementary provisions on time limits, place of litigation, enforcement of judgments and subrogation.

The Fund acquires its funds under Article 10 from contributions raised by levying crude oil and fuel oil received by persons in the territory of contracting states; hence, the people who pay for the compensation distributed by the Fund under Articles 4 and 5 are the oil companies, and not the governments who are party to the Convention (unless, of course, such a government receives contributing oil itself and in its own name). It is in this way that the

---

7. See generally L. A. W. Hunter, 'The Proposed International Compensation Fund for Oil Pollution Damage' (1972) 4 *J Mar L & Comm 117*.

Convention distributes the overall burden of pollution damage between the shipowner and cargo interests.

Articles 11 to 36 deal in detail with administrative matters, and will not be examined in this book. Articles 37 to 48 contain the final clauses, of which only those dealing with eligibility and entry into force are of interest here.

11.2.2 ARTICLE 3(1) AND ARTICLE 4

11.2.2.1 The duty to compensate

By Article 3(1), compensation under Article 4 applies exclusively to 'pollution damage[8] caused on the territory including the territorial sea of a Contracting State, and to preventive measures[8] taken to prevent or minimise such damage'. It would therefore appear that a claimant may claim under Article 4, irrespective of where the ship causing the damage is registered, although the damage in respect of which he may claim must have been caused on the territory or territorial sea of a state party to both CLC and this Convention (for no state may be party to the Convention which is not already party to CLC[9]). The conference rejected a proposal[10] that the scope be extended to cover damage suffered on the high seas by a contracting state or person resident therein. The scope of Article 4 is therefore identical to that of CLC[11].

Article 4(1) provides as follows:

> 'For the purpose of fulfilling its function under Article 2, paragraph 1(a), the Fund shall pay compensation to any person[12] suffering pollution damage if such person has been unable to obtain full and adequate compensation for the damage under the terms of the Liability Convention,
>
> (a) because no liability for the damage arises under the Liability Convention;
>
> (b) because the owner[12] liable for the damage under the Liability Convention is financially incapable of meeting his obligations in full and any financial security that may be provided under Article VII of that Convention[13] does not cover or is insufficient to satisfy the claims for compensation for the damage; an owner being treated as

8. Both pollution damage and preventive measures are defined by Article 1(2) as in CLC: see section 10.2.1.
9. See section 11.2.5.
10. LEG/CONF. 2/3, p. 12.
11. See Article II of CLC, above section 10.1.2.
12. Defined by Article 1(2) as in CLC: see section 10.1.1.2.
13. See section 10.5.

financially incapable of meeting his obligations and a financial security being treated as insufficient if the person suffering the damage has been unable to obtain full satisfaction of the amount of compensation due under the Liability Convention after having taken all reasonable steps to pursue the legal remedies available to him;

(c) because the damage exceeds the owner's liability under the Liability Convention as limited pursuant to Article V, paragraph 1, of that Convention[14] or under the terms of any other international Convention in force or open for signature, ratification or accession at the date of this Convention[15].

Expenses reasonably incurred or sacrifices reasonably made by the owner voluntarily to prevent or minimise pollution damage shall be treated as pollution damage for the purposes of this Article.'

The major requirement is that the claimant has suffered pollution damage, which is defined by Article 1(2) as having the same meaning as in CLC[16]. It has been seen that, subject to exceptions contained in Articles III(2) and XI(1), CLC compensates pollution damage[17]. Hence, without more, paragraph (a) of Article 4(1) would apply in the case of all those exceptions. However, Article 4(2)(a) exempts the Fund from liability in two cases: (1) where the pollution damage resulted from an act of war, hostilities, civil war or insurrection, and (2) where Article XI(1) of CLC applies (oil pollution damage caused by warships etc.). Paragraph (a) of Article 4(1) therefore residually applies where (a) the damage resulted from a natural phenomenon of an exceptional, inevitable and irresistible character, (b) the damage was wholly caused by an act or omission done with intent to cause damage by a third party (e.g. terrorist action) and (c) was wholly caused by the negligence or other wrongful act of any government or other authority responsible for the maintenance of lights or other navigational aids in the exercise of that function. The decision to compensate victims in these situations was taken despite detailed and cogent argument by OCIMF[18] against placing such liability on the Fund: the Conference clearly took the view that the need for compensation in these cases, excluded from CLC because they were uninsurable by the shipowner, outweighed the consideration of logic that cargo and shipowning interests should be liable in identical situations.

14. See section 10.2.2.
15. E.g. the 1957 Brussels Convention, section 9.8.2.2, or the 1924 Brussels Convention, section 9.8.2.1, but not the 1976 London Convention.
16. See section 10.2.1.
17. See for Article III(2), section 10.1.4 and for Article XI(1), section 10.1.1.2 under the heading *State-owned vessels*.
18. LEG/CONF. 2/5, pp. 4 to 6.

Paragraph (b) of Article 4(1) would cover the situation where the owner is insolvent and either he is uninsured against his CLC liability or that insurance has failed (for instance due to the unlikely event of the insurer's insolvency or the more likely event of the wilful misconduct of the owner). The most likely situation in which this paragraph would come into operation is where an incident has been caused by a small ship carrying less than 2,000 tons of oil in bulk as cargo, and which is uninsured because it does not need to be under CLC. In such a situation the shipowner, who may be in a small way of business (or who may even be a one-ship company) could easily become insolvent.

Paragraph (c) is the one under which most claims against the Fund are likely to arise. The operation of the first limb is fairly obvious; the second limb would apply in the following situation. A ship registered in State A causes pollution damage in State B. State B is a party to CLC and to the 1957 Limitation Convention (or the 1924 Limitation Convention). State A is not a party to CLC but is a party to the 1957 Convention (or 1924 Convention). Here, State B is still obliged to allow the ship to limit under the 1957 (or 1924) Convention, even though it has made the ship strictly liable in accordance with CLC. Hence, the liability of the Fund under Paragraph (c) can begin at the 1,000 Poincaré francs per ton level, or even the 8 pounds per ton[19] level, just as under paragraphs (a) and (b) it can begin at the beginning (i.e. the Fund can bear the whole burden of the pollution damage, up to its maximum limit).

Perhaps the most significant provision for shipowners and plaintiffs alike is the final sentence of Article 4(1). This was absent from the draft Convention, and was proposed by Norway[20]: it was argued that, just as such measures were to rank as claims for limitation purposes under Article V(8) of CLC[1], so they should equally rank as claims against the Fund. The adoption of the provision provides an important incentive to the shipowner to take immediate action following a spill, an incentive which, as was noted before[2], had been completely lacking prior to 1969. The duty to compensate the shipowner applies even though he has been negligent, and even, it seems, where he has been guilty of wilful misconduct[3].

The precise intent of this provision is clear only when taken in the context of Article 2(1)(a) (which states that the aims of the Fund include the compensation of claims to the extent that CLC is

---

19. This may well mean something nearer £32 per ton nowadays: see section 9.8.2.1.
20. LEG/CONF. 2/3, p. 25.
 1. See section 10.2.2.4.
 2. Section 9.8.2.4.
 3. Article 4(3), proviso to the first sentence. A. L. Doud, 'Compensation for Oil Pollution Damage', (1973) 4 J Mar L & Comm, 525 at 535 argues from the way the paragraph was evolved that the final sentence of Article 4(3) should not detract from this conclusion.

whichever the less; Article 5 reimburses the shipowner down from that limit to 1,500 francs per ton or 125 million francs, whichever the less; and Article 4(1) compensates the shipowner for clean-up costs he has incurred which are not notionally compensated in the CLC limitation fund.

It would seem that the right to relief is not dependent on the shipowner having been able to limit his liability under CLC itself, so that he may still qualify for relief where he has been able to limit under the provisions of, say, the 1957 Convention[13]. This follows from the reference in Article 5(1) to indemnifying the shipowner against his liability under CLC: It does not talk about bearing a portion of any limitation fund.

There are, however, strict limitations on the right to shipowner relief under Article 5 which do not pertain in respect of compensation for voluntary clean-up costs under Article 4(1). These limitations are designed to encourage compliance with the major oil pollution prevention and ship safety conventions. Article 5(3) provides that

> 'The fund may be exonerated wholly or partially from its obligations under paragraph 1 towards the owner and his guarantor, if the Fund proves that as a result of the actual fault or privity of the owner:
>> (a) the ship from which the oil causing the pollution damage escaped, did not comply with the requirements laid down in:
>>> (i) the International Convention for the Prevention of Pollution of the Sea by Oil 1954, as amended in 1962[14]; or
>>> (ii) the International Convention for the Safety of Life at Sea 1960[15]; or
>>> (iii) the International Convention on Load Lines 1966[16]; or
>>> (iv) the International Regulations for Preventing Collisions at Sea 1960[17]; or
>>> (v) any amendments to the above-mentioned Conventions which have been determined as being of an important nature in accordance with Article 16(5) of the Convention mentioned under (i), Article 9(e) of the Convention mentioned under (ii) or Article 29(3)(d) or (4)(d) of the Convention mentioned under (iii), provided, however, that such amendments had been in

---

13. This could happen where the ship was registered in a state party to the 1957 Convention but not to CLC – see above, section 10.2.2.2.
14. See above, section 2.3.2.1.
15. See above, section 3.2.1.
16. See above, section 3.4.
17. See above, section 3.2.1.

force for at least twelve months at the time of the incident[18];

and

(b) the incident or damage was caused wholly or partially by such non-compliance.

The provisions of this paragraph shall apply irrespective of whether the Contracting State in which the ship was registered or whose flag it was flying, is a Party to the relevant Instrument.'

The Fund must therefore prove three things to escape liability wholly or partially under Article 5(3): first, that an event occurred (or failed to occur) which constituted the actual fault or privity of the owner; second, that as a result of that event or failure the breach of a provision of one of the named Conventions occurred; and third, that that breach wholly or partially caused the incident or damage. What at first seems a fairly wide opportunity for the Fund to escape liability is, therefore, rather narrow on closer examination. While a breach of these Conventions would probably be quite common, and while such a breach can be imagined to be likely to have at least partially caused the incident, it will be rare that the breach will have occurred with the actual fault of privity of the owner – subject, however, to the noted tendency of courts to interpret that phrase very widely[19].

11.2.4   ARTICLES 6 TO 10

11.2.4.1   Jurisdictional provisions

Article 6(1) makes provision as to the time limit for actions against the Fund similar to that of Article VIII of CLC[20]: the basic period is three years from the date of damage.

The provisions of Article 7, dealing with the place of action against the Fund, are complicated. A reason for such complexity is the possibility that an action can be brought against the Fund in respect of damage suffered in a state party to CLC but not to this Convention: see Article 3(2)[21]. Another reason for the complexity is that a single incident can give rise to claims against the owner (under CLC) and the Fund (under this Convention) in respect of damage suffered in several states, some of which are party to both Conventions and some of which are party only to CLC.

18. By Article 5(4) the Assembly of the Fund has power to replace any of the Conventions referred to with Instruments in force designed to replace them (e.g. SOLAS 1974 for SOLAS 1960).

19. See section 9.8.2.2 under the heading *Denial of the right to limit*.

20. See section 10.3.2.

21. Section 11.2.3.

The object of jurisdictional provisions limiting the place of action should be to facilitate the litigation and to draw it all before one court. This was quite effectively done by Article IX of CLC[1] in respect of that Convention, but for the above reasons the same could not be achieved in respect of this Convention. The rules elaborated in Articles 7(1) and (3) accordingly provide that, if possible, a claim against the Fund in respect of any damage should be made in the same jurisdiction as the claim in respect of the same damage is made against the owner under CLC; but that if that jurisdiction is one where the Fund Convention is not in force, then the claim against the Fund must be made either before a court of the state where the Fund has its headquarters[2] or before the courts of a contracting state in which pollution damage has also been suffered as a result of the incident.

The Convention does as much as it can to keep the litigation in the court where the CLC limitation fund has been established, but could not, of course, make any very simple provision for the case where this court is in a jurisdiction in respect of which the Fund Convention is not in force, nor for the case where there was no limitation fund under CLC (because, for instance, Article III(2)[3] exempted the owner from liability).

The detailed provisions of Articles 7(2) and 7(4) to (6) need no discussion here, and it need merely be mentioned in passing that Article 8 makes provision for recognition and enforcement of judgments as in Article X of CLC[4], and Article 9 makes provision for subrogation of rights and rights of recourse.

11.2.4.2 Contributions

Contributions are made to the Fund each year in amounts calculated in accordance with Articles 11 and 12, the details of which are outside the scope of this work. The important provision for present purposes is Article 10, which identifies the persons who are to make the contributions. These are those persons[5] who have received contributing oil[6] in total quantities exceeding 150,000 metric tons[7] during the calendar year specified in Articles 11 and 12, in specified places and in specified manner. Put simply, the oil must have been received in a

---

1. See section 10.3.1.
2. The venue of the Fund's headquarters will probably be decided at the first Assembly of the Fund, to be held in London from 13 to 17 November 1978.
3. See section 10.1.4.
4. See section 10.3.3.
5. Person is defined by Article 1(2) as in CLC: see section 10.1.1.2 under the heading *Owners and others*.
6. Contributing oil is defined by Article 1(3) to be crude oil and fuel oil of specified types.
7. Article 10(2) makes special provision for where the total received by two associated persons exceeds 150,000 tons.

Contracting State either directly by sea or by some other method (e.g. pipeline or railway wagon) bringing in oil which has been carried by sea to a non-contracting state.

Therefore, it is not the whole of the oil industry receiving oil which contributes, but only that section whose oil is carried by sea – an appropriate limitation in the circumstances. But it is noticeable that it is the consignee of the oil who pays: the consignor who has produced it pays nothing. It is therefore largely the oil companies in the West who will be the direct contributors to the Fund. It is further noticeable that the small companies are relieved from contributing at all. Thus, in places importing only small quantities of oil the benefits of being able to claim under Article 4 may be obtained free of cost to the companies operating in those countries.

11.2.5 ELIGIBILITY AND ENTRY INTO FORCE

By Article 37(4), the Convention may be ratified, accepted, approved or acceded to only by states which have ratified, accepted, approved or acceded to CLC[8]. To have opened the Convention to any other states would have made a mockery of the whole scheme of the Convention, which is to supplement CLC liability.

Article 40 contains the entry into force requirements. Now that CLC has entered into force, the requirement of Article 40(2) that this take place before the Convention enters into force has been fulfilled, and on 4th May 1976 the Tunisian accession completed the requirement of Article 40(1)(a) that at least eight states deposit instruments of ratification, etc. But the Convention had to wait until 16 October 1978 before it entered into force because of the requirement contained in Article 40(1)(b), namely that entry into force could not take place until the Convention had acquired parties in which a total of at least 750 million tons of contributing oil were received in the preceding year.

It was important that a minimum contributing oil tonnage be built into the entry into force provisions of the Convention, otherwise, as OCIMF pointed out to the Conference[9], a single early claim against the Fund could have very serious effects on the economics of the few early contributors. The Forum pointed out that the industry scheme CRISTAL[10] had avoided this problem by requiring that companies importing 50% of the oil transported by sea be party to the agreement

8. See Article XIII of CLC for eligibility to become a party thereto.
9. LEG/CONF. 2/5, pp. 16–17.
10. See Chapter 12.

Each party must establish his financial capability to fulfil his obligations to the satisfaction of the International Tanker Owners' Pollution Federation Ltd, a company set up to administer the agreement. This may now be done by entering vessels in a specially-formed mutual insurance association, the International Tanker Indemnity Association Ltd (ITIA) or in a conventional Protection and Indemnity Club. The arrangement of such cover would have been impossible without limiting the liability of a party; under the old forms of the agreement, this was US $100 per gross ton or $10 million (whichever the less), but now by Clause VII the limits roughly mirror those of CLC – US $160 (say £85) per limitation ton or US $16.8 million (say £8.9 million) (whichever the less).

A most important characteristic of the agreement is that the company set up to administer it ('the Federation') does not itself provide any insurance. Hence, when a person files a claim in response to being informed by the Federation that the tanker involved is subject to TOVALOP, any payment made comes from the insurer and not the Federation. The liabilities of parties are to each other, and consist of mutual promises. Insurance against the cost of having to fulfill them must be taken out by parties, and the beneficiaries are the claimants and, in respect of their own voluntary clean-up costs, the parties themselves.

The main intention of the parties in making the fundamental changes in May 1978 was to provide in those areas not protected by CLC benefits and protection generally comparable with those available under CLC. How, then, does TOVALOP now differ from CLC?

The main difference is that TOVALOP, being voluntary, covers only those tankers owned by the parties thereto. It has just been seen that there are in fact very few tankers in the world not covered by TOVALOP, but it is always possible that a particular incident will be caused by a vessel owned by a non-party. For this reason it is often said that TOVALOP is *vessel specific*. CLC, being a legal regime, applies to all vessels within the scope of its provisions, although it is limited to pollution damage caused on, and measures taken to prevent or mitigate pollution damage in, the territory or territorial sea of a contracting state. Hence it is said by way of comparison that CLC is *territory specific*.

While such a distinction is inherent in the form of the two schemes (namely, a voluntary agreement amongst shipowners and an international agreement between sovereign states) there are differences not so caused. Perhaps the most important of these is the coverage by TOVALOP of the pure threat situation. TOVALOP allows a person who takes reasonable preventive measures while no oil has yet been spilled to recover his costs in many situations, whether he be the tanker owner or the potential victim, whereas CLC would neither reimburse such costs nor allow them to rank against a limitation fund set up because a spill subsequently took place[8]. It has already been noted[9] that it is probably not desirable to extend CLC to mirror this provision. Another important difference is that TOVALOP covers a spill from a tanker in ballast (a development with which CLC may well catch up in due course[10]). The third major difference from a legal point of view, although in practice it will be relatively insignificant, is that the limits to TOVALOP liability apply in all cases, not just those (as in CLC[11]) where the owner has not been guilty of actual fault or privity. The absence of such a restriction from TOVALOP, being a purely voluntary arrangement, is necessitated by insurance considerations.

A further significant difference is that TOVALOP covers the bareboat charterer, by providing that he shall be deemed to be the owner. This means that, unlike the CLC regime[12], there is no question of there being two (voluntary) payments where the tanker is subject to such a charter. However, it is not clear from Clause VIII(E) that a claimant could not accept a TOVALOP offer from the bareboat charterer and then sue the registered owner under national legislation. Such action would, of course, be highly unconscionable, and is most unlikely, but a simple drafting amendment to TOVALOP could put the matter beyond doubt.

There are, of course, minor differences – for instance the limitation period under TOVALOP is shorter than that under CLC, disputes must be settled by arbitration and TOVALOP does not cover whale oil – but these do not call for comment here. The striking conclusion to emerge from comparison of the two systems is that claimants are better protected by TOVALOP (when available) than by CLC. This was not always the case – before the changes made in May 1978, CLC was undoubtedly the more beneficial of the two from the claimant's point of view. TOVALOP was not based on strict liability, its limits were lower and it applied only to governmental claimants.

One thing which the two systems have always had in common is the method of handling claims: in practice, the entity behind the owner will be a Protection and Indemnity Club (or ITIA) in both TOVALOP and CLC claims. Once the liability of the owner under either system is agreed, the only matter of contention is likely to be the reasonableness of the costs claimed. In the past negotiations on this question have almost invariably been handled on an amicable basis and a settlement reached without recourse to litigation or arbitration.

A government not yet party to CLC is therefore faced with a choice of schemes, one purely voluntary which does not cover every tanker in the world but which provides very wide protection in respect of those

8. See section 10.2.2.4.
9. Section 10.6.2.
10. See section 10.6.1.
11. See section 10.2.2.2.
12. See sections 10.1.1.2, 10.5.1 and 10.6.6.

vessels which it does cover, the other a legal scheme which does cover all laden tankers but which does not offer such wide protection in respect of them. It must now be a considerable temptation to a government not yet party to CLC to remain so, so that TOVALOP will continue to cover incidents off its shores. Of course, TOVALOP is likely to be voluntarily terminated one day, when CLC becomes so widespread in its application as to obviate the need for TOVALOP, but until that date the attractiveness to a state, particularly one with an exposed coast but a small fleet, of not becoming a party to CLC must be admitted. This is regrettable because it could mean that the global application of CLC will be delayed. The irony would be that the delay would be caused by the existence, not necessarily of a lack of environmental concern by states, but of an industry-run alternative which is better than CLC.

12.2 CRISTAL

Just as the 1969 CLC was preceded by a tanker industry scheme to compensate the victims of oil pollution, so the 1971 Fund Convention was preceded by an oil industry scheme. The 1971 Fund Convention was adopted on 18 December 1971 and entered into force only on 16 October 1978[13]; the Contract Regarding an Interim Supplement to Tanker Liability for Oil Pollution (CRISTAL) was adopted on 14 January 1971 and came into effect on 1 April following, when oil companies receiving over 70% of the world's crude and fuel oil had become parties[14]. Currently this figure is about 92% (comparable with TOVALOP). CRISTAL is a voluntary scheme adopted originally to compensate only the victims of oil pollution who had obtained insufficient compensation under existing laws or under TOVALOP, the compensation being provided within carefully defined limits by a fund, administered by an Institute set up under CRISTAL and contributed to by the oil company parties. The original CRISTAL was therefore limited to helping only the victims of oil pollution, and not shipowners.

It was recognised early on that where a shipowner failed to take voluntary clean-up measures himself, the oil would be far more likely to cause damage compensable under CRISTAL; whereas if these measures had been taken, CRISTAL offered the shipowner nothing in the way of reimbursement. The expenses incurred by the shipowner were therefore borne by him, but they had the effect of reducing the liability of the CRISTAL fund. Shipowners and their insurers

13. See section 11.2.5.
14. Under Clause III(A) a minimum of 50% was required.

therefore entered into negotiations with the oil company parties to CRISTAL, as a result of which CRISTAL was changed, as from 19 June 1972, to offer shipowners reimbursement of a top slice of their voluntary clean-up costs; in return, the P and I Clubs formally undertook to encourage their members to take prompt and effective voluntary clean-up action. Hence from that date, CRISTAL contained the two main elements of the 1971 Fund Convention – reimbursement of victims and shipowners.

When TOVALOP was amended as from 20 February 1973 to cover preventive measures taken prior to a spillage of oil upon the water, it became logical to make a similar amendment to CRISTAL. This was effected on 25 May 1973. So as from then, in contrast to the 1971 Fund Convention, CRISTAL covered the pre-spill situation insofar as measures taken by the shipowner to prevent pollution were concerned. Hence the industry voluntarily put right what the law had not done.

CRISTAL was amended again, this time fundamentally, in May 1978, so that with effect from 1st June 1978 it mirrored the provisions of the Fund Convention as far as was desirable: hence TOVALOP and CRISTAL between them now form an integrated voluntary scheme just as CLC and the Fund Convention form an integrated legal scheme, whereby the cost of a pollution incident is shared between the shipowning and the cargo interests. The older versions of CRISTAL[15] will not be further mentioned here, save where to do so would cast light on the current provisions.

CRISTAL sets up a fund which is held by the Oil Companies Institute for Marine Pollution Compensation Limited, a company incorporated in Bermuda, and it is to this company and to each other that the parties owe their duties. The Institute collects the funds necessary to meet claims made under CRISTAL by raising a levy from the oil company parties based upon their receipts of crude and fuel oil. This fund will pay out to compensate any person (either private or governmental) who has suffered pollution damage or who has taken threat removal measures[16] as a result of an incident[16]. There are, however, numerous prerequisites, exceptions and qualifications to this rule, all of which are contained in Clause IV.

It is a prerequisite to the Institute's liability that the oil[16] involved in the incident was 'owned' by an oil company partly to CRISTAL. Clause V provides an extended definition of ownership so that, even if title was not in an oil company party at the time of the incident, the oil is nonetheless considered to be owned by such a party if the shipment in question had been sold by or is under contract to be sold to such a party, or if it is carried in a tanker owned by or chartered to such a

15. For comment, see G. L. Becker, 'A Short Cruise on the Good Ships TOVALOP and CRISTAL' (1974) 5 *J Mar L & Comm*, 609. The first version of CRISTAL is reproduced at 10 ILM 137; the latest edition is obtainable from Marine Pollution Compensation Services Ltd, 51 Berkeley House, 15 Hay Hill, London W1.
16. Defined as in TOVALOP.

party, and that party has elected in writing to have the shipment so considered. Such an extension of the concept of ownership enables an environmentally conscious company which has a close connection with the shipment to ensure that it is covered by CRISTAL, even though it is not owned by a party thereto. It also enables such a company to eradicate the anomaly which would have arisen where oil is sold on c.i.f. or c. and f. terms; under such contracts property in the oil usually passes on receipt of documents by the buyer, so that, if one was party to CRISTAL and the other was not, the cargo would have been covered by CRISTAL for part only of the voyage.

The other important prerequisite is that the tanker concerned is entered in TOVALOP.

The Institute is absolved from liability altogether if any of the events described in Article III(2) of CLC[17] caused the incident. Hence, CRISTAL follows the same policy as that followed in respect of shipowners' liability by the 1969 Conference, but diverges from that adopted in respect of the Fund Convention. It will be remembered that the Fund Convention does compensate where the incident was caused by 'a natural phenomenon of an exceptional, inevitable and irresistible character' and it also does compensate where the incident was caused by an intentional act or omission on the part of a third person (e.g. terrorist action).

CRISTAL is designed to compensate those who have suffered pollution damage only insofar as they have been unable to get adequate compensation from other specified sources – like the Fund Convention, it comes in on top of other provisions. Hence, it does not compensate a person in respect of pollution damage compensatable under the Fund Convention itself[18]: one cannot prefer CRISTAL to the Fund! But this does not mean that CRISTAL will not pay up where the CLC applies but the Fund Convention does not. Clause IV(E)(1) provides for the Institute's liability in such cases to the extent that the claimant has been unable to obtain full compensation by taking all reasonable steps to pursue the remedies available to him. Clause IV(F)(1) makes similar provision in respect of an incident to which CLC does not apply.

It has already been mentioned that the other major object of CRISTAL since June 1972 has been to compensate the shipowner himself. These provisions are now contained in Clauses IV(E)(2), (F)(2), (G) and (H). The first limb is constituted by the provision that the Institute shall compensate the shipowner[19] for the cost of preventive measures[20] and threat removal measures[1] taken by him to the extent that he has been unable to actually or notionally compensate

17. See section 10.1.4.
18. Clause IV(A)(1).
19. Including in most cases the bareboat charterer.
20. Defined as in CLC.
 1. Defined as in TOVALOP.

himself for them without resorting to CRISTAL. The second limb is
constituted by the provision that the Institute shall indemnify the
shipowner for that portion of his liability to others which exceeds US
$120 per ton of the tanker's tonnage or $10 million (whichever the
less) and which does not exceed $160 per ton or $16.8 million
(whichever the less)[2]. These limits are of course designed to mirror the
equivalent provisions of Article 5 of the 1971 Fund Convention. It is
noticeable, however, that under CRISTAL, while there is no proviso
relating to breach of the various International Conventions relating to
oil pollution and safety at sea, there is a proviso that 'no such
indemnity shall be paid to an Owner whose recklessness or willful
misconduct caused the Incident'. Recklessness is an unfortunate
concept to have brought in here. It is unknown in civil maritime law
in the common law countries, and hence it is not easy to see exactly
how it will be interpreted.

The second limb would still leave the shipowner bearing all the
liability to others above $160 per ton or $16.8 million in cases where
the legal regime relating to the incident did not entitle the shipowner
to limit his oil pollution liability at that level or at all. Clause IV(H)
therefore provides that in such a case, so long as the shipowner has not
been guilty of causative wilful misconduct or privy to unseaworthiness,
the Institute shall bear the excess of his liability over $160 per ton or
$16.8 million (whichever is less).

CRISTAL of course has to have a limit, and this was raised in May
1978 to be comparable to that of the Fund Convention – US $36
million. There is also provision for raising this limit by up to $72
million if the Institute considers such an increase advisable in the light
of experience.

It can therefore be seen that CRISTAL now closely mirrors the
Fund Convention – but how closely? CRISTAL is of course limited to
incidents where the oil concerned is 'owned' by an oil company party
to the contract, whereas the Fund is limited by reference to the
territories and ships of states party to the Convention. In practice this
means that, until the Fund Convention is ratified by nearly all the
states in the world, CRISTAL would cover far more incidents than
would the Fund Convention (unless CRISTAL suffers the unlikely
withdrawal of major oil companies or TOVALOP suffers the
withdrawal of major tanker owners). CRISTAL does not cover
incidents caused by natural phenomena of an exceptional, inevitable
and irresistible character, or those caused by terrorist acts, whereas
the Fund Convention does. In practice this is unlikely to be a
significant difference, since few such incidents can be expected. The
criteria for shipowner relief are more generous in CRISTAL's case
than in the Fund's, although again this is unlikely to be a serious
difference.

2. Now the TOVALOP limit as well as the CLC limit.

Undoubtedly the most significant difference, from the point of view of coverage, is that CRISTAL applies to pure threat situations whereas the Fund Convention does not. From the point of view of procedure there is also likely to be a significant difference. Claims under CRISTAL are handled swiftly and with the minimum of bureaucracy; claims under the Fund Convention are bound to take longer, and they could even become involved in litigation (an impossibility under CRISTAL).

The inevitable conclusion must be that on balance, CRISTAL is a significant improvement on the Fund Convention – a fact which may deter some governments from ratifying that Convention: since CRISTAL can operate quite happily on top of CLC, and since the Fund Convention contains the unfortunate defects mentioned in Chapter 11, one cannot say that this would be a bad thing.

The existence of TOVALOP and CRISTAL has transformed the practice of claiming compensation for oil pollution damage far more than has the adoption of the CLC and Fund Conventions. They are undoubtedly two of the most important developments in the history of oil pollution prevention and clean-up, and they will remain of pre-eminent importance until the international conventions become really widespread. Their existence probably owes more to the environmentalist lobby following the *Torrey Canyon* disaster than to anything else, although their development must be seen as largely due to concerned opinion inside the oil and tanker industries, and, perhaps to a healthy fear of more draconian measures than strict but limited liability. They have filled wide gaps in the law quicker and better than legal developments have been able to do. One must applaud those responsible, and encourage every company in each industry to become a party for their duration.

Part three
Salvage

13 Salvage

At many points in this work the question of salvage has been touched upon. For instance, in section 5.1 the ability of private interests to deal with a stricken tanker in most situations, and in sections 9.8.1.3 and 10.6.2 the need for early preventive measures in a casualty situation, were mentioned. In sections 9.8.2.4 and 10.2.2.4 it was seen that the cost of taking pre-spill preventive measures (which, of course, in many cases would consist of or include salvage services) could not be offset against a limitation fund set up under any of the Limitation Conventions or under CLC, although it was seen in Chapter 12 that TOVALOP and CRISTAL do cover such expenses and so enable the shipowner to recover them. In section 10.1.1.2 the salvor's liability for oil pollution damage under CLC and the related legislation of several countries was dealt with.

The recent incident of the '*Amoco Cadiz*' in March 1978 has centred so much attention on the process of engaging professional salvors and on how the relationship between salvor and salved operates, that a chapter on salvage was felt necessary. It is not, however, the purpose of this chapter to provide a comprehensive exposition on the English and International law relating to salvage, for that would be to merely summarise the many detailed works already written on the subject[1], and also to provide far more than is relevant to this work; rather, attention will be focussed upon some of the legal problems which oil pollution risks create for salvors and on the shortcomings of existing law and practice from the oil pollution point of view.

---

1. E.g. *Kennedy's Civil Salvage* (4th ed. (Ed. K. C. McGuffie) London, 1958); *Carver's Carriage by Sea* (12th ed. (Ed. R. Colinvaux), London, 1971) Chapter 13; and *Halsbury's Laws of England* (3rd ed., London, 1961) Vol. 35, Part 9.

13.1 The salvage contract

Although in most cases a contract of some kind will be entered into between the master of the stricken ship and the master of the salving ship, such a contract is not necessary to enable the salvor to claim salvage reward. This principle is of ancient origin, and has been embodied in the Convention for the Unification of Certain Rules of Law Respecting Assistance and Salvage at Sea 1910[2], Article 2 of which states that 'Every act of assistance or salvage of which has had a useful result gives a right to equitable remuneration.' Hence in English law, even where the master of the stricken vessel declines the services of the salving vessel, there will be a right to salvage reward if a prudent owner of the salved property would have accepted the services[3]. Article 3 of the Convention embodies this principle in the following way: 'Persons who have taken part in salvage operations notwithstanding the express and reasonable prohibition on the part of the vessel to which the services were rendered, have no right to any remuneration.'

In most circumstances, however, a contract will in fact be agreed. The two most common forms are a towage contract and a salvage agreement. The former is not strictly a salvage agreement, for it provides for the towing vessel to be remunerated on a fixed rate basis, usually that of the number of miles towed or the time taken in towing: it is fundamental to the concept of salvage that the reward is only for success. Hence Article 2 of the 1910 Convention provides that 'No remuneration is due if the services rendered have no beneficial result', and Article 4 provides that 'A tug has no right to remuneration for assistance to or salvage of the vessel she is towing or of the vessel's cargo, except where she has rendered exceptional services which cannot be considered as rendered in fulfillment of the contract of towage'.

The most common form of salvage agreement, which is in use throughout the world, is Lloyd's Standard Form[4]. Under this agreement the salvor agrees to use his best endeavours to salve the

2. UKTS No. 4 of 1913 (Cd. 6677). As at 1 January 1978, the Convention had been ratified or acceded to in respect of most of the coastal territory in the world. The 1967 Protocol to the Convention, UKTS No. 22 of 1978 (Cmnd. 7095), which extends the operation of the Convention to services rendered by, and to warships or other ships owned, operated or chartered by, a State or Public Authority, entered into force on 15 August 1977 and as at 1 January 1978 had been ratified or acceded to by six states.

3. See e.g. *The Vandyck* (1881) 7 PD 42; on appeal (1882) 5 Asp MLC 17, CA; *The Auguste Legembre* [1902] P 123; *The Emilie Galline* [1903] P 106; *The Port Caledonia and The Anna* [1903] P 184; *The Kangaroo* [1918] P 327.

4. The latest addition is dated 23 February 1972, although it is expected that a Committee reviewing the form will before long recommend changes. For commentary on many of the clauses contained in the current form see K. C. McGuffie, P. A. Fugeman and P. V. Gray, *Admiralty Practice* (London, 1964) Chapter 38. For a more up to date analysis, see D. R. Thomas, 'Lloyd's Standard Form of Salvage Agreement – A Descriptive and Analytical Scrutiny', [1978] *LMCLQ* 276.

vessel and/or her cargo and to take them into an agreed place of safety, on the principle of 'no cure – no pay' just described.

The basis of the amount of reward under Lloyd's standard Form is the same as that for any salvage award under maritime law, namely, it must be sufficient to encourage people to take risks in the saving of life and property. As Willmer J put it in *The Sandefjord*[5],

'the awarding of salvage is governed largely by considerations of public policy and by the desirability of encouraging seafaring folk to take risks for the purpose of saving property.'

Accordingly, many factors are taken into account; as Article 8 of the 1910 Convention states,

'The remuneration is fixed by the court according to the circumstances of each case, on the basis of the following considerations:

(a) firstly, the measure of success obtained, the efforts and deserts of the salvors, the danger run by the salved vessel, by her passengers, crew and cargo, by the salvors, and by the salving vessel; the time expended, the expenses incurred and losses suffered, and the risks of liability and other risks run by the salvors, and also the value of the property exposed to such risks, due regard being had to the special appropriation (if any) of the salvors' vessel for salvage purposes;

(b) secondly, the value of the property salved.'

But, by Article 2, 'in no case shall the sum to be paid exceed the value of the property salved'. In practice, more than half the value of the salved property is rarely awarded.

No one with salvage experience could deny the risks habitually run by professional salvors, or the skill and daring so often exhibited. Further, no one who appreciates the amount of time a salvage tug spends waiting in port (during which period all the normal expenses of running a ship, with the exception of bunker consumption, are incurred) could deny the equity of allowing the salvor a high reward in the cases in which there is success. There is no doubt that the law outlined above, and Lloyd's Standard Form which utilises it, normally enables a salvage operation to get under way swiftly and the remuneration to be fixed later in a just manner. There is no question of professional salvors being the 'vultures' they are taken by the popular press to be, or that the law relating to salvage is, as a whole, out of date. This is not to say, however, that there are no problems or that a potential oil pollution situation does not present special difficulties – on the contrary, it does, and it is to these that attention is now directed.

5. [1953] 2 Lloyd's Rep., 557 at 561.

13.2 Particular problems associated with the risk of oil pollution

13.2.1 SALVORS' LIABILITY FOR OIL POLLUTION: INDEMNITIES

It was seen in section 10.1.1.2 that CLC had failed to deal with the question of salvors' liability for oil pollution damage, and so it had fallen to individual states to rectify the position for their own national law. Not all states, by any means, have chosen to either partially or wholly exempt salvors from liability for pollution. Before CLC came into force in 1975, this was even more true.

For a long time P and I Clubs had felt unable to offer insurance cover to salvors for oil pollution liability, and traditional markets would only rarely grant it. As tankers grew larger and as public emotions about oil pollution grew more volatile, salvors became more and more reluctant to attempt salvage of a tanker without taking full indemnities from the owner of the tanker in distress. The P and I Clubs, in their turn, would not cover the shipowner for his liabilities under such indemnities until they had approved the form of the individual indemnity demanded by the salvor. Consequently, arranging salvage of a tanker in some cases involved vital delay, increasing the risks run by the tanker.

In 1972 a standard form of indemnity was therefore agreed•by the major salvors of the world and the majority of the P and I Clubs of the world: it was known as the P and I Oil Pollution Indemnity Clause (PIOPIC)[6]. This clause was suitable for insertion into both towage and salvage agreements. However, the existence of PIOPIC led not unnaturally to a demand for its use in almost every case. The P and I Clubs felt that this was wrong, and that it should be confined in its use to cases where there was a grave danger of the salvor suffering claims for oil pollution damage. In all other cases the P and I Club would have effectively taken a risk in a situation where the benefit of the salvage accrued to other underwriters (namely hull and cargo).

---

6. 'The Owners shall be responsible for and shall indemnify the Contractor, unless guilty of personal wilful misconduct, in respect of all claims for oil pollution damage, including preventative measures, howsoever arising (including contractual liabilities to sub-contractors) out of the services performed hereunder provided always that the Owners' total liability arising under this indemnity shall in no circumstances exceed (a) US $15 million less the aggregate amount of all liabilities, costs and expenses for or in respect of oil pollution damage, including preventive measures (otherwise than under this indemnity or similar indemnities given to other persons performing salvage operations in connection with the vessel) incurred or to be incurred by the Owners arising out of or in connection with the casualty to the vessel or the consequence thereof or (b) US $10 million, whichever is the greater; Provided always that if the Owners' total liability arising under this and any other similar indemnities given or to be given to other persons performing salvage operations in connection with the vessel exceeds the amount of the applicable limit of liability referred to above such amount shall be distributed rateably among the Contractor and such other persons and the Owners' liability hereunder shall be reduced accordingly. This Clause shall be construed in accordance with English Law.'

Consequently as from 20 February 1975, the P and I Clubs arranged to cover professional salvors for oil pollution risks incurred while engaged in salvage, whether or not a tug is used. All the world's leading professional salvors are thought now to be entered in a P and I Club for this cover. This does not mean, however, that PIOPIC is completely redundant: a salvor not entered in a Club for this cover may still require it, and other salvors may require it in cases where oil spillage is almost certain.

13.2.2 LIMITATION OF SALVORS' LIABILITY FOR OIL POLLUTION

In section 9.8.2.2 it was seen that the right to limit under the 1957 Limitation Convention was not available in respect of acts neither performed on board the ship in respect of which limitation was sought, nor performed in connection with the management or navigation of it. The recent decision of the House of Lords in *The Tojo Maru*[7] has highlighted the importance of this restriction in the case of tanker salvage.

A salvage company were employed to salve a tanker, the '*Tojo Maru*'. The salvors' chief diver left the tug from which he was operating, and negligently caused an explosion aboard the '*Tojo Maru*' by firing a bolt through her plates into a tank which had not been gas-freed. The salvors were held unable to limit their liability under s. 503 of the Merchant Shipping Act 1894 (as amended) because the negligent act of their diver was not done either 'in the management of' or 'on board' the salving tug. Thus, had oil pollution damage resulted, and had the salvors been held liable to third parties for breach of duty of care, limitation would also have been denied.

The fact that the 1924 Limitation Convention[8] might have afforded a different result, on the grounds that the diver might be considered as being 'in the service of the vessel' while performing the salvage, within the meaning of Article 1(1), affords cold comfort because of the very few countries where it is still in force. Nowadays, salvors operate increasingly in a manner which would, on the reasoning in *The Tojo Maru*, deny the right to limit – e.g. when men are put aboard the vessel being salved by a helicopter.

These difficulties were at the heart of the special provisions relating to salvors adopted in the 1976 Limitation Convention[9]. These provisions expressly enable a salvor to limit his liability in accordance with the terms of the Convention by defining a salvor in Article 1(3) as 'any person rendering services in direct connexion with salvage operations[10]', and by providing in Article 6(4) a special basis for

7. [1972] AC 242, [1971] 1 All ER 1110.
8. See section 9.8.2.1.
9. See section 9.8.2.3. Discussion of the principle of salvors limiting their liability when not operating from a ship is recorded in LEG/CONF. 5/C. 1/SR. 13.
10. 'Salvage operations' include certain specified operations defined in Article 2(1)(d), (e) and (f).

limitation when the salvor is not operating from any ship, or is operating solely on the ship to or in respect of which he is rendering salvage services. While these provisions will undoubtedly help salvors in most cases, they are of no avail where a claim for oil pollution damage is made against them, for, as was seen in section 9.8.2.3, Article 3(b) of the Convention excludes from its application all 'claims for oil pollution damage within the meaning of the International Convention on Civil Liability for Oil Pollution Damage, dated 29 November 1969 or of any amendment or Protocol thereto which is in force.' The position is, then, that any state ratifying the 1976 Convention is free to, but not bound to, make special provision for salvors' limitation of oil pollution liability. It is desirable that this is done by exempting salvors from such liability altogether: this would remove the current difficulty in which salvors are placed and which could lead to a salvor not wishing to undertake a particular salvage operation.

13.2.3 THE SMALL PRIZE

It was seen in section 13.1 that rarely, in practice, will the salvor receive more than half the value of the property saved as a salvage reward, and that there is a legal limit of the whole value of the property saved. These limits could lead in practice to a reluctance on the part of a professional salvor to undertake the salvage of a tanker, which, together with the freight at risk and the cargo, is worth less money than may be needed in order to salve her successfully. The fact that oil cargoes are now very often worth more than the ship (this likelihood increases with the deadweight capacity of the ship), due to the high price of oil and the currently low market values of oil tankers, does not in fact relieve this situation; for if the cargo is lost or partly lost in the salvage process, the salvor will be unable to benefit to the extent of the lost cargo. Reward is based upon the value of property actually saved.

This problem will be more apparent than real in many cases because salvors are, notwithstanding what was said in section 13.2.1, used to taking risks. But where there is also a risk of oil pollution damage being caused, these considerations may tip the balance in favour of refusing the opportunity to salve. The need to take specifically anti-pollution orientated measures is another, but related, problem, exacerbated by the small tanker.

13.2.4 SPECIFIC ANTI–POLLUTION MEASURES

The duty of the salvor under Lloyd's Standard Form is to use his best endeavours to salve the ship and/or her cargo. Sometimes, the need to avoid oil pollution conflicts with this. The most extreme example is where, in order to refloat a grounded tanker, the salvor would, but for oil pollution considerations, be inclined to jettison cargo. The taking of anti-pollution measures by the salvor may be costly, and the question is whether the law affords any ground for the recovery of such expense.

As has been seen in section 13.1, a salvage award is only payable where property is salved: so, if the salvage operation ultimately fails, the expense of the anti-pollution measures will remain with the salvor taking them. If the operation is a success, the question is, would the salvor be able to claim an award enhanced by at least the cost of those measures taken exclusively to avert the risks of oil pollution? Take the simple case where, instead of jettisoning cargo to refloat a stranded tanker, the salvor succeeds at great expense in lightening her[11]: would the costs of the lightening be added to the salvage award which would otherwise have been made?

The answer to this will, of course, depend on the law applicable to the salvage – which, in the case of Lloyd's Standard Form, is likely always to be English law[12]. There would appear to be at least some scope for such an enhanced award in jurisdictions governed by the 1910 Salvage Convention, for Article 8 thereof provides that the reward is to be based, inter alia, on '. . . the risks of liability and other risks run by the salvors'. Another, perhaps much better, basis for finding such scope is that, if the anti-pollution measures succeed in reducing or averting oil pollution, by definition cargo must thereby have been saved.

However, there appears to be no English authority directly in point, and so the basis for an enhanced award in such circumstances must at best be regarded as doubtful. Of course, the salvor does not know before the anti-pollution measures are undertaken whether or not they will be successful; the legal basis for a recovery of anti-pollution expenditure where such measures are not themselves successful but where some property (e.g. the ship) is nonetheless saved is even more doubtful than in the case where such measures are successful. It would be unreasonable to expect anyone to undertake such special measures with such a doubtful chance of obtaining reimbursement.

Where the shipowner himself, as opposed to the salvor, expends money on taking anti-pollution measures, the position might well be different in practice, if not in law. It was seen in Chapter 12 that TOVALOP and CRISTAL cover what are defined therein as threat

11. Lightening is a very common operation, the most recent well-known case being the '*Venoil/Venpet*' collision on 31 December 1977 off the South African coast. In the '*Amoco Cadiz*' case the plan was to lighten her, but it proved impossible because of the shallow water surrounding her, the uncertain nature of the depth information on local charts and the bad weather precluding a special hydrological survey.

12. In *The Tojo Maru* [1972] AC 242, Lord Diplock said (at 290) '[The parties'] use of Lloyd's Standard Form of Salvage Agreement, which provides for many functions to be performed by the Committee of Lloyd's and by Lloyd's arbitrators, negatives any intention of the parties that their rights and liabilities thereunder should be determined by the internal municipal law of any country other than England.'

removal measures. Consequently, a shipowner whose ship is entered in TOVALOP and carries a cargo owned by a party to CRISTAL should be able to recover these costs in most situations under those schemes in the manner described in Chapter 12. If TOVALOP does not apply because the incident is covered by CLC, the shipowner's Sue and Labour clause in his P and I policy should enable him to achieve the same result[13].

If for some reason the shipowner does not have recourse to these methods of recovery, and indeed, even if he does, there is only a slim chance that he could claim a general average contribution towards the costs he has incurred, always assuming that the maritime adventure has not completely failed. In order to successfully claim such a contribution the shipowner will, of course, have to show that what he has done is indeed a general average sacrifice. Rule A of the York-Antwerp Rules[14] expresses the essence of such a sacrifice[15] as follows: 'There is a general average act when, and only when, any extraordinary sacrifice or expenditure is intentionally and reasonably made or incurred for the common safety for the purpose of preserving from peril the property involved in a common maritime adventure.' Hence, the purpose of the measures is all-important, but there does not appear to be an English decision directly in point as to whether the main purpose of the action must be to save the common property or whether this may be a subordinate purpose – still less is it clear what would be the position where the shipowner did not have it clear in his mind at the time why he was taking the particular measures, but he simply reacted instinctively and ordered that they be taken. However in America there is some authority for the view that the purpose of saving the property imperilled must be the sole purpose for the act to qualify as a general average act[16].

In conclusion, at present there are at best doubtful grounds on which a shipowner who has taken anti-pollution measures for the purpose of saving oil pollution and who in so doing has saved cargo and freight at risk can obtain a contribution towards the cost of such measures from those who have benefitted. Further, the fact that he can recover the cost from his insurers, either under the voluntary industry

13. The fact that CLC imposes strict liability must make the chances of recovery under Sue and Labour much greater than if the legal liability sought to be avoided by the measures was based on fault.

14. The York-Antwerp Rules, which first appeared in 1887, are incorporated into most charterparties and Bills of Lading by choice of the parties. The 1974 York-Antwerp Rules were adopted by the Comite Maritime International at their Hamburg Conference in 1974.

15. Cf. the Marine Insurance Act 1906, s. 66(2): 'There is a general average act where any extraordinary sacrifice or expenditure is voluntarily and reasonably made or incurred in time of peril for the purpose of preserving the property imperilled in the common adventure.' For a classic common law statement of the principle, see *Birkley v Presgrave* (1801) 1 East 219 at 228, per Lawrence J.

16. *Ralli v Troop* (1895) 15 Sup Ct 657; *Armour v Northern* [1928] AMC 606; but cf. *Andree v Moran* [1930] AMC 631 where the point was left open. I am grateful to Mr M. J. Mustill QC, and Mr R. J. L. Thomas for these references.

schemes or under the Sue and Labour Clause in his P and I policy, while being of great importance from the oil pollution point of view, is of cold comfort to the insurers of such risks. Lastly, there are disincentives under the no cure – no pay system of salvage to a salvor taking anti-pollution measures. All these points illustrate the inability of current legal concepts to overcome with certainty the difficulties posed in this area by and in connection with the risk of oil pollution, and hence there is a need for the solution of these problems either by international legislation or by widening the scope of current voluntary arrangements.

13.3 The French proposals for change

Following the '*Amoco Cadiz*' incident off the coast of Brittany in March 1978, the government of France made wide-ranging and radical proposals for changes in international standards relating to control of ships, navigation, design and construction, and salvage[17]. These proposals were put first to the Maritime Safety Committee of IMCO[17], then to the Marine Environment Protection Committee[18], then to IMCO's Council[19]; insofar as they relate to salvage, the proposals have been taken up by the Legal Committee[20].

The proposals relating to salvage start from the proposition, partly illustrated above in section 13.2.4, that 'the régime which is set out in the Brussels Convention of 1910 may have been satisfactory at a period when the loss of a ship's cargo involved only the interests of the shipowner and the shipper as well as the interests of the party rendering assistance. The system of "no cure/no pay" contracts no doubt provided a framework within which the interests of the two parties to the contract coincided. There is now another party concerned who is the potential victim of pollution...'[1]

However, in developing directions for the possible solution of this problem, a number of suggestions of doubtful utility are made. The first is that 'a new obligation should be created which would be additional to the obligation laid down in Article 11 of the 1910 Convention[2]: every ship's master should in future be obliged to render assistance to a ship creating a danger of pollution even if no human life

17. See MSC XXXVIII/21/Add. 1.
18. See MEPC IX/15.
19. See C XL/25.
20. See LEG XXXV/4, paras. 40–68 and Annex IV.
 1. MSC XXXVIII/21/Add. 1, p. 11.
 2. Article 11 states: 'Every master is bound, so far as he can do so without serious danger to his vessel, her crew and her passengers, to render assistance to everybody, even though an enemy, found at sea in danger of being lost.' This has been enacted into UK law by the Maritime Conventions Act 1911, s. 6.

is at risk[3].' If this suggestion were to be taken to the length of imposing on a private professional salvor the duty to salve without a contract, it is quite possible that there would quite suddenly be no professional private salvors. Only a salvor who is an agent of government could tolerate operating under such a régime. One must also ask whether such a duty implies a duty on the part of the vessel in distress to accept the salvage services to be imposed.

The existence of government salvors may, in fact, be in the minds of the French delegation, for the major proposal put to the Legal Committee was that coastal states should be able to take measures (inferredly against the wishes of the private interests involved) where the 1969 Intervention Convention[4] would not at the moment allow this – i.e. before the threat of oil pollution became 'grave and imminent'. The French delegate to the Legal Committee explained that what was envisaged here was that the coastal state 'should have the power to impose on ships in distress compulsory measures of assistance and salvage': contracting states to a new Convention embodying this principle should be able to apply such measures 'to all ships whether or not flying the flag of a contracting state to the new instrument[5].'

It was seen in Chapter 5 that the 1969 Intervention Convention was a codification of rights existing in customary international law; as such, it was justified, and, indeed, welcome. Any extension of rights granted thereunder can only be justified, therefore, if they can be shown to be absolutely necessary to aid the fight against oil pollution: every such extension is an encroachment on freedom of the seas. The *Amoco Cadiz* case is not evidence of such need. A careful reading of the daily transcript of evidence given at the Liberian Inquiry[6] reveals that even if the French authorities had had such powers, the accident would not have been prevented. It is at best doubtful that increased powers of intervention by the coastal state would help in other cases.

It does appear from the '*Amoco Cadiz*' incident that there was considerable delay in the sending of a request for tug assistance. This fact has led the French government to suggest that it should be made mandatory for 'any master, owner or charterer of a ship involved in seeking assistance, or where assistance is necessary or envisaged, to notify immediately the designated authorities of coastal states within 200 miles of the ship[7].' As the observer of the International Chamber of Shipping pointed out to the Legal Committee[8], there are elaborate provisions on reporting contained in the 1973 International Con-

3. MSC XXXVIII/21/Add. 1, p. 12.
4. See Chapter 5.
5. LEG XXXV/4, para. 45.
6. At the time of printing, the Official Report of the Liberian Marine Board of Investigation has not been published.
7. MSC XXXVIII/21/Add. 1, p. 12.
8. LEG XXXV/4, para. 63.

vention for the Prevention of Pollution from Ships[9] which there may be merit in augmenting. The Legal Committee agreed to investigate this aspect[10], although one must wonder whether by law alone one can improve the standard of seamanship exhibited by masters of ships.

These propositions all proceed on the assumption that the best way in which the interests of the potential victims of accidental oil pollution can be protected is to increase the powers of their government and the duties of the private interests concerned, whereas it was seen in sections 13.2.3 and 13.2.4 that the proven problems in this area of the law are basically financial in character, and concern the inter-relationships of the private interests concerned – shipowner, cargo owner, salvor and their respective underwriters. For this reason, the French initiative following the '*Amoco Cadiz*' incident may have missed the mark, although it is possible that the ensuing work of the IMCO Legal Committee may nonetheless encompass the problems mentioned above.

9. See section 6.3, above.
10. LEG XXXV/4, para. 68 and Annex IV.

Index

References are to page numbers; superior figures refer to notes